Art and Cognition

Art and Cognition

INTEGRATING THE VISUAL ARTS IN THE CURRICULUM

Arthur D. Efland

Teachers College, Columbia University
New York and London

National Art Education
Association

Published simultaneously by Teachers College Press, 1234 Amsterdam Avenue, New York, NY 10027 and the National Art Education Association, 1916 Association Drive, Reston, VA 22091-1590

Library of Congress Cataloging-in-Publication Data

Efland, Arthur, 1929-
    Art and cognition : integrating the visual arts in the curriculum / Arthur D. Efland.
        p.   cm.
    Includes bibliographical references and index.
    ISBN 0-8077-4218-X (pbk. : alk. paper) — ISBN 0-8077-4219-8 (cloth: alk. paper)
        1. Art—Study and teaching—United States.   2. Art—Psychology.   3. Cognitive learning—United States.   4. Curriculum planning—United States.   I. Title.

    N353 .E34 2002
    707'.1'073—dc21   2001060391

ISBN 0-8077-4218-X (paper)
ISBN 0-8077-4219-8 (cloth)

Printed on acid-free paper
Manufactured in the United States of America

09   08   07   06   05   04   03   02   8   7   6   5   4   3   2   1

To David and Amy

Contents

Acknowledgments   xi

1 The Uneasy Connection Between Art and Psychology   1

    The Positivist Legacy   2
    Objectivism in the Sciences   5
    Purpose of Book   6
    Organization of Book   12

2 Artistic Development in Cognitive Developmental Theories   14

    The Legacy of Behaviorism   14
    Piaget's Theory of Cognitive Development   23
    Sociocultural Cognition: The Vygotskian Perspective   30
    Difficulties with Piagetian and Vygotskian Theories
       of Cognitive Development   38
    Theories of Development in Children's Drawings   41
    Implications for Art Education   48

3 The Cognitive Revolution and Conceptions of Learning   52

    Three Cognitive Orientations   52
    Cognition as Symbol Processing   55
    Sociocultural, or Situated, Cognition   69

Toward Integrated Theory   72
Requirements of an Integrated Cognitive Theory
    for Education in the Arts   78
Implications for Education in the Arts   79

4   Cognitive Flexibility Theory and Learning in the Arts   82

Differences Between Introductory and
    Advanced Knowledge Acquisition   85
Complex Domains and Learning   86
Instruction That Promotes Cognitive Flexibility—
    Hypertext Technologies in Instruction   89
Misconceptions Resulting from Reductions of Complexity:
    The Reductive Bias   91
The Complexity Riddle and the Application of
    Curriculum Models   99
The Integrated Curriculum   103
Implications of Cognitive Flexibility Theory for Art Education 104

5   Obstacles to Art Learning and Their Assessment   107

Misconceptions in Learning About Art—The Koroscik Analysis   107
The Lifeworld and Cultural Cognitive Mapping   120
Implications for Instruction and Assessment   130
Instructional Prompts in Instruction and Assessment   130
Designing Curriculum Contexts for Improving Art Understanding 131

6   Imagination in Cognition   133

Imagination in Philosophy   134
Psychological Studies of Mental Imagery   136
Categorization in Cognition   138
Some Implications—Experience, Abstraction, and Metaphor   142
Toward a Theory of Imagination—Categorization,
    Schemata, and Narratives   150
Relevance to Art Education   152
Implications for General Education   154

7   The Arts and Cognition: A Cognitive Argument for the Arts 156

Cognitive Flexibility   159
Integration of Knowledge Through the Arts   164
The Imaginative in Cognition   167

The Aesthetic Experience   168
In Summary: The Purpose of the Arts   171

Notes   173

References   179

Index   189

About the Author   201

Acknowledgments

THIS BOOK TOOK ROOT in a particular social environment—my academic home, the Department of Art Education at Ohio State University. The references listed in this book attest to this, as they include numerous works by my colleagues Judith Koroscik, Michael Parsons, and Georgianna Short, and the works of graduate students too numerous to mention here. Together these provided a research base to help me search for a more adequate account of learning in the arts as seen from a cognitive perspective.

Other influences also have contributed to this foundation, namely, the work on cognition undertaken by Howard Gardner, David Perkins, and Rebecca Simmons at Harvard's Project Zero for more than a quarter-century. In my effort to find a view that can accommodate the sociocultural perspective in cognition, I have strayed from the symbol-systems view of cognition they have advanced, yet without the foundation their work has provided, the integrated view put forth in this book would not have been possible. The work on cognitive flexibility theory by Rand Spiro, Paul Feltovich, Richard Coulson, and Daniel Anderson, although initially developed for medical education, offered a set of conceptual tools for clarifying the nature of problems occurring in learning the arts. George Lakoff and Mark Johnson's work on metaphor and imagination enabled me to revisit the landscape of the imaginative in learning and the arts. I also acknowledge my debt to theoretical work occurring in other subject fields such as science and mathematics education as providing a basis for dealing with similar educational problems in the arts.

During the spring quarters of 1998 and 1999, early drafts of the manuscript were tried as texts in graduate seminars on cognition in the arts, presented by Michael Parsons and myself. Our students ranged from art teachers in local school districts working on graduate degrees to international students pursuing doctorates. On several occasions the questions posed by these students challenged me to clarify ideas, to fill gaps in the arguments, and to render intelligible what may have been unclear in initial formulations. This resulted in burning the midnight oil as whole chapters and sections underwent repeated revision. Michael, in particular, helped me see the strengths, weaknesses, and gaps in the early drafts and offered numerous suggestions. Without his trenchant and thoroughgoing critique, this book would not have been possible.

Finally, I owe much to my son David, who taught me that city plans, like curriculum plans, embody the aspirations and hopes of communities for a better life, and that maps like curricula embody metaphoric visions of human potential and possibility. Lastly, I can never acknowledge completely the fullness of my debt to my wife Jenny, whose art and life personify the belief that true understanding emerges when thinking, feeling, and willing are in balance.

1

The Uneasy Connection Between
Art and Psychology

THE BELIEF THAT THE ARTS are intellectually undemanding occupations, suitable for amusement and diversion, is deeply ingrained in the Western psyche. When asked to list the intellectual giants in Western cultural history, most people will list Einstein or Newton before Rembrandt or Picasso. Artistic genius is the stuff of legend—an extrahuman gift, not a measurable mental trait. In ranking the fields demanding brain power, the physicist is placed before the painter, the molecular biologist before the poet, the mathematician above the composer of symphonies. But are these judgments grounded in actual assessments of the intellectual requirements of these fields? And more to the point, what is the conception of mind that leads so many to think of the arts as "lightsome vocations" (Snedden, 1917, p. 805)?

These are psychological questions concerning the nature of intelligence. However, the assumption that the arts are intellectually inferior as modes of knowing and understanding antedates psychology by at least 2,000 years, reaching back to Plato. In favoring the "ideal forms" as the supreme source of true knowledge, Plato argued for the lesser status of the arts. The archetypes that the rational mind can grasp in their cold purity, he presumed to be free of the distortions of the senses and hence superior to the knowledge given in perception. Sensory knowledge based on the actuality of nature was made up of imperfect copies or imitations of these ideals. Furthermore, the objects appearing in works of art were "imitations of imitations," hence doubly inferior.[1]

Platonic ideals are highly abstract, beyond the reach of average minds. Pure, sense-free thinking is hard. For this reason we enlist sensory aids for assistance: maps, diagrams, pictures, statues, and the instruments of science. Teachers and parents stimulate the minds of the young by providing models of the good and the true, often with songs, stories, or pictures—all because the realm of the abstract is difficult to grasp!

Yet, there are occasions when the image of a work of art is itself a source of puzzlement, mystery, or bewilderment. For example, in looking at Rene Magritte's 1963 painting *The Telescope* [*La lunette d'approache*], we see a casement window with two panels of glass, and looking through the glass we see a field and a serene blue sky with fleecy clouds (Figure 1.1). One of the panels is shut; the other is slightly ajar, opening into the room. But, there is a problem here, which appears in the opening between the two halves of the window. If the artist's representation of the window is right, we should see a continuation of the scene in the space between the window panes, but instead we see darkness—total darkness! Did the artist make a mistake? Did he forget to finish this work? If not, is there a logical explanation for this illusion? What could Magritte have had in mind when he painted this picture?

I can't answer these questions, except to illustrate the point that works of art often make heavy cognitive demands on thinking. Such works, in my view, awaken intellectual inquiry, for thought does not begin in the abstract, but with images directly sensed or recalled in memory. Abstraction is an "achievement of the imagination" (Brown, cited in Lakoff, 1987, pp. 32–33), and the meanings derived from this effort may bear on our lives in the social and cultural worlds we inhabit. Indeed, this is their educative function.

If so, why are the arts accorded such scant attention in schooling? Unfortunately, there is no short answer to that query, for educational policies and practices rest on what is valued in society, and on conceptions of intellectual accomplishment and what it entails. The bias persists that the arts not only make lighter demands on the intellect but actually may take time and resources away from "serious" endeavors. I take vigorous exception to this view and argue throughout this book that encounters in and with the arts can widen the powers of understanding in growing minds, and that the neglect or omission of the arts in education narrows the cognitive potential of tomorrow's adults.

THE POSITIVIST LEGACY

To make matters worse, the bias against the arts also is deeply ingrained in the history of psychology. Scientific psychology has had a relatively short history, less than 130 years from the time of this writing.[2] Before

Figure 1.1. Magritte, Rene. *La lunette d'approache* [The Telescope]. 1963. Oil on canvas, 69-⁵/₁₆ × 45-¼". The Menil Collection, Houston, Texas. © 2001 C. Herscovici, Brussels/Artists Rights Society (ARS), New York.

then, the intellectual status of the arts was a matter for endless philosophical debate. No definitive, scientific answer was expected that would determine whether the cognitive processes involved in understanding works of art were any more or less demanding than those involved in understanding anything else. Philosophy waffled on the question, and if Plato questioned the primacy of the arts as modes of knowing, there was Aristotle, who valued poetry as a truer source of knowledge than history. Later, in Roman times, Plotinus believed that artistic inspiration was a gift from the gods and hence a source of knowledge truer than that achieved by reason alone. No decisive answer was likely ever to come from philosophy and hence philosophy represented no real threat (Beardsley, 1966).

But then, psychology aspired to become an empirical science, supplanting metaphysical speculation. Psychologists dedicated themselves to the objective observation of phenomena, presumably without bias, including the creation of and response to works of art. Yet certain philosophical assumptions permeated the practices of psychological investigation. One was the notion that the ability to think in the disciplined logic of the sciences required a higher level of intellect than sonnet writing, painting, and the like, a bias that reflects Plato's contention that abstract thinking is a higher form of thought than knowledge given in perception.[3]

In particular, positivism shaped the character of psychological thinking and research during the late nineteenth and early twentieth centuries. It provided the philosophical ground for behaviorism as it developed in North American universities. The model of research adopted by experimental psychologists was borrowed from the natural sciences. The purpose of these sciences was (and still is) to discover the laws of nature as revealed by carefully controlled observations and experiments. However, beliefs about nature and its laws were guided by a deterministic model of nature, a reality independent of human purposes.

Objects in nature were conceived like billiard balls that followed certain predictable laws of motion. Every observable effect had its cause. In applying this principle to human behavior, psychologists reasoned that every behavior had its cause, that every human response was determined by a stimulus, and that general laws like the laws of motion could be found to explain behavior. This principle assumed that human purposes implied by such actions were wholly determined by such laws and hence were not freely chosen. Luk Van Langenhove (1995) said that the problem with such a view is that it does not take into account the fact that "human behavior is meaningful behavior that involves active agents with intentions and expectations and [who are] able to communicate with other equally active agents" (p. 14).

In its infancy, psychology not only borrowed methods from the natural sciences, but assumed that science itself was the only way to procure reliable knowledge. Scientific forms of understanding were presumed to be more advanced than nonscientific or prescientific forms. It was no accident, then, that the first psychological accounts of intelligence either attempted to reduce human behavior to specific laws, for example, Thorndike's laws of learning, or equated the high end of intellect with the capacity to engage in logical, scientific thought, as Piaget believed. Indeed, Piaget's stage of formal operations is characterized by this capacity, not growth in narrative, or symphonic composition. So certain was he about the place of science in human development that he rarely evinced interest in questions pertaining to artistic or aesthetic development. On occasions when he studied children's drawings, it was for the purpose of demonstrating what they knew, not what they saw or imagined (Piaget & Inhelder, 1967). Such assumptions contributed to the marginalization of the arts as intellectual endeavors.

OBJECTIVISM IN THE SCIENCES

Accompanying the philosophy of positivism is a philosophical theory of meaning identified as objectivism. This philosophy assumes that the symbols used in thinking or in linguistic utterances get their meaning solely by virtue of their capacity to stand for objects, people, properties, and the connections between them as they actually exist in the world. In short, these symbols represent the world. Such symbols often are described as "disembodied" concepts, in that they are not tied to any particular mind that experiences them. This abstract and general nature of symbolic concepts is what presumably makes them shareable. Objectivists insist that meaning "must be given ultimately in terms of literal concepts" (Johnson, 1987, p. xxiii). Metaphorical or figurative use of language may have ornamental value but such expressions usually involve what Mark Johnson (1987) calls "category crossings" that do not exist objectively in the world (p. xxiii). Yet, the symbolic character of most works of art is not limited to representation; they are also expressive; they transcend representation.

In taking exception to the objectivist view, George Lakoff and Mark Johnson (1980) cite a typical metaphor that occurs in daily speech, namely, "time is money," which communicates the notion that time has economic value in our society. But literally speaking, time is not money. The objectivist insists that to understand what is meant by such figurative expressions we reduce them to literal terms. Yet it is clear that users of this metaphor understand it quite readily without any reduction to literalism, and so patently obvious is its meaning that most users scarcely regard it as a metaphor.

Unfortunately, objectivist assumptions tend to pervade the cognitive sciences. If cognition can be reduced to symbols that represent the world, as many cognitivists insist, then thinking becomes akin to computation. It is a process governed by the conventions of logic and grammar. The human capacity to think metaphorically thus becomes a stumbling block in failing to explain why so much speech is metaphorical or figurative. What motive would impel the truly rational mind to fashion expressions that are neither literally true nor false? Why would it attempt to deceive or obscure our understanding? Computational models of the mind also have difficulty explaining the role of mental imagery in cognition.

PURPOSE OF BOOK

The time has come to undo the damage caused by the biases of the past and to look at more recent understandings of the mind and the nature of human intelligence, and at how these bear on the question of the intellectual status of the arts. This is the central mission of this book. A second mission is to identify reasons for teaching the arts within a view of general education dedicated to expanding cognitive development. It asks, How does a cognitively oriented conception of art teaching change the ways that the arts were taught in the past?

Works of art are complex and valued human achievements capable of providing knowledge, aesthetic experience, and enjoyment. They also can provide occasions for thought-provoking encounters into problems and concerns affecting individuals and society. Unfortunately, too many students grow into adulthood unable to understand what they see in works of art. While it is true that most schoolchildren are not likely to become professional artists or scholars of the arts, my purpose in examining the cognitive implications of education in the arts is to see how or whether individuals can develop their powers of thought more fully through widening their understanding of art and the ideas one encounters in the study of art. The educational task is to build a foundation for lifelong learning inclusive of the arts.

Problem Areas Affecting Education in the Arts

There are at least three problems that affect the arts as subjects in general education. The first is the tendency to think of them as modes of entertainment, frivolous occupations, and elective options—"nice" cultural experiences to have if time and resources permit, but not major contributors to the cultivation of the mind or personality formation. Although the arts are prized as cultural capital, they are not accorded the importance in education given to those subjects that might lead to economically productive lives in the world of occupations.

The second is a serious lack of awareness of the substantive roles the arts can play in overall cognitive development. Even those who teach the arts often characterize their efforts as fostering creative expression—as if the power of imagination were devoid of thinking or knowledge acquisition.

Third, were it possible to overcome the biases inimical to art, educators are unsure of how to use the arts to develop cognitive abilities in children or of the means for assessing such attainments. The purpose of this book is to shed light on these problem areas.

Reconceptualizing the Cultural Importance of Arts Instruction

The public at large sees the arts not as an academic necessity but as "a delightful seasoning of life rather than a certified component of the educated mind" (Broudy, 1987, p. 17). Changing this public perception is one objective of this book. I will attempt to show the contributions educational activity in the visual arts might make to the overall development of the mind, the cognitive abilities that grow through the individual's efforts to create, understand, and interpret works of art.

Meaning making. Throughout this book, the discussion of learning focuses on the development of general cognitive ability. It assumes that the development of artistic interests and abilities is a regular part of learning and cognition, not limited to the highly gifted. This learning enables individuals to construct cultural meanings that permit social communication to take place. Not only does art learning involve the acquisition of knowledge about works of art, and strategies for the deployment of this knowledge to construct meanings and understandings; it also includes a capacity for "culture building," as suggested by literary critic James Sosnoski (1995, p.12). He suggests that certain intuitive forms of understanding, which he also refers to as "configurations," rely more heavily on narration than on logical deduction, a point also made by Jerome Bruner (1986), who identifies "two modes of cognitive functioning, two ways of ordering experience, of constructing reality." He claims that the two "are irreducible to one another" and terms them the "narrative" and the "paradigmatic" or logical-scientific modes of reasoning. The latter verifies truth "by even-tual appeal to procedures for establishing formal and empirical proof, while narrative modes of reason may not establish truth as such but verisimilitude," that is, "good stories, gripping drama, believable (though not necessarily true) historical accounts" (pp. 11–13).

Current educational practice is skewed to favor the paradigmatic form of dealing with reality, and this necessarily limits the capability of today's youth to participate in the creation and communication of cultural meanings. Moreover, the effects of such deficits are not limited to high culture. They also affect the lives of students in the practical world of work.

An article in the October 13, 1996 *Los Angeles Times* attests to this: Several prominent California executives from major film studios and digital production companies complained about the lack of a skilled work force trained in simple aesthetics, let alone digital art tools. In their view, the schools of California have not adequately educated their children in the arts, and this shortage of qualified artists had its origins in 1978 when California passed the Proposition Thirteen ballot measure, which rolled back property taxes, the key funding source for schools. This forced many schools to lower their arts standards. Now, a generation later, corporations must look overseas for workers trained in the arts, and since the entertainment media, including film, TV, and multimedia, are among California's chief exports to world markets, the current situation has grave economic implications. These complaints uttered in 1996 about the need to import trained workers from abroad sound remarkably like the concerns of New England textile manufacturers of the 1870s. The arts and industrial economic concerns are connected.

Although many schools offer art education, most students experience the arts as a world of precious things, sheltered and isolated from the real world by their accession to museums. They will likely see modern art as the butt of jokes, a world given to madness—distorted by feelings and emotions. Personal art making often is regarded as having private relevance, not to be shared with others. Discussions of contemporary art often are couched in the arcane or esoteric terminology of the elite, which bear no apparent relevance to the lived experience of the learner. Yet artworks are also sources of powerful revelations about local culture, the cultures of others, and other historical times.

The educational task is to enable learners to form connections with these works, including works by artists from other cultures not widely understood in the Western world. One must learn about the cultural setting in which the artist lived and worked and from which the work of art emerged. Indeed, if one really wants to understand the human social world, one has to draw upon the arts that are part of that world. We need to adopt curricular forms that cultivate and encourage the formation of such linkages.

Importance of context in learning. To understand a work of art requires that one see it in relation to its context. Indeed, to understand anything, whether it consists of the individual components of economic systems, or whole ecosystems comprising multiple plant and animal species, one must be able to grasp things holistically—in their interconnectedness. Moreover, there are multiple forms of interconnectedness. Key ideas in the form of propositional knowledge have the power to link together many cases or examples, as in the sciences, to form explanations. However, many subject fields link cases and examples through narrative to form understandings or interpretations. The understanding of history relies more on narrative structures than cause–effect explanations. Moreover, individuals are inclined to experience their own lives as the unfolding of a story, and that story cannot be told in isolation from the environment in which it takes place, so that in understanding oneself, one also learns about the people, objects, and events that make up one's social world. The emphasis on context is particularly crucial in learning about art, for works of art cannot be fully understood apart from the social and cultural context in which they were created.

Overcoming compartmentalization. Understanding art involves the establishment of linkages between areas of knowledge to which it is related. For many generations, art educators strove for subject-matter autonomy and wanted to teach art for its own sake in isolation from other subjects constituting the culture. Moreover, art often is taught in isolation from aspects of itself. Students tend to learn studio technical skills, but not the history of the media they are using, the social needs that were met by the invention of these media, or the cultural meanings expressed by the work's symbolic content. They might learn to describe works in terms of their formal elements, but rarely can they explain how these function to contribute to a work's expressive power or how the expressed content reflects the perceived realities that fit its cultural location. They may know about the effect of warm and cool colors from experiences in a painting class, but not recognize how such colors create meanings within works of art by others.

Cognitive Implications for a Learning Theory in the Arts

There are multiple views of the learner in theories of cognition, just as there are multiple theories of the nature of art. Some portray the learner as a lone individual trying to make sense of a work of art or, for that matter, the world. Others picture learners as living within a social or cultural context from which knowledge derives its meaning. Such different views of the learner have consequences for teaching the arts. At the same time, if works of art are to be understood in terms of their social and cultural origins and purposes, then it would make sense to integrate the knowledge of the artwork into those subjects, such as the social studies or history, where knowledge of the culture and society is collaterally provided. But if works of art are thought of as autonomous structures whose meaning is set by the artist, where there is one "objective" or "right" interpretation, independent of its social context, then it might make more sense to pair this conception of art with the view of the learner as lone individual.

The view of cognition adopted for teaching the arts would have to be one that can explain mental imagery, metaphor, and narrative, and that can identify the cognitive operations that make these functions possible. Computational models of the mind tend to be adequate to account for subjects that rely heavily on propositional thinking, such as language and mathematics, but tend to have difficulty accounting for cognitive operations that rely on perceptual images and nonpropositional forms of thought.

Differences in the Structure of Knowledge Domains

In addition, the structural differences between knowledge in various domains is compared and contrasted with structures of knowledge in and about art. One of the legacies of the behavioral tradition in learning was its tendency to assume that learning in all cognitive subjects was essentially the same (Gagné, 1977), that learning to read, or do long division, or study the U.S. Constitution differed only by content. Behaviorists also assumed that certain subjects like the arts were noncognitive in nature and resided in the domain of affect. From the time of Thorndike and Watson, behaviorists sought general laws that would apply to all learning situations. They did not look for differences in learning peculiar to specific domains. Difficulties like math anxiety were ascribed to personal attitudes or phobias and were not considered an intrinsic feature of the domain undergoing study.

Current views of cognition have largely dissolved the distinction between cognitive and noncognitive subjects (Parsons, 1992). All subjects, including the arts, are now seen as having their cognitive and affective components (Scheffler, 1986). Yet art often is taught as though it were only about feelings and emotions and not ideas. Moreover, feelings often are seen as factors that inhibit the capacity to develop objectivity in judgments. In the "normal" course of cognitive development, such feelings are presumably supplanted by reason.

Although behaviorists were aware that early learning paved the way for later learning, they tended to ignore the differences between introductory knowledge acquisition and advanced knowledge acquisition. Recent research has made it increasingly apparent that certain forms of introductory learning, such as rote memorization, while initially successful in procuring factual knowledge in the short run, actually may set the stage for later comprehension failure (Feltovich, Spiro, & Coulson, 1993; Perkins & Simmons, 1988; Spiro, Coulson, Feltovich, & Anderson, 1988).

It is also the case that cognitive psychologists began making advances in their understanding of learning by researching the *domain-specific* character of expertise. They realized that high levels of competence in sonnet writing would not necessarily enable individuals to solve math problems, while computational ability might not enhance the learner's capacity to interpret a work of art. Moreover, domains of knowledge are organized differently and require differing approaches to instruction. The physical sciences are organized around general concepts or principles, whereas domains like law, medicine, the arts, and humanities tend to rely on the study of cases rather than overarching principles. Some contemporary psychologists (Feltovich, Spiro, & Coulson, 1993) characterize these as differences between "well-structured" and "ill-structured" domains of knowledge.

Failure to recognize and accommodate for these differences leads to two kinds of difficulties. First, those who do not recognize the case-based structure of domains like the arts, have a tendency to misrepresent their level of complexity, making them seem simpler and more regular than they are. When instruction misrepresents the level of ambiguity that may be characteristic of a work of art, its possible meanings are lost to the learner. Spiro and colleagues (1988) note that textbook writers and lecturers often make the mistake of "artificially neatening" a domain to simplify the learning task.

Second, as students construct knowledge with such oversimplified concepts, they are unprepared for the kinds of complex issues they are likely to encounter at more advanced levels of learning, or in life itself! Well-structured representations of knowledge often are experienced as being easier to teach and learn, and thus textbooks tend to be biased in their favor. In effect, this misrepresents the inherent complexity (ill-structuredness) of learning in many domains, including the arts and humanities.

This is seen in definitive statements about the characteristics of a given art style, such as the idea that Gothic architecture has pointed arches when, in fact, there are such notable exceptions as Chartres Cathedral, or in statements suggesting that there are definitive meanings in works of art, known by experts, and hence not subject to alternative interpretations. Expert opinion, itself, is represented as a consensus, widely shared within specific domains of knowledge when, in fact, there may be wide divergences of opinion and interpretation. The tendency prevails that there is one— and only one—"right" interpretation of a work of art.

A cognitive perspective must consider why art learning sometimes remains undeveloped or goes wrong, why people who are knowledgeable in the sense of possessing facts, end up forming misconceptions about art. Examples might be the belief that abstract art is either without meaning or that its meanings are like those derived from cloud watching, leaving observers free to devise any interpretation that pleases their fancy. Another might be the view that artworks have exact definitive meanings intended by the artist and such works need to be deciphered, like a code comprising symbolic forms, before the work can be fully apprehended and appreciated. The acquisition of naive beliefs, or garbled or wrong knowledge in one's prior learning, may compromise the ability to understand an unfamiliar work encountered for the first time.

Issues Related to the Assessment of Art Learning

Traditional modes of assessment in the visual arts have been dedicated largely to studio skills, or slide identification in art history courses. Teachers see how drawing or painting abilities improve over time. In art history, student performance is measured by the ability to recall names and dates. The emphasis in testing is usually on determining the quantity of knowledge acquired, not the quality of its organization that would enable students to apply it in other situations to further their understanding. What art teachers have yet to do is to find ways of assessing changes in students' ability to handle complex learning tasks, such as the ability to relate isolated bits of information into larger contexts where it can fit.

The definition of understanding used throughout this book relies heavily on a learner's ability to situate the knowledge learned in appropriate contexts and to organize it for a given purpose. Rarely does testing assess a student's ability to transfer knowledge learned in one situation to other situations where it may be relevant. And this is because transfer is far more difficult to assess since the range of potential uses to which existing knowledge can be put cannot be fully known in advance.

ORGANIZATION OF BOOK

This chapter introduces the book project and provides summaries of the chapters that follow. Chapter 2 offers a history of the uses of cognitive developmental theory to explain learning in the visual arts. It describes behaviorism as a long-standing tradition in North American psychology and the gradual transition to the cognitive view that currently is dominant in contemporary psychology. The contributions of Jean Piaget and

Lev Vygotsky to cognitive developmental theory are emphasized. The chapter also surveys various theories of children's artistic development.

Chapter 3 contrasts the major theoretical strands within contemporary theories of cognition, including *symbol processing* and *sociocultural* perspectives. Also examined is the idea that individuals construct their own views of reality. These traditions can be traced to differing aspects of Piagetian and Vygotskian psychologies.

Chapter 4 explores cognitive flexibility theory as it has emerged in work on learning by Rand Spiro, Paul Feltovich, Richard Coulson, Daniel Anderson, and their associates. Differences in the structures of various domains of knowledge are explained, with particular attention to differences in learning strategies required in what they call "well-structured" as compared with "ill-structured" domains. While their work does not specifically address learning in the arts, reasons for characterizing the arts as ill-structured are offered, as well as the cognitive importance of having experience with both well- and ill-structured domains.

Chapter 5 identifies the components of learning theories in accounts provided by Judith Koroscik and her associates. A major portion details the types of conditions that lead to misconceptions, including problems that might either arise in the organization of the learner's knowledge base or result from the inappropriate choice of strategies used to procure new knowledge. The chapter also introduces the concept of the *lifeworld* as the learner's map of his or her culture, society, and sense of self.

Chapter 6 provides a cognitive account of metaphor, imagination, and narrative both in the production of artworks and in the interpretation of works by others. Imaginative thinking as characterized throughout this chapter deals with the cognitive characteristics of metaphor that can form relationships between and among unlike things to create novel meanings. Imaginative thinking is especially characterized as allowing alternative pathways for interpretation, enabling thinking to go "beyond the information given," as Jerome Bruner (1973) once characterized the use of hypotheses to venture into the unknown.

Chapter 7 summarizes the curriculum implications of various cognitive perspectives for teaching the visual arts. It discusses the need for a more complex approach to learning to build the kind of knowledge structures required in a postmodern age, where the future is likely to change at a faster rate than previously, requiring high degrees of cognitive flexibility. In such a world the arts will acquire greater significance than they were accorded in the past two centuries.

2

Artistic Development in Cognitive Developmental Theories

THE CONTRIBUTIONS OF Jean Piaget and Lev Vygotsky become the central preoccupation of this chapter. Piaget, in particular, offered the prototype for cognitive developmental studies and provides the benchmark against which all developmental theorizing is compared. Piaget's work is compared with the developmental psychology of the Russian psychologist Lev Vygotsky, who was Piaget's contemporary. Although less well known, his work has begun to capture the attention of psychologists in Europe and North America despite the fact that his principal contributions were made more than 60 years ago. In the remaining portion of the chapter I review several developmental studies of children's drawings to link artistic development more closely with general cognitive development. I seek to nullify a long-standing tradition in art education of discussing artistic activity apart from cognition as a whole and favor the idea that such activities are an integral part of such discourse. The chapter opens by recalling the behavioral psychological tradition.

THE LEGACY OF BEHAVIORISM

Throughout the 1950s, psychological behaviorism dominated the educational scene and its influence on schooling still persists. Beliefs and practices implied by behavioral psychology have to a large extent become an unquestioned part of the conduct and culture of schooling, as seen in the widespread use of achievement and intelligence tests. The theories advanced by its most influential proponents, such as Clark L. Hull and B. F.

Skinner, explicitly excluded all reference to mental processes and aspired to reduce all forms of learning to conditioning. The topic of learning was reduced to the precise description of stimulus conditions that would produce specific responses. It aspired to become a psychology of cause and effect as opposed to one that would consider human purposes and intentions as mediating factors in learning. However, the objective observation of stimulus conditions, as the background against which to observe responses, was more complex than it was assumed to be.

For example, in a series of revolutionary experiments (called the "new look" in perception—that is, new during the postwar era), Jerome Bruner and others began finding that prior knowledge could modify sensation. Patricia Greenfield (1990) described an early experiment in which a person's estimate of the physical size of coins was affected by knowledge of their value. Consequently, it was reasoned that perception does not always reveal the world as it is in objective actuality, but rather a world that our purposes, intentions, needs, and biases play a role in fashioning.

The stimulus–response bond was to be the elementary unit in learning theory, akin to the role played by the atom in physics. From these fundamental units, complex understandings were thought to develop. Yet behaviorism never explained adequately how higher-order thinking abilities emerged from bonds connecting stimulus with response. In addition, it did not adequately explain how we acquire such abilities as language learning or the ability to engage in abstract conceptualization. The idea of a bond connecting stimuli with responses might have been sufficient to explain habits and reflexes, but was inadequate to explain why certain forms of prior learning create a readiness for new learning while other forms do not. As experimental evidence mounted, psychologists began searching for better explanations than behaviorism could offer.

In his retrospective account of the cognitive revolution, Jerome Bruner (1992) referred to the year 1956 as "the mythical birthday of the cognitive revolution" (p. 783). Cognitive explanations gradually began to accord mental processes "a privileged explanatory role" in educational psychology (Rohwer & Sloane, 1994, p. 41). "Concern for the mind and the way it functions returned to scientific psychology" (Shuell, 1986, p. 411).

As noted earlier, behaviorism emerged when positivism, the prevailing philosophy of science, worked to eliminate any hint of metaphysical speculation. Behaviorists maintained that the goal of psychology as a science was simply to describe as precisely as possible the behavior of individuals as they responded to various stimulus conditions provided by their environment. However, the internal experience that is most characteristic of the human species, namely, the individual experience of consciousness, was not itself amenable to objective observation. In the early 1900s, psychologists like Edward L. Thorndike and John B. Watson were intent upon making their inquiries rigorous within the bounds of objective scientific practices as they were then understood. Concepts like "mind" were too introspective and ephemeral for the spirit of the age and were relegated to speculative philosophy—outside the legitimate bounds of scientific psychology. Watson (1914) wrote that "the time seems to have come when psychology must discard all reference to consciousness" (p. 8). The efforts of these psychologists produced a curious anomaly—a science of mind that put the mind itself beyond the limits of legitimate inquiry.[1]

Yet it is clear that we have a mental life and that it does much more than generate adaptive responses to environmental stimuli. The awe and wonder we experience when we see the starry sky on a clear, moonless, winter night is not an adaptive response in the ordinary sense. The internal process we call *thinking* seems to operate almost constantly during our waking moments, sometimes invading our dreams as we sleep. Visual, auditory, and tactile images derived from sensory perception acquire meaning as a result of thinking (Bruner, 1957; Bruner, Goodnow, & Austin, 1956).

Perceiving in Relation to Thinking

Before describing the transition from behavioral to cognitive psychology, I dwell for a moment on perceiving and thinking: The world given in perception is a multiplicity, a mass of separate details including people, objects, and events. We don't create it, but find it through the activity of our senses, suggesting that perception is a passive process, like the light-impression on photographic film. This analogy is only partial, for what we perceive is influenced also by what we elect to look at and this, in turn, is influenced by prior knowledge, interests, needs, desires, expectations, motives, purposes, curiosities—in short, by our dispositions. Much of our perceptual activity occurs under the direction of our own mental life. What is found is in large part what we set out to look for. This view of perception as an active process instigated by the learner was advanced by Jerome Bruner (1957) and reiterated by Nelson Goodman (1984), who wrote:

> What and even whether we perceive depends heavily on our state of perceptual readiness. Habit, context, explicit instruction, interests, and suggestions of all kinds can blind or activate our perception, conceal or reveal a mountain or a molehill. Far from merely recording what is before us, perception participates in making what we perceive. (p. 25)

Despite this largely subconscious tendency, we tend to believe that the world looks the way it does because that's the way it is. We are generally unaware of the extent to which prior expectations, needs, habits, and dispositions structure our perceptions. Why should we expect the world to look any other way? Seeing is equated with believing! However, once we become aware that what was learned earlier may affect *what* and *how* we perceive, the possibility exists that something else might be found than what was expected. It is often possible to change our perceptual habits if and when we suspect that they may be limiting our horizons or, as Goodman (1978b) has put it, we can engage in different "ways of worldmaking."

Our acts of perception are ordinarily quite adequate for most purposes. We scan our environment to get a general idea of the lay of the land, of what there is to be seen. Usually, this is sufficient to keep us from hitting pedestrians or other vehicles while driving a car, or stumbling over furniture in the darkness of an unfamiliar room. In such ordinary circumstances, we normally are guided by what David Perkins (1994) calls "experiential intelligence" (pp. 13–14). However, there are occasions when these customary habits are found wanting. Then, we need to deploy a more specialized type of looking. For example, in his discussion of the difference between *experiential* and *reflective* intelligence, Perkins suggests: "By cultivating awareness of our own thinking, asking ourselves good questions, guiding ourselves with strategies, we steer our experiential intelligence in fruitful directions. The steering function is reflective intelligence" (p. 15).[2]

When we look at works of art, we may find it opportune to change from an *experiential strategy* to a *reflective strategy* by taking more time in our looking. And with this change, there may be an accompanying shift in what is perceived. Details may be found that would have gone unnoticed when ordinary habits of cursory scanning prevailed. The way we choose to look is conditioned largely by expectations formed in our prior knowledge, and we change strategies when some thing or situation prompts us to search for something missed in previous encounters.

Notice what is happening here. By becoming mindful of our perceptual activity, we have made perception itself into an *object for thought,* and almost at once we discover that new possibilities for perceptual activity arise in our thinking, making new actions possible as well as new experiences, replacing or altering earlier expectations of what we might find. Add to this observation a second, namely, that the attention directed at perception has given rise to concepts and ideas about the nature of perception itself. *In becoming an object for thought, perception itself has become a concept in our thinking.* Thinking arises in our consciousness and we are no longer perceiving. *We are thinking.* The thoughts may be with images or words stored in memory, and thus present in the mind although the initial stimulus is no longer available. For example, we might think about the process of perception, as we have done here, or we could think about yesterday's sunset.

Not only can we think about perceiving as a process, and the objects we have perceived, but we can go still farther and *think about our thinking*, especially if we begin to ask ourselves when perception ended and thinking began, or whether there was a clear demarcation between them. Moreover, the activity of thinking can go on independently of the senses. If we think about yesterday's sunset, the phenomenal image we *see* in our mind's eye now exists in our thinking. Once we reach the point where the object of inquiry *is our thinking* and the instrument of inquiry *is also our thinking*, we reach a state of balance where both object and instrument are *qualitatively identical*.[3]

If we want to understand the nature of thinking in more explicit detail, we probably cannot reach beyond this point! Some cognitive scientists explain thinking as neural events in the brain and nervous system, and such explanations provide information about the biological or chemical basis of thinking, but the thoughts we are thinking and the meanings we create are not themselves reducible to biological events like neurons firing. What we experience in our consciousness is thinking itself.

Thinking sometimes is described as the process that makes symbolic representations of our external environment. It ordinarily is thought of as occurring in the brain and it is about a world existing outside the brain. At other times thinking is engaged in something else that we might characterize as imagination. It reorganizes the symbolic stuff (images, concepts, ideas, and words) in the internal landscapes of the mind. These imaginative reorderings eventually may enable us to predict new situations in our environment and thus make adaptive responses. They can lead us to create scientific conceptions of the universe, to compose symphonies, to write novels, or to make no particular response at all. "Having a mind means that an organism forms neural representations which can become images, be manipulated in a process called thought, and eventually influence behavior by helping predict the future, plan accordingly, and choose the next action" (Damasio, 1994, p. 90).

Transition from Behaviorism to the Cognitive View

The traditional behaviorist would have dismissed my description of perception and thinking as mere ephemera, hidden in a tangled web of neurons. Only objects or events may function as stimuli, and learning is determined by responses to such stimuli. That is the core of behaviorist orthodoxy. How our thinking creates concepts or finds meaning lies in a realm beyond scientific scrutiny—epiphenomena to be put in a hypothetical black box.

Gradually, this view began to change. By 1956, the year cited by Bruner as the start of the cognitive revolution, telltale signs began appearing to indicate that changes were afoot in characterizing the nature of thinking and learning. Some of these are described in the sections that follow.

Bloom's taxonomy. Indicators of change began to appear in a publication known as the *Taxonomy of Educational Objectives*[4] prepared by Benjamin Bloom and his associates (1956). In its main thrust it was compatible with behaviorism as seen in its adherence to Ralph Tyler's (1950) idea that instructional outcomes should take the form of descriptions of observable behaviors. Nevertheless, Bloom's categories of objectives were organized around the assumption that learning is both cumulative and hierarchical, two notions that require some deviation from classical behaviorism. The cumulative notion requires having a way to store knowledge, a way of remembering. The notion of hierarchy would require a mechanism whereby simple behaviors could join and coalesce to become more complex. Some notion of internal processing taking place in the brain would have to be available to account for this (Rohwer & Sloane, 1994). Also, the *Taxonomy* was filled with terminology incompatible with behavioral conceptions of learning, including such terms as *knowledge, comprehension, application, analysis, synthesis,* and *evaluation*—terms that refer more to knowledge acquisition than to the widening of behavioral repertoires.

The *Taxonomy* also established three domains called the *cognitive*, the *affective*, and the *psychomotor*. The objectives in each domain were arranged hierarchically in ascending order, from simpler to more complex. However, the domains themselves appeared to be arranged in descending order, with the cognitive appearing first, followed by the affective and psychomotor. This may be the result of the order in which they were researched. The development of these domains in isolation from each other also suggests their conceptual isolation.

Although not specifically discussing the *Taxonomy*, Elliot Eisner (1976) raised a series of questions about differences in instructional objectives that probably would not have been raised were it not for the pervasive influence of the Bloom document:

> In educational discourse cognition has become associated with thinking. So far so good. But thinking has come to be associated with what children do when they use discursive or mathematical symbols to solve problems. Thinking has become identified with mental activity mediated by discourse or numbers. Thus we tend to contrast the cognitive with the affective, and the affective with the psychomotor. Although initially we created these distinctions for purposes of intellectual precision, we find ourselves trapped and

blinded by the very concepts that were intended to free us through their power to illuminate. (Eisner, 1976, p. viii)

Although Eisner (1976) dwelt on the contrast between the cognitive and the affective, he also asked, "If work in the arts *is* cognitive or intellectual, in what way is it so? Are there such things as qualitative forms of thought and problem solving and, if so, are the processes used for such thinking the same as those used, say, in learning to read?" (p. viii; emphasis in original). Eisner's questions harbor the legacy of the arts being categorized as a noncognitive field. At the time of his writing, the disjunction between the cognitive and noncognitive was accepted as an unassailable certainty,[5] and yet it seemed to him that categorizing the arts as members of an affective domain denied their cognitive character.

Cognitive developmental theory. By the 1960s, Jean Piaget's theory and research had been available for some 35 years in North American universities, but their influence did not become widespread until the 1960s with the publication of Hunt's *Intelligence and Experience* (1961), Flavell's *The Developmental Psychology of Jean Piaget* (1963), and Bruner, Oliver, and Greenfield's *Studies in Cognitive Growth* (1966). Cognitive developmental theory, in contrast to behavioral theory, emphasized development as well as learning. Differences in a student's response to a learning situation depended as much on the student's developmental stage as on the domain of the subject being learned. Cognitive developmentalists devised the concept of stages to explain the hierarchical nature of learning. "It is the stages that are hierarchically related not the kinds of learning that characterize the stages" (Rohwer & Sloane, 1994, p. 58).

In the early 1970s, Howard Gardner worked initially in the cognitive developmental framework, although much of his later work is compatible with the cognitive science orientation, described later in this chapter. He listed several reasons for rejecting the behaviorist view as a means of studying the relation of art to human development:

I have rejected the behaviorist approach because, whatever its original uses and merits within American psychology, it has in recent years rarely led to questions, experiments, or observations relevant to the present topic. (Gardner, 1973, p. 2)

Gardner and his associates at Harvard University's Project Zero were among the principal contributors to our current understanding of artistic development. Since much of the research occurred under the cognitive developmental umbrella, that source of theory is emphasized in this chapter.

Emergence of the cognitive science orientation. Another influence is found in the rise of the cognitive sciences. These currently comprise concepts from a variety of disciplines ranging from linguistics, to philosophy, to computer science. They employ a number of methodologies ranging from artificial intelligence and computer modeling to linguistic, ethnographic, and experimental methods.

Behavioral observations continue to play an important role in the research on cognition, since mental processes or knowledge structures are still largely inferred from observations of behavior. The behaviorist is likely to focus on the environmental conditions that may have aroused the behavioral response, whereas the cognitivist is more likely to study behavior as it is situated in social contexts to draw inferences about learners and their ways of constructing knowledge. The emergence of the cognitive view has had far-reaching implications for general education, but its impact on art education has been more profound than for most other subjects in the curriculum. In 1992 Michael Parsons explained why this is the case:

> The arts were the only traditional subjects that fell clearly into the "affective" category. Most of science, mathematics, language and the social studies fell into the cognitive category. . . . In the new cognitivism, of course, all our mental activities were considered cognitive. . . . This was change enough. But with respect to science, mathematics, and most of the other school subjects, it did not involve a change in how they were categorized. These subjects were cognitive before the change and cognitive afterwards. . . . In the case of the arts, it *was* a change of category. They had been affective which meant non-cognitive. Now they were cognitive, which included the intuitive, the creative, and the emotional. (p. 71)

Unanticipated Consequences

If there are no noncognitive subjects, as Parsons suggests, what exactly does this mean for teaching the arts? And further, do the prevailing methods of teaching the arts sufficiently reflect this realization?[6] Parsons allowed that we might have liked this earlier state of affairs, when the arts were seen as lying in the affective domain beyond the traditional realms of thinking and understanding. For as long as they were situated in the warm, fuzzy realm of feeling and emotion, they could avoid the onerous business of objective testing forced on teachers of other subjects (Parsons, 1992). And since the arts were not taken seriously as means for stimulating intellectual growth, art teachers by default had a degree of freedom not available to teachers of other subjects in the curriculum. Parsons adds that "the price paid for this freedom has been the relative isolation from the rest of the curriculum" (p. 72).[7] Like it or not, teachers of art no longer have the luxury and comfort once afforded by this former status.

Bloom and his fellow taxonomists divided subjects into cognitive, affective, and psychomotor groupings. By setting these in opposition, they suggested, perhaps inadvertently, that affective objectives were noncognitive, that learning to paint or to interpret a work of art may be undertaken without serious mental engagement. Subjects situated in the affective domain thus tended to be ranked intellectually lower than subjects in the cognitive domain, although this is not a status warranted by objective, scientific verification, but is the result of a bias favoring the subjects formally organized around generalizations and principles that apply to numerous cases.[8] Behaviorists also were eager to eliminate the study of feelings from psychology. Like consciousness itself, feelings were too fleeting and ephemeral to be a proper subject for the experimental researcher. Since the arts give play to feelings, they became metaphysically suspect.[9]

Bloom's *Taxonomy* made the separation between the cognitive and noncognitive canonical in North American education, and this had two major effects. First, it led many art educators to internalize an image of their field as noncognitive, even to justify its position in the curriculum by this difference. In fact, many art educators (see Davis, 1969) welcomed this distinction. Second, drawing a line in the sand between the cognitive and the noncognitive gave credence to a structure of belief with ancestral roots in Plato, one that implied a hierarchy of subjects that placed the arts on a lower rung of the educational ladder.

However, it would be a mistake to assume that the decline of the behavioral tradition in education lessened the objectivist bias against the arts. Indeed, as the cognitive view of learning gained adherents in the 1970s, the bias assumed a different and more subtle form.

Developmental Theory as Found in Art Education Texts

Since the middle 1950s, cognitive explanations of learning have been instrumental in spurring new approaches to science and mathematics education. Indeed, the curriculum reform movements of that time period were largely justified by the rise of cognitive developmental views, which gradually supplanted behaviorist approaches to learning. Yet many, if not most, of the leading textbooks written to help prepare art teachers, have tended to neglect the topic of cognition on the assumption that it is mainly concerned with the language arts or mathematical competence. This neglect may help explain why the arts have lost ground in public education over the ensuing decades.

This omission was not wholly the result of oversight or ignorance. Cultural factors in the form of contemporary art styles like abstract expressionism have had the effect of directing attention toward Freudian or Jungian conceptions of development to explain the onset of artistic expressiveness. These selfsame theories were featured prominently in the art education texts of the 1940s through the 1960s, as exemplified by Herbert Read's *Education Through Art* (1945) and Viktor Lowenfeld's *Creative and Mental Growth*, published in 1947 (Lowenfeld, 1952).

Other texts such as Henry Schaeffer-Simmern's *The Unfolding of Artistic Activity* (1948) and Rudolph Arnheim's *Art and Visual Perception* (1954) based their accounts of artistic development on gestalt psychology, seeking to link the changes in children's graphic production to perceptual development or to perceptual learning.[10]

Still another reason for the neglect of cognitive developmental theory by art educators is that the onset of artistic development in children was not an object of inquiry by Piaget. He tended to ascribe a lesser importance to subjects like the arts that tend to involve affect. Indeed, he saw the capacity to separate emotion from intellect as a necessary step in the progress of the mind as it moves toward logical-scientific thinking. Subjects that make use of what Piaget called formal operations were thought to require a higher stage of mental development. Hence, the use of the imagination in art making, or the creation of metaphor in poetry, or storytelling, are ranked as lesser attainments. It is no accident, then, that one of the side effects of the cognitive revolution was a lowering of the intellectual status accorded the arts in education.

While there may have been good reasons to account for the neglect of cognition by art educators, the time has come to remedy this deficit. What will become clear is that there are, in fact, several developmental theories that account for the evolution of graphic ability in children. It is also the case that new studies of the factors that influence artistic development have been under way in the past two decades. These studies tend to align themselves with one or more of the general explanations of cognitive development as a whole. In fact, my conclusions take the form of suggested alignments between general theories of cognitive development and the theories accounting for artistic development.

PIAGET'S THEORY OF COGNITIVE DEVELOPMENT

According to Michael Parsons (1987), a cognitive developmental theory is founded on "the basic notion . . . that we reach the complex understandings of our maturity by a series of steps. We are not born with these abilities but acquire them" (p. 10). Parsons also identifies several features that must be present in such theories:

- A sequence of invariant steps, some of which must be acquired before others
- Plotting of the growth of constructions as learners come to understand a domain of knowledge
- Stages as clusters of ideas internally related to each other

Learning to understand art, he goes on to suggest, is an example of these stages:

> [W]hen we come to understand a painting as an attempt by an artist to express a state of mind, we also tend to think of aesthetic response as re-experiencing that state of mind and of aesthetic judgment as being largely subjective and inward looking. These ideas are related to each other, and we tend to acquire them at much the same time. Such clusters of ideas are called stages in the literature.[11] (Parsons, 1987, pp. 10–11)

Piaget's cognitive developmental views were greatly influenced by his early training and work as a biologist (Flavell, 1963). He came to realize that all living organisms constantly adapt to changes in environmental conditions and that biological acts are acts of "adaptation" to the physical environment and "organization" of the environment (Flavell, 1963). This assumption led Piaget (1952/1963) to regard cognitive acts as "acts of *organization* and *adaptation*" (p. 7; emphasis in original): Piaget claimed that the principles that govern cognitive development are the same as those of biological development. To understand the processes of intellectual development, Piaget introduced four basic concepts identified by the terms *schema, assimilation, accommodation,* and *equilibration*.

The Schema as a Cognitive Structure

We become familiar with our environment when we begin to recognize certain regularities in our experience. As this happens, less energy is required for the constant adaptation and adjustment of behavior. Increasingly, we can rely on the memory of prior encounters and the actions undertaken in response to those situations as a reasonable guide for present and even future encounters. Piaget attributed the growth of this ability to the formation of specific structures in the mind, which he called *schema*, or in its plural form, *schemata*. This concept of schema, or cognitive structure, helps explain why individuals develop relatively stable, often predictable responses to stimuli. Wadsworth describes schemata as intellectual structures that organize events grouped by similarities. "They are repeatable psychological events in the sense that the child will repeatedly classify stimuli in a consistent manner" (Wadsworth, 1971, p. 12).

Richard Anderson's (1984) definition of schema is also based on Piaget's view and is of value because it features the structure of knowledge as being broader than mere grouping by similarities. In his view,

> [A] schema is an abstract structure of information. It is abstract in the sense that it summarizes information about many different cases. A schema is structured in the sense that it represents the relationships among components. The term schema is an apt one for characterizing knowledge, because the essence of knowledge is structure. Knowledge is not a basket of facts. (p. 5)

Moreover these schemata do not remain static; in fact, they adapt and change throughout the life of the individual. These changes occur through developmental processes that constitute learning. As the child develops, his or her schemata become more highly differentiated and less dependent on the senses. They become not only more numerous but increasingly more interconnected. Thus, the infant has relatively few schemata, whereas the adult will likely have a more complex array, permitting a great number of differentiations.

Assimilation and accommodation. Since the schemata of adults are derived from those they held as children, Piaget identified two processes by which these developments take place, namely, assimilation and accommodation. Wadsworth (1971) defines *assimilation* as "the cognitive process by which the person integrates new perceptual matter or stimulus events into existing schemata or patterns of behavior" (p. 14). The process of assimilation does not result in a change of schemata but it does allow for their growth.

Since an adult's cognitive structures are different from those of a child, Piaget accounted for this process of change by the process of *accommodation*. When learners encounter a new stimulus, they may try to assimilate it into an existing schema, but this is not always possible. For example, a child may have a specific schema for animals that includes having four legs, fur, and a tail. This would apply to all dogs and cats, but eventually the child takes notice of differences between dogs and cats. Dogs bark but don't climb trees, whereas cats don't bark but climb trees. In time the child differentiates schemata by developing a mental structure for cats and another for dogs. Thus, the original schema was modified to accommodate different classes of stimuli based on similar groups of characteristics. This describes the process of accommodation, which is defined as "the creation of new schemata or the modification of old schemata" (Wadsworth, 1971, p. 16).

Once accommodation has taken place and new schemata are formed, the child might try to assimilate stimuli into the new structure. Thus the development of new and more adequate cognitive structures takes place for the purpose of enabling assimilation. And when the individual's cognitive structures are capable of assimilating all new experiences, it might be said that those structures provide a reliable representation of that individual's world. The extent to which those structures reliably match the world of the learner's experience might serve as an indication of the intelligence of that individual. Wadsworth (1971) makes the following observation:

> It can be seen that in assimilation, the person imposes his available structure on the stimuli being processed. That is, the stimuli are "forced" to fit the person's structure. In accommodation the reverse is true. The person is "forced" to change his schema to fit the new stimuli. Accommodation accounts for development (a qualitative change), and assimilation accounts for growth (a quantitative change); together they account for intellectual adaptation and the development of intellectual structures. (p. 16)

Equilibration. Both assimilation and accommodation are necessary for cognitive growth and development, but of equal importance are the "relative amounts of assimilation and accommodation that take place" (Wadsworth, 1971, p. 17). If individuals only assimilated and never accommodated, they would end up with a few large schemata and be unable to detect differences in objects or events. Reality would be represented in the mind as an undifferentiated whole. However, if individuals only accommodated and never assimilated, they would become bogged down in minute differences among schemata that would have little generality. Such persons would have difficulty detecting overarching similarities or seeing relationships between or among things. For this reason, Piaget maintained that the balance between the two is as important as the processes themselves. He referred to this balance by the term *equilibration*. Equilibration, or equilibrium, can be viewed as a state of cognitive balance that is seen as a necessary condition toward which the organism constantly strives.

It is important to recognize that Piaget was concerned primarily with describing the structure of intelligence. He was opposed to the idea that "intelligence is an 'amount' that can be measured." Rather, he assumed that it is "a structure which must be described and whose functioning must be understood" (Gruber & Voneche, 1981, p. xxxvi). These assumptions about intelligence stand in marked contrast to the notions used to guide the construction of typical intelligence tests, which tend to provide the learner with a presumably representative sample of cognitive content on the assumption that more intelligent individuals will have amassed more content than a person of lesser ability. Students who recognize the content or problem can be said to possess a designated amount of intelligence. By contrast, Piaget focused on the development of cognitive structures themselves as the means for assessing cognitive abilities.

Action in cognitive development. In Piaget's view, cognitive development is not a passive process but proceeds as a result of actions put forth by the learner. As Gruber and Voneche (1981) express the matter,

> [I]t is not through direct observation that cognitive structures develop, but through the actions we carry out upon our perceptions, not so much the actions of the body but those of the mind, mental operations, that we come to know the world. (p. xxi)

Through such actions we develop our knowledge of the world. Of greater importance is that we also develop a mastery of these cognitive operations. One can visualize an infant grasping a rattle and repeatedly shaking it to hear its sound. Grasping in this sense is a physical action, one guided by the individual's mental operations as well. Such actions are necessary for cognitive development, although with increasing maturity the operations become less reliant on physical action and more reliant on the cognitive structures already formed. Moreover, the process is continuous throughout the life of the individual. We have no enduring knowledge without actively maintaining this process (Gruber & Voneche, 1981).

Stages in Piaget's Theory

Piaget divided intellectual development into four broad periods or stages. These include *sensimotor intelligence* (0–2 years), *preoperational thought* (2–7 years), *concrete operations* (7–11 years), and *formal operations* (11–15 years). He did not claim that children move from one discrete stage to another, but suggested that stages are nevertheless useful to the observer intent upon conceptualizing the developmental process. Stages enable one to divide a long period of development into periods of shorter duration, and to direct attention to the key features undergoing development at a particular time in the life of the individual. Although stages were important devices for Piaget, he also insisted on the continuity of development over its entire course.

Parsons's Stages of Artistic Development

As noted earlier, the development of understandings in the realm of the arts, or the development of artistic skills, was conspicuously absent from Piaget's work. Other investigators working generally within a Piagetian framework have begun to fill this gap by observing the changes in individuals' responses to works of art from a cognitive developmental standpoint. Studies by Dennie Wolf (1987) and Howard Gardner (1973) have explored the characteristics of early symbolization within various artistic media.

Michael Parsons (1987) investigated the stages of aesthetic understanding that individuals undergo as they encounter works of art. Parsons views stages as "clusters of ideas" rather than "properties of persons." These clusters are patterns, or internally related assumptions, that tend to go together in people's minds by virtue of some internal or logical relationship. "To describe a stage is not to describe a person but a set of ideas. If people were consistent in thinking about paintings they would use a consistent set of ideas to interpret them" (Parsons, 1987, p. 11). And if so, they could be described as being at a particular stage of cognitive development. Stages are "analytic devices" that help us understand the learner.

By describing a stage as a cluster of ideas rather than a set of properties, Parsons assumes that certain ideas are likely to go together with other ideas and that these clusters are very likely learned together, accounting for their consistency. Moreover, these ideas tend largely to parallel the history and structure of aesthetic concepts as they have evolved in art history, art criticism, and aesthetics. In describing his project, Parsons (1987) says:

> I have tried to see art as different from science, morality, religion, as a part of the human mind distinguished by its own characteristic concepts and concerns. That is why, after all, it has its own developmental history. (pp. 12–13)

Parsons was as much influenced by artists and philosophers of art as by psychologists, and the focus of his analysis was on concepts that ordinarily are used when individuals talk about art, such as beauty or expressiveness. This suggests that developmental stages will, to some extent, recapitulate the history of ideas within the philosophy of art. The mimetic ideal of beauty, which developed early in the history of aesthetic philosophy, will most likely become available to the individual before formalist theories, which arose in the modern era. Parsons does not make this claim, although he does find that children at certain stages will more readily accept and apply certain social norms concerning what is deemed beautiful. For example, a typical 10-year-old will explain that a work of art is good when it imitates beautiful things, and bad when ugly things are pictured, values that reflect the mimetic ideal. At an earlier stage, knowledge of such values is lacking, while at a later stage, such values may be known to the observer but not deemed relevant. Table 2.1 summarizes Parsons's five stages, provides examples of verbal statements characteristic of each stage, and describes the psychological factors that operate at each stage of development.

Table 2.1. Parsons's Developmental Stages for Understanding Art

Stage	Verbal Indicators	Psychological Attributes
1. Favoritism (age 5): Little awareness of others' viewpoints; pictures as pleasant stimuli; liking is judging; concepts of good or bad art lacking	"It's my favorite color." "I like it because of the dog." "It looks like a big pickle coming down from the sky." "They're all mostly good."	Pleasure is the organizing principle.
2. Beauty and realism (age 10): Good and bad art differentiated on the basis of pictorial content	"It's gross! It's really ugly." "You expect something beautiful like a lady in a boat or two deer in the mountains." "It looks just like the real thing."	Representation becomes the operative idea. Attractive subject matter and realistic representation are objective grounds for judgments.
3. Expressiveness (adolescence): Organized around the concepts of expressiveness and empathy; rests on a new awareness of the interiority of another's experience	"You can see that the artist really felt sorry for her." "Distortion really brings out the feeling." "We all experience it differently."	Intensity and interest assure us that the experience expressed is genuine. Skill or beauty of subject matter is secondary.
4. Style and form (young adults): Perspective of a stylistic tradition becomes important	"See the grief in the tension in the lines, the pulling on the handkerchief!" "He's playing with the eyes. They are more like cups or boats; it's a visual metaphor."	Significance of the artwork is social rather than an individual achievement. Works exist within a tradition.
5. Autonomy (professionally trained adults): Questions the critical consensus that may have formed around particular works, schools, or artistic values	"In the end, the style is too loose, too self-indulgent. I want to see more self-control." "I used to think it too rhetorical; now I vibrate to it again."	One may call into question the concepts and values constructed within a scholarly tradition, and may affirm or amend accepted views in the light of one's understanding.

Although Parsons does not describe the changes in aesthetic development using the assimilation–accommodation terminology of Piaget, we could fit his observations within that paradigm. The first stage is almost lacking any form of differentiation, not even between good and bad art. However, by the time individuals reach the age of 9 or 10, they have developed very specific ideas of what is good or bad art, ideas linked to the imitation of good or bad people or things. A difference in cognitive structure thus has developed to accommodate these judgments. At stage three, which usually coincides with adolescence, it becomes possible to differentiate the expressive ideas of individual artists independent of the depiction of subject matter, while at stage four it becomes possible to differentiate further by distinguishing artists within the same artistic tradition in terms of their stylistic differences. Finally, at stage five, one can observe that art critics and historians often challenge and reappraise the collective judgments of particular works or art movements in the light of changing social values. Consider, for example, the scholarly attention given to women artists of past generations, works subjected to neglect by critics and art historians, works relegated to lesser status solely on the grounds that they were done by women. Were it not for individuals who were able and willing to question the collective judgment of their professional peers, such judgments would never have been challenged. Of course, one might argue that few people ever reach this stage of understanding, but this might be said of Piaget's stage of formal operations as well.

SOCIOCULTURAL COGNITION: THE VYGOTSKIAN PERSPECTIVE

Piaget located the mind in the brain of a lone individual. He described development as a process affecting the individual and involving interaction with the environment, including the social environment. Cognitive development is the result of a set of internal processes like assimilation and accommodation through which individuals construct increasingly more reliable representations of the outside world. As these representations become more adequate in explaining and predicting events in the environment, such cognitive structures can be said to have undergone a qualitative developmental change, increasing the individuals' competence to understand and adapt to the environment. These changes have been described as stages, and the process by which this occurs, learning.

From the standpoint of the individual's cognitive development, this explanation might seem sufficiently adequate, although it does not take into account the fact that much if not most learning is the result of the individual's interactions with others. It also imposes a dualism between the actions taking place in the individual's mind and those in the environment outside that the learner attempts to understand. The next chapter discusses the philosophical consequences of dualistic conceptions of knowledge for educational practice in more detail, but, in brief, these dualisms have the effect of separating knowing from doing, or of holding structures of knowledge apart from the social context where they were created. Such separations limit the learner's possibilities to create meaning.

However, an alternative view of development was proposed by the Russian psychologist Lev Vygotsky, whose career paralleled Piaget's. Piaget, as noted earlier, was influenced by positivist assumptions that influenced psychology and the sciences as a whole. Vygotsky, by contrast, was influenced by Marxist principles and was intent upon devising a sociohistorical psychology to serve as the foundation of a new society grounded in socialist principles, namely, the former Soviet Union. Vygotsky was born in 1896, the same year as Piaget, and would have witnessed the Russian Revolution of 1917. Unlike Piaget, his life was tragically short; he died at the age of 37 of tuberculosis. In the time given to him, he produced over 180 works, including several books (Blanck, 1990; Moll, 1990). His book *Thought and Language* was published in 1934. Two years after its initial publication, it was suppressed by the Soviet authorities and remained suppressed for more than 20 years, not making a reappearance until 1956. English translations did not become available until 1962. For these reasons, Vygotsky's psychological concepts were relatively unknown outside of the former Soviet Union.

Guillermo Blanck summarizes the major features of Vygotskian psychology that are relevant for education. Vygotsky believed that mental activity is uniquely human, that it arises as the result of social learning, through the acquisition of social signs derived mainly from language learning but also through the internalization of culture and of social relationships. What enables human beings to develop is not just their "superior nervous activity," which distinguishes them from animals, but also that this "nervous activity" carries social meanings derived from the cultural activity of human beings. Children acquire social learning in their activities with adults, who serve as "conveyers of social experience" (Blanck, 1990, p. 44).

Vygotsky's Concept of Mediation

Vygotskian psychology is "an instrumental, cultural and historical psychology" (Blanck, 1990, p. 45). Vygotsky adapted Friederich Engels's concept of tool use as the means by which human beings change their natural environment to bring it under their control, and, by so doing, *transform* themselves. This concept of mediation, as described by Cole and Scribner (1978), places emphasis on tool use as a specific human activity, an act that transforms the human being in relation to nature. Whereas the animal merely uses external nature, humans, by contrast, make it serve their ends and, with its mastery, succeed in distinguishing themselves from animals. Cole and Scribner also observe that Vygotsky applied his concept of mediation to include the use of signs. That is, when sign systems like language, writing, number systems, and artworks are internalized, they result in behavioral transformations that form a bridge between the early and later forms of development. Thus, for Vygotsky, "in the tradition of Marx and Engels, the mechanism of individual developmental change is rooted in society and culture" (Cole & Scribner, 1978, p. 7).

Signs, instruments, and tools. Vygotsky uses the terms *instruments* and *tools* to refer to ways that humans acquire knowledge that mediates their higher mental processes by modifying the stimuli they encounter, using them to both control surrounding conditions and regulate their own behavior. Vygotsky's concept of mediation anticipated by several decades the concept of *metacognition* of the 1970s and 1980s, while his notion of instruments and tools anticipates notions of *strategic or procedural knowledge* common in discussions of cognitive processes. According to Blanck, Vygotsky tried to establish how people, with the help of instruments and signs, direct their attention and organize conscious memorization to regulate their conduct. "Tools are oriented outward, toward the transformation of the physical and social reality. Signs are oriented inward toward the self-regulation of conduct itself" (Blanck, 1990, p. 45). The human social world is made up of signs. Thus, conduct "is determined not by objects themselves but by the signs attached to objects. We attach meanings to the objects that surround us and act according to those meanings" (p. 45). It was Vygotsky's view that with the internalization of such signs, consciousness itself is restructured. Thus, language becomes one of the key tools for the organization of thinking:

> Vygotsky mentioned the following as "examples of psychological tools and their complex systems: language; various systems for counting; mnemonic techniques; algebraic symbol systems, works of art; writing schemes; diagrams; maps and mechanical drawings; all kinds of conventional signs." (Blanck, 1990, pp. 45–46)

Development in Vygotskian theory. Vygotsky divided the study of development into two phases. The first is characterized by the use of lower-order mental processes, elementary attention, perception, and memory, to interact with adults as they are being socialized into the surrounding culture, including language and customs. The second stage is characterized by the use of higher mental processes acquired through the acquisition of the tools of the culture. Vygotsky did not believe that the lower processes evolved into the higher ones, but rather that they enabled one to acquire the higher processes through cultural learning. He also did not believe that the higher processes could be reduced to the inferior ones, "but that in meeting culture the natural line of development is restructured and reorganized" (Blanck, 1990, p. 46).

Internalization. The process by which higher functions are acquired is "internalization." For Vygotsky, "any higher mental function necessarily goes through an external stage in its development because it is initially encountered in a social activity or function" (Vygotsky, cited in Wertsch, 1985, p. 62). Gallimore and Tharp (1990) refer to Vygotsky's idea that "a child's development cannot be understood by a study of the individual" (p. 176). From his point of view, "cognitive and linguistic skill appears twice, or in two planes. First it appears on the social plane and then on the psychological plane" (p. 176). Blanck (1990) also comments on the significance of this idea:

> This conception implies that culture is not simply an entity independent of individuals with which they must transact. . . . *Humans are internalized culture.* Culture, the accumulation of humankind's historical legacy outside the boundaries of the organism, is interiorized as mental activity, thus becoming internal to the organism. (p. 47; emphasis added)

From the foregoing it is clear that Vygotsky's position regarding the social environment differs from Piaget's. For Piaget, the social environment was seen as a set of external influences or factors with which the individual interacted, affecting the development of that individual. In the course of cognitive development, individuals construct representations of the social environment, which take the form of personal constructions or schemata. For Vygotsky, higher forms of mental life begin *only when cultural influences are internalized!* In particular, it is language acquisition that makes conscious mental life possible. For Piaget, cultural influences may inform the content of one's mental life but they do not necessarily provide the forms of thought. The forms, what Piaget calls "operations," are determined by the individual's biogenetic development, not by the assimilation of content. As the brain grows, abstract forms of thought become possible. For Vygotsky, culture determines both form and content.

Vygotsky's zone of proximal development. Probably the most widespread of Vygotsky's educational ideas is the concept known as the zone of proximal development. According to Bruner (1985), this has to do with the ways that educators "arrange the environment to enable the child to reach a higher or more abstract ground from which to reflect, ground on which he is enabled to be more conscious" (p. 23). The zone is defined by Vygotsky as

> the distance between the actual developmental level as determined by independent problem solving and the level of potential development as determined through problem solving under adult guidance, or in collaboration with more capable peers. (Bruner, 1985, p. 24; emphasis in original)

Bruner explains the significance of the zone by contrasting it with the learning paradigms provided by behaviorism or with the Piagetian view itself, both of which depict the learner as "a lone organism pitted against nature" making repeated efforts at comprehension through essentially solitary efforts. By contrast, Vygotsky emphasized the extent to which learning is, in Bruner's phrase, "quintessentially assisted." In effect, the adult or more competent peer

> serves the learner as a vicarious form of consciousness until such time as the learner is able to master his own action through his own consciousness and control. . . . [T]he tutor in effect performs the critical function of "scaffolding" the learning task to make it possible for the child, in Vygotsky's word to internalize external knowledge and convert it into a tool for conscious control. (Bruner, 1985, pp. 24–25)

Sheldon White extends the concept of the zone of proximal development beyond the notion of scaffolding:

> The zone of proximal development is something more than the social support that some today call scaffolding; it is not just a set of devices used by one person to support high-level activity by another. The ZPD is the locus of social negotiations about meanings, and it is, in the context of schools, a place where teachers and pupils may appropriate one another's understandings. (White, 1989, p. xii)

White exemplifies such negotiations by describing an instructor's response to a student's question. The question doesn't make sense and seems obviously shallow and uncomprehending. In White's words, "Classroom discussion is a fragile flower," and "'Dumb' questions test an instructor's mind and intentions. Students watch to see how the instructor will respond, and the instructor knows they do" (p. xi). The instructor is torn between giving the question the weight it deserves, or cutting the questioner down. Instead he probes, leading the student into discussion, trying to move from the student's original question toward questions that are more worthy of discussion, more answerable, or both:

> Sometimes the instructor and the questioner find a reasonable question that can be addressed and answered with dignity and intellectual profit on both sides. . . . For a few moments the instructor has established what Vygotsky calls a zone of proximal development and what Newman, Griffin, and Cole call the construction zone. (White, 1989, p. xi)

The zone of proximal development is thus a social space. Learning and development are socially embedded, unlike for Piaget, who stressed the importance of biological maturity as a precondition for development. Vygotsky maintained that pedagogy creates learning processes that *lead* development:

> *Instruction is good only when it proceeds ahead of development. Then it awakens and rouses to life an entire set of functions which are in the stage of maturing, which lie in the zone of proximal development.* (Vygotsky, quoted in Wertsch, 1985, p. 71; emphasis in original)

Actual developmental level is that which learners would achieve by themselves, without external influence. The gap between the unassisted level of achievement and that achieved by children when given assistance thus becomes the zone of proximal development. Most, if not all, social learning has the effect of opening up zones of proximal development, whether it is the maternal prompting of infants in the toddler stage of development, the prompting of athletes by coaches, the teaching of apprentices, or the formal education provided by schools and universities.

Play and imagination. Vygotsky felt that school learning was fundamentally important to the child's intellectual development because it is the one social agency that intentionally opens up zones of proximal development, but he also discussed the role of play in development. The play of children often portrays the roles they will carry out as adults. It features developmental tendencies in a condensed form. In play children explore the roles of adults in common daily experiences. Thus they begin a process of rehearsal. They pretend to be parents, teachers, doctors, nurses, police personnel, or athletes, and because they are *only* playing, they are free to risk doing things they are not yet confident to do in real life. The Goodmans advance the notion that "in play children learn to understand the meanings of the world as they play with their representations of the world. They build concepts of mathematics and science as well as language, including literacy" (Goodman & Goodman, 1990, pp. 227–228).

Recent Applications of Vygotskian Principles

Vygotskian conceptions of learning and development have lain dormant for several generations, for reasons cited earlier. As Vygotsky's ideas became more widespread in the 1970s and 1980s, they began having an impact on educational research. One researcher who has been prominent in adapting Vygotskian ideas to educational situations is Jean Lave, who made detailed studies of the everyday cognition of "just plain folks," for example, apprentice tailors in Liberia and groups of dieters in weight-loss programs. Her work emphasized learning as it occurs in everyday situations in contrast to learning in formal schooling situations, where what is learned is experienced as being separate from how it is learned (Lave, 1977, 1988; Rogoff & Lave, 1984). Brown, Collins, and Duguid (1989) introduced what they term "the situated nature of cognition" as distinguished from the decontextualized learning often found in everyday schooling practices:

> Many methods of didactic education assume a separation between knowing and doing, treating knowledge as an integral, self-sufficient substance, theoretically independent of the situations in which it is learned and used. . . . It may be more useful to consider conceptual knowledge as, in some ways, similar to a set of tools. Tools share several features with knowledge: They can be fully understood through use, and using them entails both changing the user's view of the world and adopting the belief system of the culture in which they are used. (Brown et al., 1989, p. 33)

These recent studies of everyday cognition can be seen as embodying several facets of Vygotsky's sociohistorical psychology:

- Learning occurs in a social context, and knowledge and development are largely dependent on the social context in which these processes occur.
- When educational environments open zones of proximal development, there is mediation between the thought of two or more people, the shared perspectives of teacher and pupil.
- Language is seen as a tool created by the human species to enable developmental transformation to occur through the acquisition of culture.
- Learning is generally a form of enculturation, with knowledge conceived both as the acquisition of tools and mastery of their use.

Vygotskian Implications for Art Education

Vygotsky's ideas took shape in the 1920s and 1930s, almost exactly the same decades when the notion of creative self-expression arose in the circles of progressive educators in the United States. Then, teaching was structured around an idea of freedom, specifically freedom *from* adult intervention, which was regarded as "interference" in the genetic unfolding of the child's natural creative endowment. While Vygotsky did not refer to art education in particular, he did refer to the "botanical metaphor" in education, where the growth of the child was likened to the growth of a plant and where the teacher was the gardener. The nineteenth-century term *kindergarten*, or garden of children, is evidence of its pervasiveness in education.

It is clear that the understanding of growth and development possessed by many progressive educators was guided by this botanical metaphor, particularly those involved with teaching the arts. For them the child was born with a set of latent abilities that, if permitted to develop, would result in the flowering of the child's creative potentialities.[12] They likened the role of progressive teachers to that of the gardener providing benign nurturance, who sought to weed out such misguided social influences as rote learning, copying, pattern work, paint by numbers kits, and coloring books. Art teachers battled vainly against such pernicious influences, and generally lost the battle to free the child from their impact. Moreover, any form of social influence was deemed potentially harmful.[13]

From a Vygotskian perspective, children in these progressive schools were left at the stage of their "actual" development. What they achieved was limited to what could be done without assistance, and they were never challenged to extend their capabilities. Adult influence was limited to a shielding from social influences. It was too passive to open up zones of proximal development. There would never be a gap between the unassisted level of achievement and that which could be achieved with the help and guidance of parents and teachers. Not only were art teachers doomed to lose the battle against what they deemed to be misguided adult interference, but they also lost the child in the process, for without constructive guidance the child's interest in working in art media almost universally withered away.

In fact, Lowenfeld (1952) described a study of elementary schoolchildren who were asked to draw a picture depicting playing tag in the school yard. Ninety-five percent of them willingly participated, while only 35% of a sample of college students voluntarily participated in the same task. Lowenfeld ascribed this to a waning of interest, the result of a crisis of confidence where the individual's critical awareness of his or her limited capabilities discouraged further participation in art making. A Vygotskian educator would have anticipated this crisis in confidence and would have offered appropriate assistance to enable students to reach mastery. Teachers would have provided a critical support structure, or scaffolding, in the form of prompts or suggestions.

DIFFICULTIES WITH PIAGETIAN AND VYGOTSKIAN THEORIES OF COGNITIVE DEVELOPMENT

Problems with the Piagetian Conception of Development

Developmental theory, as conceived by Piaget, was instrumental in defining human intelligence in ways that privilege specific academic subjects employing rational, or formal, methods of thinking, such as mathematics and science. As noted earlier, Piaget ascribed lesser importance to subjects like art and music, which involve affect. Affect was seen by him as the energetics of the behavior pattern, whereas the cognitive aspect was concerned with the structure of the pattern. The evolution of cognitive structures was the principal object of his research.

The feminist critique. Indeed, the separation of emotion from intellect was seen by Piaget as a necessary step in the progress of the mind moving toward the stage of formal operations. This view was challenged in feminist theory, which has argued for the inseparability of rationality and emotion (see Belenky, Clinchy, Goldberger, & Tarule, 1986). In the view of these feminist theoreticians, the rational was misequated with the masculine and thus was privileged as the only proper path for cognitive development. Accordingly, there are deeply rooted assumptions at work in Western culture denigrating the cognitive status of the arts, since they lie in the realm of feelings and emotions. And it is clear that these assumptions also operate within the cognitive developmental theories of Piaget.

The Marxist critique. The social criticism of Piaget's work rests on the Marxist assumption that theories like Piaget's were themselves specific sociohistorical constructions grounded in a specific set of assumptions about the mind. For example, Susan Buck-Morss (1975) reviewed such Marxist scholars as Georg Lukacs, who claimed that abstract formal cognition "was the particular logical structure of Western capitalism in its present industrial stage, that it characterized both the socio-economic mode of production of the mode of consciousness" (p. 37).[14] This attacks the notion that formal structures of thought, as posited by Piaget, can claim universality on the grounds that they are content-free abstractions resulting from the mind's activity, free of social influence. Indeed, Lukacs uses Marx's view that any theory is likely to be bounded by its social location and time in history. Theories of cognitive development of necessity would be subject to this rule:

> What Lukacs tried to demonstrate was that there was a structural identity between mind and society and that the logical structure of abstract formalism, far from universal, is itself the product of history, that the *form of cognition is itself social content.* (Buck-Morss, 1975, p. 37; emphasis in original)

Gardner's critique of Piaget. Since the early 1970s, the developmental psychologist Howard Gardner has actively investigated cognitive development as seen in learning the arts. He took exception to Piaget's view that the formal operations stage is the universal end point of human intellectual capacities, suggesting that there are additional end points in human development worthy of study. Artistic development was chosen in his own work specifically because it intertwined cognitive and affective elements, as opposed to competence in logical-scientific thinking alone (Gardner, 1973).[15] A decade later he published his theory of multiple intelligences (Gardner, 1983), which promoted the view that there are seven discernible forms of intelligence. In taking this position, he took issue with Piaget's belief that logical-scientific thinking stood above other manifestations of intelligence.

Criticism of the Vygotskian Position on Development

Vygotskian notions remedy certain drawbacks of Piagetian developmental theory, namely, its tendency to legitimate formal operations as the highest form of intellectual attainment. Yet the sociohistorical developmental perspective also has its problems. In its favor is the recognition that most of what individuals learn is through various forms of social mediation. Individuals are born into specific cultural situations and acquire the accumulated knowledge structures of their culture. The significance of this point for art is underscored by Ernst Kris who, in writing about art history, observed that "we have long come to realize that art is not produced in an empty space, that no artist is independent of predecessors and models, that he no less than the scientist and the philosopher is part of a specific tradition and works in a structured area of problems" (quoted in Gombrich, 1960, p. 30).

The knowledge of art available to novice artists does not come from nature but from the social world of art itself. Moreover, the artist is a member of a culture and works within the artistic conventions of that culture. The novice does not have to reinvent the paintbrush, but is able to acquire the cultural knowledge and understandings relevant to his or her situation. What Vygotsky has suggested is that the learner acquires complex cognitive structures situated in the culture, through interaction with knowledgeable adults or peers, enabling him or her to understand or do things that he or she could not understand or do without this assistance. This does seem to describe most situations where knowledge, as it is known within the culture, is internalized by the novice through enculturation.

However, this does not explain how new knowledge is constructed, that is, how knowledge presently lacking in the culture is produced or created. Vygotsky's theory of cognition explains how existing knowledge gets internalized, but what enables individuals to construct the not yet known, where imagination and intuition enable individuals to go, in Bruner's (1973) phrase, "beyond the information given"? This is a crucial question in learning the arts because without it we encounter difficulties in accounting for the appearance of new developments in art. Vygotskian theory can account for new knowledge using the existing tools of the culture, but it does not account for the creation of new tools.

Piaget and Vygotsky Compared

Piaget recognized the explanation of creativity to be a problem with his psychology as well. While he explained the continuous modification of cognitive structures through assimilation and accommodation, the problem was that these processes provide symbolic representations of an actual world, that is, what is understood as the real world. But what about worlds that might be, worlds that don't exist but that might be possible? The existence of "possibilities" raised an interesting epistemological question because "possibilities are in fact not observable, resulting as they do from subjects' active constructions." Moreover, he suggested that "we are thus dealing with a creative process very different from the simple reading of reality invoked by empiricism" (Piaget, 1987, p. 3).

For Piaget, possibility in cognition meant essentially invention and creation, and this was an important feature of his constructivism (Piaget, 1987). Thus, Piaget's and Vygotsky's theories differ in their account of the human capacity to create higher forms of knowledge, especially those that involve imagination. Table 2.2 summarizes the differences between the developmental approaches of Piaget and those of Vygotsky.

Table 2.2. Differences Between Piagetian and Vygotskian Conceptions of Cognitive Development

	Piaget	Vygotsky
Developmental end point	Progress toward logical-scientific thinking	Progress in sociocultural learning toward culturally appropriate practices
Nature of mind	The mind is in the brain, an organization of inner structures called schemata or symbols.	Mind and consciousness are made possible by the acquisition of the tools of the culture, especially language.
Key concepts	Assimilation Accommodation Equilibration	Mediation Internalization Tools and signs
Stages of development	Sensimotor Preoperational Concrete operations Formal operations	Lower-order mental processes: elementary attention, perception, memory Higher-order mental processes: internalization, enculturation
Implications	Logical-scientific thinking is favored over affect. Overcoming feelings is seen as progress toward greater objectivity and rationality. Symbol processing invites dualism, separating learners from the situation where learning occurs. Instruction focuses on the mental operations of the learner as a lone individual.	Learning is bound to its social context. Education involves mediation between two or more people. Tools (e.g., language and pictures) foster development. Learning is enculturation. Instruction focuses on the cultural practices of the learner.

THEORIES OF DEVELOPMENT IN CHILDREN'S DRAWINGS

Precognitive Theories

From the time of the child study movement of the 1880s, a number of writers have described the evolution of children's drawings as a process passing through discrete stages (Eng, 1931/1954; Kershensteiner, 1905; Luquet, 1913; Sully, 1890; Viola, 1946). However, the stage theories that have been most influential in North American art education were drawn from the psychoanalytical traditions of Sigmund Freud and Karl Jung.

Herbert Read's *Education Through Art* (1945) and Viktor Lowenfeld's *Creative and Mental Growth* (1952) each offer descriptions of these stages, although they vary from each other. Nevertheless, they were frequently the focus of concern in the professional preparation of art teachers, especially during the post-World War II era. Read's and Lowenfeld's accounts stressed the emotional factors that unfold as children begin to develop their concepts of self and others. Their common emphasis was on the emotional growth of the individual as fostered by expressive artistic activities. Both tended to view the child's graphic expression to be the result of the mind's own activity. Their descriptions of children's art differed from each other in that Read was especially interested in classifying children's drawings in stylistic groupings defined in terms of such Jungian categories as introversion and extroversion, equating these differences with the major styles of modern art that emerged in the first 3 decades of the twentieth century. Lowenfeld, by contrast, emphasized developmental differences between stages, and deferred the discussion of stylistic differences to the onset of adolescence. Then he identified two expressive styles, which he called *visual* and *haptic*.[16]

Although influenced by psychoanalytical views of learning and development, Lowenfeld did recognize intellectual development in the evolution of children's graphic expression. For example, he counted as major intellectual attainments the evolution of pictorial space concepts such as the base-line system of pictorial organization, and the creation of the illusion of depth through overlapping. He also referred to the development of specific schema, or form-concepts, as being the result of a process of experimentation, which gradually enabled children to extend their powers of expression. However, Lowenfeld's definition of schema was not tied to Piaget's notion, that is, an abstract structure assembled or constructed of information from multiple cases. Rather, Lowenfeld's use of the term was a reference to a specific procedure or approach used for the production of a particular image such as the human figure, houses, or flowers. These appeared during the stage of development that generally coincides with the primary grades of schooling (ages 7 to 9), later to be succeeded by stages that move the child's art increasingly toward realism.

Not only did Lowenfeld identify various developmental stages in drawing ability, but his text also provided guidance to teachers based on these selfsame characteristics. While Lowenfeld's account of development can be described as an age-based stage theory, it is important *not* to equate his work with Piaget's, despite their reliance on stages to account for advances in development. Lowenfeld took the emotional aspect of development far more seriously than Piaget, whose inquiries were focused on the operations entailed in cognition, that is, logical-scientific thinking. Since Lowenfeld's views antedate the cognitive revolution, the term *pre-*

cognitive might be an appropriate way to characterize his views. This designation is also useful to heighten the contrast between Lowenfeld and Rudolf Arnheim, whose work is discussed next. Arnheim's views on children's artistic development stand closer to Piaget's in that graphic development is seen primarily as a cognitive process. Indeed, for many years Arnheim was virtually the only individual making the case for the cognitive nature of art.

Drawing as Visual Problem Solving

Rudolf Arnheim has argued quite vigorously that perception is a cognitive endeavor, that "visual perception is visual thinking and art making is a kind of visual problem solving" (Parsons, 1998, p. 81). He was an early proponent of the idea that the arts are cognitive in character, at a time when the prevalent psychology of education was behaviorism and psychological explanations of art were built on psychoanalytical views of the subconscious.

According to Parsons, Arnheim had devised two tremendously influential arguments to support the view that artistry involves cognition. The first is that sensory perception is already cognitive in that it requires the perceiver to select, generalize, and abstract aspects of the objects received by the mind. Acts of selection become the essence of perception, and this is obviously mental activity and not merely the passive reception of sensory stimuli: "It is constructive knowing, not passive reception. Cognitive powers come into play, then, not after perception has occurred but at its beginning" (Parsons, 1998, p. 81).

Arnheim's second argument is based on the idea that the representation of objects also requires the ability to think within the means provided by a given medium. In making a drawing or a painting, the artist or child does more than reproduce an image from nature; he or she also has to construct a structural equivalent of forms on a two-dimensional surface that represents the three-dimensional world of nature. For example, a circle, which is two-dimensional, may be used to represent the three-dimensionality of the head. As Parsons (1998) puts it:

> It is as if each medium sets a puzzle for the artist or the child: how to create an image in the particular terms of the medium which will yet be taken as representing some aspect of reality. The artist is therefore a problem-solver. (p. 81)

Having made the case for the cognitive nature of the visual arts, Arnheim also maintained that visual thinking is a self-sufficient means for

understanding works of art. In his view, the beholder does not need para-
graphs of text to explain the cultural symbolism in the work. The meaning
can and should be read in the form. Moreover, written or spoken accounts
of the work can in no way substitute for the encounter with the work on its
own terms. The power of Arnheim's ideas, in Parsons's (1998) view, "rested
on the fact that [they fitted] so well into the assumptions of the artworld of
[their] time, that is, with the assumptions of modern art" (p. 81).

Arnheim (1954) observed that the first geometric shape that children
can draw successfully is the circle, and that following the circle they tend
to organize pictorial elements in terms of right-angle relationships. In drawing the human figure, children will place arms and legs either vertically
or horizontally from a central shape, usually a circle. This vertical–horizontal method of organization greatly expands the pictorial options made
available by the circle alone. These simple devices used in combination
enable the child to form images of objects such as people and animals. The
images themselves are not copies of nature but structural equivalents that
represent objects in nature within the limits imposed by the medium.
Somewhat later the child becomes dissatisfied with the expressive possibilities of the vertical–horizontal organization and makes use of oblique
lines and angles, which enable the depiction of bending limbs to differentiate people running from people standing still.

The question arises, why do children make these successive differentiations? Arnheim's (1954) first answer is his belief that the differentiation
impulse is not "motivated solely by the results of . . . formal experimentation . . . [that] children grope for higher stages of differentiation because they
are dissatisfied with the limitations of lower ones" (p. 150).

His second answer is that the differentiation of form is also the result
of the progressive mastery of the medium in which the expression is taking place. The child will draw the frontal view of the head of the human
figure because it is easier for most children to draw than the profile view.
Consequently, one may find drawings of figures showing the figure in
profile, while the head appears in the frontal position. Each medium imposes its own set of constraints upon the differentiation of form, and the
attempt to depict a three-dimensional figure like the human form with a
two-dimensional medium like pencil and paper presents the learner with
a difficult set of problems to be mastered.

Claire Golomb (1992) studied the problem of frontality in the figure drawings of children by making systematic comparisons of children's
graphic representations in a two- versus three-dimensional medium, that
is, drawing versus clay modeling. Most children using the latter medium
had little difficulty representing the third dimension. For example, a ball
of clay becomes the head of the person, which is structurally equivalent

to the circle that the child draws in making the figure with paper and pencil. On the other hand, the medium of clay imposes its own set of limitations. When children try to use clay to make the kind of lines that pencils make, they will experience difficulty. For example, clay has to be rolled out into thin rods to produce a close approximation of the lines that are possible with pencil or crayon.

According to Golomb (1992), Arnheim has been "the most articulate spokesman for a position that stresses the internal logic of representational development as a meaningful problem-solving mental activity," and his view of children's graphic development "embodies a universalist orientation to developmental phenomena and looks for general principles that cut across time and space" (p. 325), and that presumably transcend culture as well. She suggests that Arnheim's theory of graphic development is compatible with Noam Chomsky's linguistic theory, with its notion of a universal grammar.[17] Whether one learns to draw or to model in clay or to use words in daily speech, one is in each case learning to think in a symbolic medium. And although Golomb sees this aspect of Arnheim's work to be the source of its strength, it also becomes the basis for its vulnerability, as the formalist aesthetic assumptions that were prominent during the first half of the twentieth century recede into history. For example, Parsons suggests that Arnheim's "universalist implications and individualist views of learning sit uneasily with our awareness of the diversity and importance of cultures." In addition, Arnheim's aversion to the use of written explanations or critical discussions as potential resources for understanding works of art "fits poorly with our postmodern interest in meaning and context" (Parsons, 1998, p. 84).

My own view is that works of art are also social conventions that are somewhat arbitrary in character. The dragon in Chinese art and culture will mean something quite different from the dragon in Western art, and these differences are not limited to differences in arrangements of formal elements. The work and what it means are not wholly evident in the form nor can they be found in the organizing principles that guide visual perception. One grasps meaning in various ways, including the social context, often through verbal mediation—through teaching.

A Sociocultural Explanation of Drawing Development

The position taken by Brent and Margery Wilson (1982) is one that challenges key elements of Arnheim's views and also serves as an alternative to the Lowenfeld position discussed earlier. Unlike Lowenfeld, who saw the imitation of comic book characters as a destructive practice, Wilson and Wilson, for more than two decades, have studied the self-tutored drawings of children, which often feature such images. They claim that the graphic representations of children are efforts to mirror the social conventions provided by their culture. These are forms learned in a social context largely by imitation. In their view, children are concerned not with representing objects in the real world but with the production of the visual signs of the culture. Thus, it can be said that *art comes from art* and not from the effort to depict the images given in perception within the limits set by graphic media, as Arnheim characterized it. Children learn to make signs by observing others at work and by studying the graphic models available in the culture. The graphic language of art, like the verbal one, consists of artificial signs that are mere conventions. Wilson and Wilson reject the notion of "an autonomously guided development in the arts and view the imitation of existing models as the major vehicle for the acquisition of graphic skills" (Golomb, 1992, p. 326).

A second aspect of the Wilsons' work is their finding that drawing usually takes the form of visual narratives that are centered upon themes or issues raised by the problems children are likely to confront in their daily life. For example, it is not uncommon for children to draw superheroes, which may serve to compensate for their lack of independence and power, owing to their juvenile status. A recent example of this is revealed in a conference presentation by B. Wilson on the influences that Japanese comic books have on children growing up in Japan. According to Wilson (1999) these images deal with such themes as good and evil, conformity and rebellion, danger and opportunity, and the like. Since this comic book art is imitative in character, most Japanese art teachers deem such efforts unworthy of serious consideration, despite the seriousness of the thematic content touched upon by these efforts.

Wilson argued that "Japanese children who draw graphic narratives following models based on comic books called *manga* devise a more potent and influential form of art education than is found in textbooks based on the Japanese national curriculum." School art[18] as prescribed by the national curriculum will more likely focus on the development of such aesthetic considerations as good composition and color, avoiding the issues and themes raised by imagery appropriated by children into their own work from comic books.

Hence, the Wilsons raise important questions about the ultimate purpose of art education. If the official curriculum as perceived by the children has little or no relevance in their lives, what then is its ultimate purpose? And if these children find that they need to resort to the popular culture to find graphic tools suitable for communication to their peers, it should raise the further question of why the forms provided within the setting of formal education often fail to do this.

Multiple Repertoire Theories

For a number of years, observers commented on the fact that children's artistic development did not appear to follow the stage-like progression first described by early students of child art such as James Sully (1890) or Earl Barnes (1896–1897, 1902). In the postwar era, Lowenfeld's *Creative and Mental Growth* (1952) was probably the most widely used stage theory by art educators in North America. Herbert Read's (1945) account,[19] although contemporaneous with Lowenfeld's, differed in one important way in that it dealt with the presence of stylistic differences in children's art, differences that were relatively independent of developmental stages. As noted before, Lowenfeld did not discuss stylistic difference as a distinguishing factor in children's art until the onset of adolescence.

Read's discussion of stylistic differences might have been driven by an effort to justify modern art, by showing that such styles appear to arise spontaneously in children's art if it is unfettered by external social influences. Although it may not have been his intention, his work also underscores the point that stage theory never adequately explained the many differences in the graphic forms produced by children. Stage theory explained differences as the result of maturation, but when maturation is allowed to run its course, it is evident that different styles appear. Read attributed these stylistic differences to personality variables such as introversion or extroversion.

Most studies of the development of drawing have assumed that the achievement of pictorial realism was the end point toward which children's graphic development aimed. However, Dennie Wolf and Martha Perry (1988) have argued that "we might want to reconceive drawing development as yielding not one type of drawing, but a repertoire of visual languages, as well as the wit to know when to call on each" (p. 18). For example, children also devise mapping systems to represent on a two-dimensional surface the location of objects in three-dimensional space.

Similarly, Bernard Darras and Anna Kindler extend the typology of images made by children on different occasions for different purposes. They build upon Wolf and Perry's notion of "multiple repertoires" to explain that variations in image making will change depending on the expressive intent or purpose of the drawing, and even the setting in which it is made. Their model for the development of pictorial representation is one that regards it "as a semiotic process that occurs in an interactive social environment" and that results in what they call "pluri-media manifestations" (Kindler & Darras, 1998, p. 148).

In their view, children develop repertoires of graphic forms, and thus they question the tendency to characterize artistic development as a "unilinear phenomenon," as most stage theories do. In one instance they indicate that lines on a page may not be an effort to depict objects but to document actions like a car in motion, whereas in another instance the visual image is an icon that stands for an object. In proposing the idea that development can follow more than a single well-defined path, they also suggest that cultures tend to select certain aspects of the child's repertoire of graphic possibilities for fuller development, while other aspects are allowed to atrophy or remain dormant (Kindler & Darras, 1998). They also raise the question of whether it is possible that students narrow their drawing repertoires in response to perceived cultural preferences.

IMPLICATIONS FOR ART EDUCATION

For many years behaviorism was the dominant paradigm accounting for learning. Knowledge and skills were reduced to elementary units—bonds connecting specific stimuli to specific responses. From these fundamental building blocks complex understandings were thought to develop. Yet behaviorism never adequately explained the emergence of higher-order thinking abilities through the formation of such connections, nor did it explain the specific factors in stimuli that activate the arousal of feelings and emotions given play by works of art.[20]

Consequently, art educators have tended to combine psychological theories—using behaviorist theories to account for the acquisition of factual knowledge and skills, while psychoanalytical theories were used to account for feelings and emotions expressed through art making. Indeed, when Benjamin Bloom (1956) developed his taxonomy of instructional objectives for the *cognitive*,[21] *affective*, and *psychomotor* domains, he, in effect, reified this artificial separation. This served to classify certain subjects as cognitive or noncognitive, with the arts falling into the latter grouping.

The shift toward cognitive developmental theory did not necessarily improve the educational climate within which the arts had to operate in schools, especially during the latter decades of the twentieth century. As we saw, Piagetian theory also had its biases in tending to view logical-scientific thinking as the highest form of intelligence.

Other implications became apparent as raised by the sociocultural ideas of Vygotsky. His zone of proximal development construct contrasted sharply with practices of nonintervention or noninterference that operated for many decades in North American art education. I called attention to this developmental tradition because it has profoundly imposed a long-standing mind-set within the culture of practice in art education, where the best teaching is thought to be no teaching at all, and where artistic accomplishments are judged primarily for their therapeutic rather than their educative value. Such long-standing historical biases have made it difficult to recognize the study of art as a cognitive endeavor.

Vygotskian notions have at least three implications for learning in the arts. First, like all learning, the study of art should *not* be studied in isolation but seen in relation to its social context. This, in turn, raises the question of whose social context is given credence in instruction, the teacher's view of the culture or the student's? The existence of this question raises the idea that educational situations should be occasions where interpsychological mediation, or negotiation between two or more people, should occur. This happens when the instructor and the student interact to find a reasonable topic that can be addressed and answered with dignity and intellectual profit on both sides.

The second implication is the idea that language and other cultural symbols are tools that enable human development to advance, and that humanity is the species that makes culture through its use of symbols.

The third is that learning entails the internalization or enculturation of cultural knowledge, suggesting that the focus of instruction should be on the cultural practices operating in the learner's environment rather than on domains of knowledge per se.

The preceding section of the chapter compared differing theories accounting for the emergence of children's graphic development. It took issue with a prevalent tendency among art educators to divorce graphic development from overall cognitive development. Indeed, if we place in chronological sequence all the theories that have attempted to explain why children draw the way they do, a familiar pattern emerges, namely, the theories of drawing development tend to parallel the changing theories of cognitive development that emerged throughout the last half of the twentieth century. Lowenfeld's and Read's developmental accounts, being precognitive theories, were compatible with the assumptions of psychoanalytical theory. Arnheim's view found its counterpart in the cognitive developmental views of Piaget and Chomsky. Wolf's version of multiple repertoire theory reflects a symbol-systems orientation consistent with the research program of Harvard's Project Zero, which will be described in the next chapter. The Wilsons' view of drawing development has its counterpart in Vygotskian sociocultural conceptions, as does the multiple repertoires view of Kindler and Darras, in that the visual forms provided by the popular culture become tools enabling the young to come to terms with their society. I maintain that this set of parallels is not coincidental. The development of graphic potential is also a cognitive endeavor. As cognitive developmental theories became more inclusive, they should be able to account for the development of graphic ability as well, suggesting that graphic development is

Table 2.3. Theories of Children's Graphic Development

Theory	Aesthetic Orientation	Psychology Orientation	Cognitive Claim	End Point
Lowenfeld's stages of expression	Art is creative self-expression.	Freudian psychoanalytical view: personality and creativity as reflections of a repressed subconscious	Works of art are the result of the mind's own activity, the wellspring of creativity.	Development proceeds in stages, showing an increase in the capacity for visual realism.
Read's child art styles	Art is creative self-expression.	Jungian psychoanalytical view: artistic symbols as universal—expressions of a collective unconscious that transcends local cultures	Works of art express and communicate universal values.	Development moves toward different individual styles of art making.
Arnheim's differentiation of form	Art is significant form or formal order.	Gestalt psychology of perception as predecessor of cognitive developmental theory	Art is visual problem solving or thinking in a medium.	Development is based on the law of differentiation; i.e., formal organization becomes increasingly sophisticated.
Wolf's multiple repertoires	Each medium gives rise to a unique symbol system.	Symbol-processing view of cognition; development of multiple repertoires	Art making entails problem solving in various art media.	Development of multiple repertoires facilitates differing symbolic representations.
Wilson and Wilson's visual signs and narrative	Art is a form of cultural production.	Sociocultural view of cognition: knowledge as situated in the social context and learning as enculturation	Acquisition of cultural tools enables higher levels of consciousness.	Development is progress toward culturally mediated practices.
Kindler and Darras's semiotics of multiple repertoires	Art is a form of cultural production.	Sociocultural view of cognition: knowledge as situated in the social context and learning as enculturation	Acquisition of cultural tools enables higher levels of consciousness.	Development is progress toward multiple repertoires and avoidance of a narrowing of repertoires.

explained by cognitive development or, better yet, that it is evidence of such development!

Unfortunately, this correlation was neither studied nor voiced by researchers. While this pattern is not hard evidence, it does suggest that graphic or artistic development is accounted for by the development of cognition as a whole. Table 2.3 summarizes the key points in each theory of graphic development.

The chapter that follows looks at competing perspectives within cognitive theories of learning. First is the view of mind as a computational process that tends to liken mind and brain to the central processing unit of the computer and to equate thinking with symbol processing. The second perspective is a sociocultural or situated view of cognition, which says that knowledge becomes meaningful to the extent that it is linked to the social or cultural context or situation in which it arises. The third is an integrated view in which the individual creates his or her own particular understanding of reality, one that combines aspects of symbol processing and sociocultural views to form understandings of the world that are of the person's own making.

3

The Cognitive Revolution and Conceptions of Learning

WITH THE GROWING INFLUENCE of Piaget in the 1960s, learning and the mind itself began to be described as symbol-processing operations. Attention shifted from the *behavior* of the learner to *structures* of knowledge, to the idea that schemata, images, and concepts are symbolic entities created by the mind to represent reality, with learning itself portrayed as the accumulation of these structures.[1] Throughout the 1970s, a second trend developed that was an outgrowth of Vygotsky's view that learning is grounded in a social context, especially the idea that the higher levels of mind and consciousness are social in origin, that they are acquired through the mediational processes of socialization or enculturation—processes relying heavily on language.

Although Piagetian and Vygotskian perspectives were foundational for the cognitive revolution, an additional impetus was provided by Allen Newell and Herbert Simon's (1972) introduction of the computer analogy as a model and testing ground for such intellectual functions as problem solving and logical reasoning (Davis & Gardner, 1992; Gardner, 1987). The interdisciplinary movement known as *cognitive science* was one outcome of this development. There were also changes afoot within behaviorism proper, as notions of mediating or intervening variables began elaborating classical stimulus–response theory. The stimulus–response bond was no longer taken to be the whole story.

THREE COGNITIVE ORIENTATIONS

In what follows I trace the emergence of three cognitive orientations in learning. They are the *symbol-processing* and *sociocultural* perspectives, and the view that individuals construct their own views of reality. These traditions have their foundation in differing aspects of Piagetian and Vygotskian psychologies. What distinguishes them are differences in their epistemologies, and the research programs that gave rise to each theoretical perspective. The symbol-processing view rests on the assumption that there is an objective reality that exists independent of the knower, and that it is represented in symbols formed and manipulated by the mind, located in the head. Mind, itself, is the constructive activity that creates symbolic representations of the world and through which one comes to know the world.

When these symbolic structures become well organized, they are assumed to correspond to the various domains of knowledge, or disciplines. Symbol-processing views characterize themselves as constructivist theories because they represent structures of knowledge in symbolic form. Since computers also process symbols, the computer serves as an apt metaphor for the mind and its operations.

Sociocultural cognitive theories, by contrast, assume that reality is socially constructed, that it emerges in and through the communicative transactions individuals have with one another. The mind is thus *not* in the head, but emerges in the social interactions of individuals, and it is through these that knowledge of cultural norms and practices is both constructed and acquired. Sociocultural cognition also views knowledge as a constructive process. Knowledge as cultural content also consists of symbolic tools (language) that enable social interaction to take place. In addition, knowledge is likely to be organized around social purposes, for example, work and occupations, or around problems confronting society rather than by disciplines. Learning is a process of construction but it is also enculturation through which growing individuals become initiated into their society.

A third constructivist notion emphasizes the idea that reality is a construction of one's own making, that individuals construct their views of reality guided by their own knowledge-seeking purposes. Emphasis is placed on human agency where meaning making is guided by personal interest and effort. This assumption also tends to be embedded in the other two perspectives, and serves as the basis for what I will call an *integrated theory* of cognition, outlined at the close of this chapter.

Symbol-processing theories often tend to portray the learner as a lone individual whose interests and purposes guide his or her symbol-processing endeavors, whereas sociocultural theorists tend to use the anthropological metaphor of the learner undergoing an initiation process or apprenticeship to enter the culture of the community. Initially, the neophyte must rely on help and guidance provided by knowledgeable members of the culture. The integrated view of learning put forth at the conclusion of this chapter draws strength from these three perspectives, which are not pictured as rival viewpoints but as partial theories that place emphasis on differing aspects of learning. According to Douglas Kellner (1995), "A multiperspectival approach holds that the more theories that one has at one's disposal, the more tasks one can perform and the more specific objects and themes one can address. Further, the more perspectives that one brings to bear on a phenomenon, the better one's potential grasp or understanding of it could be" (p. 26).[2]

The view of mind to be advanced is thus a threefold one: First, mind is characterized as a *symbol-creating and processing function*, with the symbols themselves being created in the brain to represent knowledge or reality. Second, it is portrayed as a *sociocultural practice* among interacting individuals, and third, it is portrayed as *the meaning constructed from one's experience*. In turn, knowledge also can be viewed in a threefold way: first, as a symbolic structure in the mind; second, as the meanings and skills derived from social experiences and situations; and third, as a personal construction of one's own making.

As independent perspectives, each has its range of applicability from which educational practice can derive benefit. Each is not likely to be refuted by empirical evidence favoring it over its rivals. These are metaphorical representations of mind and knowledge. Their value lies in where and to what they direct attention within the learning process. As Carl Bereiter (1994) put the matter: "There is no basis for claiming that one view or another gives us an account of how things really are, and so we are free to choose or to mix-and-match in whatever way gains us an advantage in solving problems" (p. 21).[3] Admittedly, Bereiter was not satisfied with this picture of cognitive theory, for such eclecticism invariably invites contradiction. He also observed that *constructivism*[4] already assimilated the *sociocultural* perspective in the math and science disciplines, which can be taken as evidence that an eclectic approach is at least feasible in practice, if not wholly desirable in theory (Bereiter, 1994).

In what follows, each cognitive orientation is elaborated and critiqued, with common points of agreement emphasized and presented in summary form. Since educational systems pursue multiple purposes, it stands to reason that a given perspective will be more compatible with some domains than with others. Learning in mathematics will likely involve systems of numerical symbols and rules for their proper manipulation. Learning in this view is both the acquisition of a computational process and the formal logic that enables users to determine the truth or falsity of mathematical expressions. A view of mind as a symbol-processing entity is likely to be compatible with mathematical learning.

By contrast, learning in the visual arts utilizes abstract forms fashioned from lines and colors used in specific combinations, but these elements are an expressive compilation, which is not computational in character.[5] Yet it is expressive of something. The lines and colors refer to something other than themselves as lines and colors, such as a person, place, thing, feeling, or event. No two compilations of formal elements are likely to have the same formal organization or meaning. Moreover, interpretations voiced *about* works of art utilize verbal symbols, the everyday language of the individual's lifeworld, so that what is said about the work of art is not in the art media undergoing discussion but registers in everyday language. These do not take the propositional form characteristic of mathematical expressions, where such statements are either true or false. Instead, they are interpretive in character, often relying on such devices as narrative or metaphor. Moreover, interpretations can be expected to vary from one individual to another.

I am saying that each cognitive orientation differs in its theory of meaning and offers different criteria for what can have status as knowledge. A cognitive learning theory that satisfies the truth conditions that obtain in mathematical learning, where learning is likely to be characterized as computation, will likely draw strength from an objectivist theory of meaning, whereas the same theory could wreak havoc in the arts. The question confronting us is which orientation in cognition accommodates learning in the arts? A partial answer to this question is provided by the study of the structural differences of knowledge in various domains. This is the central topic of the chapter that follows.

The integrated account of cognition that is described at the end of this chapter should accommodate the ways that learning occurs in both the arts and other domains. If it would account for mathematical learning but not accommodate learning in the arts, it would fail to offer a comprehensive explanation of learning in its varied forms, and, by the same token, a theory that would account for learning in the arts but fail to account for learning in other subjects is likely to be of little use.

COGNITION AS SYMBOL PROCESSING

Historical interpretations vary on the exact origin of the cognitive revolution. Some writers (Davis & Gardner, 1992; Gardner, 1987) identify its start with Newell and Simon's use, in 1958, of the computer to model the processes of thinking and problem solving. Bruner (1990, 1992) aligns it with the effort "to bring 'mind' back into the human sciences after a long winter of objectivism" (1990, p. 1), and marks its beginning with the 1956 publication of Bruner, Goodnow, and Austin's *A Study of Thinking*. While the difference between the two dates is small, there are notable differences separating Bruner's initial research interests from those of Newell and Simon, differences that become more pronounced in later writings (see Bruner, 1986, 1990, 1992, 1996).

Cognition as symbol processing is also associated with the terms *information processing, symbolic computation,* and the *rule-based manipulation of symbols*. These terms refer to processes that happen in the brain (or any device, such as, a computer) that forms and manipulates symbols. Jessica Davis and Howard Gardner (1992) explain the character of the symbol-systems approach to cognition and identify two core assumptions that serve as major tenets of this theoretical orientation:

> One core assumption is that the computer serves as a relevant model of human thinking, that is, that the computer shapes our understanding of internal processes of thought. The other is that for scientific purposes, human cognitive activity must be described in terms of symbols, schemas, images, ideas, and other forms of mental representation. (p. 97)

One of the positive features of the cognitive science perspective is its interdisciplinarity, which is seen in the contributions of computer scientists, linguists, philosophers, as well as psychologists; yet another is "the rootedness of cognitive science in classical philosophical issues" (Davis & Gardner, 1992, p. 98). For example, Davis and Gardner (1992) refer to Piaget as having roots in classic philosophy as seen "in the Kantian concerns of his inquiry" (p. 98), while critics of symbol processing (Bredo, 1994) cite its Cartesian dualism—its tendency to separate mind from body, or isolate the knower from the known.

An additional feature of the symbol-processing view is that it establishes the activities involved in making and interpreting works of art as *cognitive* activities, whereas the previous behaviorism tended to classify the domain of the arts as noncognitive or affective endeavors. This has greatly expanded the conception of cognition beyond theories antedating the symbol-processing view, including Piaget's cognitive developmental theory. Davis and Gardner (1992) define the characteristics of a symbol-systems approach:

> A symbol-systems approach to cognition begins with a view of a symbol as an entity (material or abstract) that denotes or refers to any other entity. Numbers, words, and musical notes are all discursive which *denote* reality, that is, they are in themselves arbitrary indicators for specific physical entities or concepts. Other equally important symbols like drawings or gestures in dance, have meaning above and beyond the object or concept they denote; they are

non discursive or presentational symbols and aspects of their own construction (e.g., the direction or shape of a line in drawing) are integral to their containment and communication of meaning. (p. 101; emphasis added)

These writers also list several attributes of the cognitive science orientation less congenial to the arts, these being its tendencies to *de-emphasize both context and affect*. To illustrate the first, they refer to Noam Chomsky's notion of an "inborn 'language acquisition device' which was destined to unfold *regardless* of specific cultural stimuli and environmental interaction" (Davis & Gardner, 1992, p. 97). The de-emphasis of context is consistent with the view that the mind is located in the brain, that it is a nonmaterial entity distinct from the body, and that the fashioning and manipulation of symbolic representations of the real world existing outside the brain is its principal activity.

The tendency to de-emphasize affect is seen in the separation of the knowing function from the feeling function.[6] In the previous chapter we saw a dichotomy between the cognitive and the affective in behaviorist theory, and saw it anew in Piagetian theory, where the control of affect was viewed as a necessary step to promote attitudes of objectivity, a characteristic requirement of the stage of formal operations. Such tendencies are consistent with an objectivist theory of meaning.

A symbol-processing system functions well when its symbols "appropriately represent some aspect of the real world and the information processing leads to successful solution of the problem given to the system" (Varela, Thompson, & Rosch, cited in Bredo, 1994, p. 25). However, the phrase "given to the system" begins to problematize this view. A problem can be given to a system like a computer. It would need to have a program configured to accept the information and process it accordingly. But the computer merely carries out the computation. The analogy that likens the brain to the central processing unit of a computer is partial, for the computer neither selects the problem nor sets the goal to be achieved by the process, nor does it understand or appreciate the significance of the results. Unlike learners, computers don't have purposes. The analogy fails to explain how the learning problem is identified and recognized, how such symbols are created, and how they acquire meaning.

The Cognitive Revolution

Ideas about the nature of learning as involving the construction and manipulation of symbols began to enter the curriculum reform literature in the late 1950s and early 1960s, when the notion of basing reforms on the structure of the disciplines got its start. This more or less coincided with the onset of the cognitive revolution in psychology.[7] For example, in 1960 Jerome Bruner introduced what he termed the "spiral curriculum." This was based on his idea that children could be introduced to a leading idea at quite an early age, provided that it was *represented* in a symbolic form that they could assimilate at their stage of development. Kindergarten children may not understand the principle of balance that underlies algebraic equations, but preparation for that understanding may be had through experiences with the see-saw on the school playground, where balance is achieved physically with the placement of equal weights on either side. Somewhat later, the problem of balance can be represented in diagrammatic or pictorial form, in what Bruner called the *iconic stage* of learning. And still later, on reaching the *symbolic stage*, older children can grasp the structure of the equation where different numerical symbols can be said to represent the same quantity (e.g., $2 + 2 = 4$; but also $2 + 1 + 1 = 4$).

What changes throughout the curriculum is the *form* of the representation used, not necessarily its *content*.[8] One can move from learning about physical objects, to pictorial symbols representing these objects, and then to abstract symbols that do not look like the ideas or things they represent. For Bruner, cognitive growth is the increase in symbolic competence, a progress toward abstraction that enables the mind to deal with broad universals and increasingly powerful generalizations. He stated his well-known hypothesis, which became the hallmark of curriculum reform efforts of that epoch, when he asserted that "any subject can be taught effectively in some intellectually honest form to any child at any stage of development" (Bruner, 1960, p. 33). In elaborating this idea, he described some of the basic differences in children at different phases of their intellectual growth:

> [A]t each stage of development the child has a characteristic way of viewing the world and explaining it to himself. The task of teaching a subject to a child at any particular age is one of representing the structure of that subject in terms of the child's ways of viewing things. The task can be thought of as translation. The general hypothesis that has just been stated is premised on the considered judgment that any idea can be represented honestly and usefully in the thought forms of children of school age, and that these representations can later be made more powerful and more precise the more easily by virtue of this early learning. (Bruner, 1960, p. 33)

The main difference in the stages of learning was in the forms of representation available to the learner for use in constructing knowledge. Learning in early childhood is largely grounded in the senses and thus instruction at this level would make use of concrete objects. Older students, who are less dependent on sensory stimuli, will employ increasingly abstract symbols. They are encouraged to discover general categories that make use of verbal or mathematical symbols that express the broad generalizations or leading ideas of a discipline. No domain of knowledge was deemed too complex for early learners. Planners of curricula could begin to build readiness in some intellectually honest form, provided that they honored the limits set by the forms of thought available to the child at a given stage of development. Moreover, these structures of knowledge could be presented quite early.

For Bruner, solving the riddle of curriculum meant finding ways of representing the leading ideas of a discipline in concrete ways at the early stages of learning, thus creating readiness for abstract learning to follow. If what distinguished the early learner from the advanced learner was no more than a difference in the forms they could utilize to represent knowledge, the curriculum task entailed finding those leading ideas around which a curriculum should be built, "the great issues, principles, and values that a society deems worthy of the continual concern of its members" (Bruner, 1960, p. 52), with the ideas themselves coming from the best minds of each discipline. It also consisted in finding the appropriate forms of representation for each stage of the child's development.

Bruner's *The Process of Education* (1960) was the report on the Woods Hole Conference, whose purpose was to review the educational research supporting the reforms of math and science education. There was much interest in this report since the country was still reeling under the impact of the Russian space achievements. Much of the initial research summarized by the report was about disciplines rich in formal logic, such as mathematics and physics, subjects compatible with Piaget's view that the end point in human development is the attainment of formal operations that enable one to engage in logical-scientific thinking. Although this was not his intention, this reduced thinking and intelligence to the narrower conception of symbol processing.

Project Zero at Harvard University and Gardner's Multiple Intelligences

In 1967, a research project involving learning and cognition was proposed by Nelson Goodman, who became its first director. The research program was guided initially by the type of developmental considerations of interest to Piaget, although it attempted to supplement Piaget's work by directing attention to developmental issues in the arts, an area left untouched by Piaget. As the work of the project progressed, the research program gradually incorporated aspects of the symbol-processing orientation in cognition. This direction was compatible with Goodman's (1978a) notion of mind as a symbolic function.[9] I suspect that Goodman would have been less comfortable with the computer analogy since his own definition of the cognitive also included the emotions. Geahigan (1992) summarized Goodman's philosophical perspective in the following way:

> In establishing that the arts constituted distinct kinds of symbol systems, Goodman argued that they had an essentially cognitive function in human life. . . . A persistent critic of the epistemological tradition inherited from Descartes and Locke, Goodman argued that experience of works of art is not a matter of passive reception, but rather one of active inquiry. Unlike epistemologists who distinguished between science and art on the basis of a difference between cognition and emotion, Goodman argued that perception, cognition, and the emotions are involved in both domains, and that emotion itself, has a cognitive component. The symbol systems of art, like those of science, are used in constructing different versions of the world, and none of these systems can be reduced to another. (p. 15)

The initial emphasis in the early studies was on developmental issues involving the acquisition of symbolic competence. Gardner's publications *The Arts and Human Development* (1973) and *Artful Scribbles* (1980) embodied this perspective. As Gardner (1983) moved closer to his multiple intelligences theory, the initial emphasis on developmental issues began shifting to a concern with understanding the differences among the forms of symbol processing in cognition. Davis and Gardner (1992) offer this explanation:

> Initial exploration in the symbol-system mode approached the various symbol systems in much the same way as Piaget had approached the Kantian categories of, for example, time and space. Indeed early research into the impact of media and materials, on the construction of meaning through symbols contributed to an understanding of the various symbol systems as different "problem spaces," each offering unique challenges and potentials to the user of symbols. Accordingly, where Piaget had dismissed décalage as an anomalous aside, symbol-systems researchers became keenly interested in whether and when "knowing how" in one symbol system might predict performance in another. (p. 102)

Piaget never explained adequately the gap between cognitive stages, what has been termed his décalage problem, which asks why it is that the same individual apparently can operate simultaneously at different stages in differing domains of knowledge. The existence of different symbol systems, each representing differing intelligences, was Gardner's way of explaining this. Davis and Gardner (1992) explain how symbol-systems research was instrumental in leading to the development of multiple intelligences (MI) theory:

> Symbol-systems research contributed to the development of the theory of multiple intelligences, which further illuminates a view of drawing as a cognitive process. The theory acknowledges that a vast range of human experience is not divorced from cognition as may have been supposed, but rather demonstrates highly distinctive cognitive forms. Seven different intelligences are posited as distinctive "frames of mind," potential cognitive resources for negotiating one's way (finding, creating, and solving problems) in different symbolic domains (problem-spaces). These intelligences constitute seven different sets of know-how: (1) linguistic; (2) musical; (3) logical mathematical; (4) spatial; (5) bodily-kinesthetic; (6) intrapersonal; (7) interpersonal. (pp. 102–103)

Piaget's décalage problem arose because he had adopted the concept of stages, each with differing forms of representation to mark the development of cognition. If the mind's development evolves from one stage to another, why does the change in intellectual growth affect some domains more than others? Conceiving of mind as a variety of symbol systems enabled Gardner to get around this problem. Learning can occur within a specific symbol system such as math, and with increased experience, a higher level of math competence is likely to follow. But an increase in math is not likely to improve learning in other areas. Other psychologists (Prawat, 1989; Shuell, 1986) accounted for differential cognitive abilities with the construct known as "domain specificity," which will be discussed in the following chapter.

Parsons (1992) noted that the research program of Project Zero was largely indebted to Goodman's idea that each art medium is a symbol system in its own right, being in some way analogous to a natural language. This idea contributed to the recognition of the arts as cognitive areas, each operating with discrete symbol systems. Indeed, MI theory greatly extended the categories of cognitive activity that general education should strive to cultivate. Recognizing that schools favor the cultivation of logical-mathematical and linguistic intelligence at the expense of the other intelligences, Gardner has steadfastly advocated that schools dedicate more time to the intelligences typically neglected in public schools, including learning in the arts.

However, Parsons (1992) questioned MI theory for its tendency to reduce "the notion of intelligence to the ability to work within a medium" (p. 73). In Gardner's view, a comprehensive education would enable individuals to develop competence in a wide array of educational media.

The curriculum would be constructed around the several intelligences as posited in his theory. This would stress the identification of problem-spaces, or patterns of thinking, within each of the various symbol systems. Parsons (1992) found this feature of MI theory troublesome and stressed the idea that several symbol systems should be integrated to construct understandings:

> [W]hen the object is unclear, we need access to ideas that can be developed only within language. . . . In practice this means we must try to say it as well as see it . . . we must be able to discuss what is hard to see, and to see what is hard to say. And then the two kinds of thinking—that is, thinking in the two different media—will be interactive and combine to form one understanding. (p. 82)

Eisner's Forms of Representation

Elliot Eisner (1982) argued for a balanced curriculum on grounds somewhat similar to MI theory. He wrote as an educational theorist and critic rather than as a psychologist, although his argument was couched largely in the language of cognitive psychology. Because his and Gardner's conceptions have a number of common threads, a discussion is appropriate at this point.

Eisner postulated that the essence of mind is the process of forming representations of one's experience. Since symbols are created for purposes of representation, his particular view is essentially a symbol-processing view. These "forms of representation" have their origin in the experience gained through the senses, with some representations grounded in visual perception, while others originate in auditory or tactile sources. The virtue of having multiple forms is clear since "some aspects of human experience are simply better expressed through some forms than through others. If it were possible to convey everything that humans wanted to convey with one or two forms of representation, the others would be redundant" (Eisner, 1982, p. 50).

For Eisner, the mind is biologically rooted in the senses, whereas Gardner's ideas about the various intelligences are linked to regions in the brain rather than to the eye or ear. Gardner's idea of mind is akin to the central processing unit of the computer, whereas for Eisner, the mind begins with the senses as inputting devices. As Gardner (1983) comments:

> The review of recent work in neurobiology has again suggested the presence of *areas in the brain that correspond, at least roughly, to certain forms of cognition*; and these same studies imply a neural organization that proves hospitable to the notion of different modes of information processing. At least in the field

of psychology and neurobiology, the Zeitgeist appears primed for the identification of several human intellectual competencies. (p. 59; emphasis added)

Concept formation, as conceived by Eisner, begins with experiences picked up by the various senses. However, the meanings individuals secure are also affected by the purpose of their inquiries. "What we experience depends in part on what nets we cast" (p. 41). The notion of purpose suggests that a human agent directs this perceptual activity, not a disinterested and disembodied brain or central processing unit. Unlike Gardner, who tends to portray *each* intelligence as an autonomous system in its own right, Eisner recognizes the interactions among concepts arising in differing sensory modalities. In fact, this is one of the major differences between Eisner and Gardner.

A second major difference is that Eisner's forms of representation are socially situated, that is, human beings create representations both to further their own understanding and to communicate these understandings to others. In this respect Eisner's view is closer to Vygotsky than is Gardner's.[10] For example, as Goodman and Goodman (1990) have pointed out, when we compare Eisner's passage below with Vygotsky's ideas about play and imagination as rehearsal, we see many points in common:

> The ability to employ different forms of conceptualization simultaneously has, of course, extremely important assets. Being able to visualize, to hear, and to feel, through imagination, aspects of a situation or problem with which we have to cope provides us with opportunities for rehearsal. We can play out in our imaginative life what we would otherwise have to act upon in order to know. (Eisner, 1982, pp. 42–43)

Eisner characterized the concepts derived from purely sensory experience as essentially "personal aspects of human experience" that cannot be shared socially until they are made public. Forms of representation thus are posited as the devices through which these personal concepts are made communicable. In his emphasis on the personal "nets we cast," Eisner (1982) anticipated certain features of the theory that individuals construct their own views of reality:

> Forms of representation are the devices that humans use to make public conceptions that are privately held. They are the vehicles through which concepts that are visual, auditory, kinesthetic, olfactory, gustatory, and tactile are given public status. This public status might take the form of words, pictures, music, mathematics, dance and the like. (p. 47)

Learning, in Eisner's model, thus moves from sensory perception to conception and then to representation in forms that can be shared publicly.

The skills we possess in the use made of particular forms of representation influence the extent to which what we know conceptually can be represented publicly. Here he cites David Olson's definition of intelligence as "skill in a medium," which echoes Nelson Goodman's idea that each medium is a symbol system in its own right. Eisner's (1982) assertion that *"the choice of a form of representation is a choice in the way the world will be conceived"* (p. 50; emphasis in original) also echoes Goodman's (1978b) view that each symbol system gives us different ways of "worldmaking." Thus, in spite of some notable differences with Gardner, this is an area where Eisner and Gardner are essentially in agreement. Eisner's conception of mind is more fluid and flexible, anticipating aspects of sociocultural constructivism.

Eisner's and Gardner's pleas on behalf of the arts in education are in several respects quite similar. Both base their arguments for the arts in education on the notion of cognitive balance, the idea that some aspects of experience are better expressed than others through certain media or symbolic forms. Formal education tends to be limited to verbal or numerical forms of representation. The more forms of representation that we can cultivate in the schooling of the young, the more ways that are available to extend their intellectual horizons. However, both Gardner's and Eisner's conceptualizations fall heir to a similar host of difficulties, as will become clear in the critique of symbol-processing theories that follows.

Critique of Symbol Processing

This critique of the symbol-processing view is structured around five major, overlapping characteristics of the cognitive sciences: (1) the limitations of the computer analogy; (2) an inherent dualism; (3) the de-emphasis of context; (4) the de-emphasis of affect; and (5) the lack of human agency (Davis & Gardner, 1992).

Limitations of the computer analogy. In his retrospective account of what he called the first cognitive revolution, Bruner (1990) recalled that the intended purpose was "to bring 'mind' back into the human sciences after a long winter of objectivism" (p. 1). Pointing to the cognitive sciences as a whole, Bruner (1990) maintained that its more recent developments have

> become diverted by success, a success that technological virtuosity has cost dear. Some critics, perhaps unkindly, even argue that the new cognitive science, the child of the revolution, has gained its technical successes at the price of dehumanizing the very concept of mind it had sought to reestablish in psychology, and that it has estranged much of psychology from the other human sciences and the humanities. (p. 1)

Emphasis began shifting from "meaning" to "information" from the construction of meaning to the processing of information. These are profoundly different matters. The key factor in the shift was the introduction of computation as the ruling metaphor and of computability as a necessary criterion of a good theoretical model. (p. 4)

The computer analogy as an extension of behaviorism. Echoing similar complaints, Rom Harré (1995) characterized the introduction of the computer analogy as an extension of the behavioral tradition, and the cognitive science position, as a whole, as a continuation of the experimental program of behaviorism, in particular the idea that cognitive processes are reducible to forms of *symbol processing*. Harré's view accords with Bruner's critique that the cognitive revolution had digressed from its initial project of determining the nature of *meaning making* in learning. Although Harré identifies the symbol-processing notion of mind with behaviorism, it is important not to overlook its affinity with Piaget. For example, Newell and Simon (1972), who are credited with having originated the computer analogy, referred to thinking as *formal operations* on symbols that represent objects and their properties and relationships, a definition that underscores a bond with Piaget.

As noted earlier, the analogy that likens the brain to the central processing unit of a computer is only partial, since it fails to explain how the learning problem is identified and recognized, how symbols are created, and how they acquire meaning. In addition, it does not adequately account for how new and more complex knowledge emerges from less complex antecedents. If symbol construction creates representations of reality through processes like assimilation and accommodation, these may become more extensive and more differentiated, and even have increased levels of reliability through the gradual elimination of error, but such activity provides representations of an actual world. It could not symbolize alternative possibilities, or go beyond the real world given in perception to deal with hidden or underlying patterns, or with what the physicist David Bohm calls the "implicate order" of reality (Bohm, 1980; Bohm & Peat, 1987) or what Kincheloe and Steinberg (1993) refer to as "tacit forces, the hidden assumptions that shape perceptions of the world" (p. 305). It is unclear how symbol processing, which produces representations of an actual world, would permit this to happen. Piaget (1987) had allowed for the concept of *possibility* in cognition, which, for him, meant essentially invention and creation.

Finally, the computer analogy is constrained by an objectivism that limits the creation of meaning to the formal operations of classical reason where words and symbols have stable, designated meanings, and where metaphor is banished or relegated to the ornamental fringes of linguistic communication. This raises the question of how a cognitive view can purport to be comprehensive when it fails to explain why the mind bothers to construct meanings through metaphor, which lack precision.

Dualism: the inside-outside problem. According to Eric Bredo (1994), symbol-processing views of cognition tend to portray the individual and the environment as a dualism. A problem may be said to exist in the real world, but solving it requires a capacity to represent that situation symbolically, that is, to put it in propositional form with words, numbers, or scientific formulae in a self-contained logical system. The mind can know its own representations, but how can we be certain that our representations of external reality are accurate and reliable when the only way we can think about them is through these representations themselves? This suggests that there is something wrong with a system of knowledge where we, literally, "have to climb out of our minds" to find answers.[11] Modern dualism has been challenged since the time of Descartes and by such contemporary philosophers as Richard Rorty and Nelson Goodman. It is also challenged by research accounts on the neurophysiological nature of the brain. Damasio, whose book *Descartes' Error* (1994) is an exposition on the biological bases of mind, reason, and emotion, essentially took issue with the mind–body dichotomy inherited from Descartes:

> [T]he comprehensive view of the human mind requires an organismic perspective; that not only must the mind move from a nonphysical cogitum to the realm of biological tissue, but it must be related to a whole organism possessed of integrated body proper and brain and fully interactive with a physical and social environment. (p. 252)

De-emphasis of context. Bredo also notes that by locating the mind in the brain, in isolation from the external world, symbol-processing views tend to de-emphasize context. Concepts are disembodied and not tied to any particular mind that experiences them. Symbol processing detaches the learner's mind from the object undergoing study. It separates the symbolic forms operating in the brain from the world outside the brain. "The educational analog of this view is the belief that students can learn by passively sitting still and absorbing knowledge rather than by actively manipulating things and testing the results of their inquiries" (Bredo, 1994, pp. 26–27).

In addition, Bredo (1994) comments that in symbol-processing approaches there is a "tacit separation of the individual and group. Thinking, learning, and development often are thought of as processes taking place inside the individual, with social influences coming from the outside" (p. 27). This is seen in standardized test situations that compare individuals from many situations on the same task on the presumption that the extent of learning, development, and intelligence can be determined by such comparisons.

Bredo explains how this can be misleading because students from different social situations will organize their learning activities in different ways. For example, I once observed an art appreciation lesson where the teacher showed a reproduction of a Millet painting to a middle school class with a large percentage of African American students. The teacher asked the students to describe the central figure, a farmer, and to explain what he was doing. One of the students interpreted the painting as being about slavery because the man was working in the fields and appeared to her to have dark skin. If that work of art appeared as a test item asking for an interpretation, older Black children, who have awareness of the legacy of slavery, might well respond to this work in a different light than White children.

Lack of context for learning also is revealed by the example of the student given a word problem in an algebra class. If the student selects the appropriate algorithm, and enters the right numerical values and manipulates the symbols with the appropriate rules that apply to their use, it is probable that the right answer will be produced, with the learner having little or no understanding of the reality being represented or how to apply the result in contexts where it may be relevant. Perkins and Simmons (1988) use the term *equation cranking* to describe students who rely on a type of ritualized guessing where they might obtain the right answer without understanding why it was right or its potentialities for real-world applications.

De-emphasis of affect. Symbol-processing views tend to separate feeling from knowing. Israel Scheffler (1986) questioned the tendency to separate cognition from emotion:

> I hold that cognition cannot be cleanly sundered from emotion and assigned to science, while emotion is ceded to the arts, ethics and religion. All these spheres of life involve both fact and feeling; they relate to sense as well as sensibility. (p. 347)

> It does not follow . . . that emotion as such is uniformly hostile to cognitive endeavors, nor may we conclude that cognition is, in general, free of emotional engagement. Indeed, emotion without cognition is blind, and I shall hope particularly to show . . . [that] cognition without emotion is vacuous. (p. 348)

He then illustrates how emotions can serve cognition. First, there are what he calls *rational passions*, such as a love of truth and contempt for lying. There are also *perceptive feelings* that are interwoven with our cognitive ideals. When we perceive our environment in a certain light, we ask whether it is beneficial or harmful, promising or threatening, fulfilling or thwarting. Such feelings, he explains, serve as cues for interpreting situations. Third, emotions can promote one's *theoretical imagination*. Scheffler used the well-known story of a dream had by the nineteenth-century chemist F. A. Kekule that enabled him to represent the structure of the benzene molecule as a hexagonal ring. When the model of thinking uses the computer analogy as its foundation, linkages between facts and feelings would be either overlooked or minimized.

Lack of human agency. As the cognitive sciences moved toward a computational model of mind, they also moved away from meaning making as the focal point of the cognitive revolution. Bruner (1990) noted that promoters of the computational model also came to reject the notion of intentional states, purposes, or motives possessed by the learner. He complains:

> But cognitive science in its new mood, despite all its hospitality toward goal directed behavior, is still chary of the concept of agency. For "agency" implies the conduct of action under the sway of intentional states. So action based on belief, desire, and moral commitment . . . is something to be eschewed by right-minded cognitive scientists. It is like free-will among determinists. (p. 9)

Similarly, Harré (1995) found that there was a tendency in the cognitive sciences to characterize human beings as passive, mere spectators of processes over which they had no control, rather than as active agents in the construction of their own knowledge.

Roots in Enlightenment Philosophy

The discussion of dualism from the time of Descartes continues within the cognitive sciences. Descartes separated the *sense-free* or inside-the-mind part of our consciousness from the objective world out there and declared these two realms to be inviolably separate (Schlain, 1991). Cartesian rationality is essentially disembodied since mind is an immaterial substance.

Although the computer analogy is identified with the cognitive sciences, many working in this field, such as Bruner, Johnson, and Goodman, do not necessarily endorse that particular characterization of mind and, in particular, the objectivist theory of meaning it embodies. In Chapter 6

I make extensive reference to Lakoff and Johnson's (1980) work on nonpropositional forms of symbol processing, especially those involving metaphor, to posit a richer view of mind and rationality than that which is characteristic of symbol-processing views of cognition.

SOCIOCULTURAL, OR SITUATED, COGNITION

An alternative to symbol-processing views of cognition is typified in work by John Brown, Allan Collins, and Paul Duguid (1989), who introduced a theoretical perspective they termed *situated cognition*. Drawing on research in cognition as manifested in everyday activity, these authors argued that "knowledge is situated, being in part a product of the activity, context, and culture in which it is developed and used" (Brown et al., 1989, p. 32). Other writers, such as Paul Cobb (1994a) and Carl Bereiter (1994), identify this view with the term *sociocultural cognition*. Those adopting the latter term criticize symbol-processing views for separating "knowing how" from "knowing what." They also tend to describe learning as enculturation (Brown et al., 1989). Brown and colleagues (1989) write:

> Many methods of didactic education assume a separation between knowing and doing, treating knowledge as an integral, self-sufficient substance, theoretically independent of the situations in which it is learned. The primary concern of schools often seems to be the transfer of this substance part of what is learned. Situations might be said to co-produce knowledge through activity. Learning and cognition, it is now possible to argue, are fundamentally situated. (p. 32)

Brown and colleagues (1989) also introduce the notion of *cognitive apprenticeship*, which they define as "embed[ding] learning in activity and mak[ing] deliberate use of the social and physical context" (p. 32), and they tend to be critical of prevalent school practices that treat knowledge as a set of abstractions bearing little or no relation to life outside the school. Their idea of cognitive apprenticeship is patterned after the craft apprenticeship mode of instruction common in pre-industrial times:

> Cognitive apprenticeship methods try to enculturate students into authentic practices through activity and social interaction in a way similar to that evident—and evidently successful—in craft apprenticeship. (Brown et al., 1989, p. 37)

The authors illustrate their point by citing studies by Miller and Gildea (1987), who contrast children's learning of vocabulary through dictionaries and sentence-writing exercises with the ways that vocabulary normally is learned outside of school, where "people generally learn words in the context of ordinary communication." They continue:

> Miller and Gildea note that by listening, talking, and reading, the average 17-year-old has learned vocabulary at the rate of 5000 words per year (13 per day) for over 16 years. By contrast learning words from abstract definitions and sentences taken out of the context of normal use, the way vocabulary has often been taught, is slow and generally unsuccessful. (Brown et al., 1989, p. 32)

In place of abstract exercises as a basis for teaching, Brown and colleagues (1989) suggest that it may be more useful

> to consider conceptual knowledge as, in some ways, similar to a set of tools. Tools share several significant features with knowledge: They can only be fully understood through use, and using them entails both changing the user's view of the world and adopting the belief system of the culture in which they are used. . . .
> Learning how to use a tool involves far more than can be accounted for in any set of explicit rules. The occasions and conditions for use arise directly out of the context of activities of each community that uses the tool, framed by the way members of that community see the world. (p. 33)[12]

The view of situated cognition put forth by Bredo (1994) characterizes learning situations as made up of "contributions both individuals and environments bring to a learning activity rather than seeing them as separate entities. . . . The inside-outside relationship between person and environment which is generally pre-supposed in the symbol processing view, is replaced by a part–whole relationship" (p. 28). Bredo characterizes a learning performance as the product of a history of relating in which the learner and the environment both undergo change as a result of transactions involving learning. He sees parallels between the situated views undergoing current discussion and the transactional view of knowledge in Deweyan pragmatism that appeared early in the twentieth century. To exemplify the learning process in transactional terms, Bredo (1994) uses drawing as an analogy for learning situations in general:

> One draws, responds to what one has drawn, draws more, and so on. The goals for the drawing change as the drawing evolves and different effects become possible, making the whole development a mutual affair rather than a one-way determinism. Writing can similarly be seen as a mutual matter of composition rather than simply the transfer of ideas from brain to paper. One writes,

responds to what one has written, and so on, altering interpretation and aim in the process. The same may be said for conversing or for thinking itself. Each is the result of a dialogue, a way of relating or mutually modulating activity, in which person and environment (ideally) modify each other so as to create an integral performance. . . . the production of a well-coordinated performance involves a kind of dance between person and environment rather than the one way action of one on the other. Such performances are quite naturally described in artistic terms that acknowledge interplay, such as "concerted," "orchestrated," or "composed." (pp. 28–29)

Sociocultural cognition succeeds in avoiding the dualisms of symbol-processing views by binding knowledge construction closely to its embedding context, and provides a useful critique of schooling practices that often try to teach concepts independently of authentic situations, overlooking the ways that understandings develop through continued, situated use (Bredo, 1994).

Yet sociocultural theory is not exempt from certain epistemological difficulties of its own. Although sociocultural cognitivists are able to explain how learning occurs in everyday situations with just plain folks such as apprentice tailors, groups of dieters, and milk delivery men (Lave, 1977, 1988; Lave & Wenger, 1991; Rogoff & Lave, 1984), they have relatively less to say about the ability to categorize or generalize about our experiences in ways that transcend the particulars of everyday social situations. A cognitive learning theory also should be able to explain how abstract generalizations might arise from particular, situated experiences that are neither present in the culture nor yet in the mind of any particular individual. For example, an anthropologist studying many cultures may categorize sets of observations under generic headings like child-rearing practices or puberty rites, but where do such categories come from? One may argue that they are imposed on the data by the discipline of anthropology itself, acquired as discursive tools devised by the anthropological community to impart consistency and structure to independent observations. However, new categories often arise spontaneously in the mind of the anthropologist from collections of local, multiple observations, and since these do not have a history of use in the discipline, they are newly formed. But how would a situated cognitive theory explain the rise of such newly formed categories? Current theory is relatively silent on this point.

In my view, Lave and Wenger's (1991) work embodies this very difficulty. For example, they study a number of discrete instances of everyday learning situations to arrive at a principle they identify as *legitimate peripheral participation*. I have no quarrel with this particular concept, but it is an abstraction, a generalization assembled from multiple cases, a type of ability their theory would tend to eschew. Moreover, if situated theory cannot explain where our capacity for mental abstraction comes from, it will have difficulty accounting for the transfer of learning, where learning in one situation finds applicability in other situations.

There is also a second and more telling limitation of sociocultural cognition, namely, that its research on learning has tended to focus on what might be called *low-tech* situations, where craft apprenticeship is pictured as the educational ideal. But this ideal is taken from a romanticized view of European medieval guilds, or from situations where the teacher is guru, as in pre-industrial cultures, and I question whether these practices are likely to be useful to emulate in future situations in industrialized contexts. Lave and Wenger's critique of current schooling practices has focused on their aridity and abstractness, with justification, but it is unlikely that the demands for increasingly complex knowledge required in future occupations will be satisfied by resorting to educational practices that antedate the industrial revolution. Rather, that knowledge will begin to flower when nonpropositional forms of social communication are studied as ways in which cognitive structures are formed and acquire meaning. And these abound in the arts.

Nevertheless, notions of cognitive apprenticeship and the enculturation of novices into specific knowledge communities are emergent ideas that show promise in overcoming the difficulties within symbol-processing views. In particular, there are affinities between notions of cognitive apprenticeship and notions to be introduced in the next section, having to do with learning as enculturation into specific knowledge communities like the scientific community or the art world.

TOWARD INTEGRATED THEORY

Both the symbol-processing and sociocultural theories are constructivist theories. In the symbol-processing view symbols are manipulated, modified, constructed and reconstructed. In the sociocultural view knowledge is constructed in and through social transactions, but it is constructed, nevertheless. There is a third family of theories which take as their central premise the idea that knowledge is not passively received but is actively constructed by the learner, where learners are portrayed as active human agents with motives and purposes for learning, rather than passive receivers of information. The construction of meanings occurs through their own efforts at knowledge-seeking. Piaget believed that the processes which enable cognitive development to take place were primarily individual affairs, with intellectual reconstruction occurring throughout life (Driver, Asoko, Leach, Mortimer, & Scott, 1994, p. 6).

Conceptual Change

Some constructivists characterize learning as a process of conceptual change, in which the knowledge and prior understandings held by the learner undergo intellectual reconstruction when these are found to be flawed or conceptually inadequate in some way. As this happens, such learners construct better representations of their environment or of the material being learned. When learners find that their presently held understandings are inadequate, they may experience cognitive conflict or "cognitive discomfort"[13] enough to raise questions about the adequacy of presently held knowledge. The learner may feel impelled to reconstruct or reorganize his or her personal knowledge and understanding.[14]

And indeed, the task of the teacher is to raise questions that challenge students to examine their presently held assumptions if they are judged to be conceptually inadequate. Dewey discussed the process of inquiry as beginning with "a felt difficulty," that is, a challenge that induces a level of cognitive conflict so that the researcher feels impelled to develop schemata better able to accommodate his or her experience. Instructional practice attempts to influence the individual's personal construction of meaning by inducing dissatisfactions with presently held understandings.

The problem with the conceptual change approach to learning, especially as it has been followed in the sciences, is that the more conceptually adequate states of knowledge tend to reflect the teacher's view of the *right* answer. In the teaching of science, commonsense ways of explaining phenomena that represent structures of knowledge in the everyday world tend to be systematically replaced by the knowledge and understandings of the scientific community. Wrong answers are greeted with prompts leading to right answers, until the understandings sought by the teacher are set in place.

The problem is twofold: First, in the context of the everyday world, commonsense ways of understanding actually may work quite well. The statement, "The sun is rising in the east," is not wrong knowledge. Although it is an illusion caused by the earth's rotation, in ordinary conversation one does not refer to that fact to understand what is meant by the sentence. It is not necessary to explain away the expression, "There is a full moon tonight." Everyone knows what is meant by that expression and is not likely to conclude that the moon is physically changing its shape. Second, the practice of devaluing commonsense understandings in favor of the knowledge of science proper tends to isolate science from the lifeworld of the learner.

Lessons from Science and Mathematics

However, researchers in the teaching of science and mathematics have begun to integrate sociocultural approaches to instruction into their practices. What distinguishes current applications of theory from the classical constructivism of Piaget, is that the progress the individual makes toward becoming a disciplined professional, like a scientist or an artist, is *not* undertaken in isolation. Individuals do not have to invent the tools with which they work, and even when working on problems in relative solitude or isolation, they make use of the "cultural tools" of the specific knowledge domain where their activities take place. Rosalind Driver and her associates (1994) describe learning in the sciences as a case in point:

> [T]he symbolic world of science is now populated with entities such as atoms, electrons, ions, fields and fluxes, genes and chromosomes; it is organized by ideas such as evolution and encompasses procedures of measurement and experiment. These ontological entities, organizing concepts and associated epistemology and practices of science are unlikely to be discovered by individuals through their own observations of the natural world. (p. 6)[15]

The theoretical approach taken by Driver and associates incorporates elements from both the symbol-processing and sociocultural cognitive traditions, with the latter providing the cultural tools of the subject field undergoing study. Once acquired, these tools can be manipulated symbolically, while the domains of knowledge themselves are likened to cultural communities with distinctive practices. The emphasis on cultural practices does not necessarily deny the possibility of independent discovery learning, but recognizes that fields of knowledge such as science have their social dimension, and that teaching within these domains enculturates learners into the specific discourses of a field. The objects of scientific study thus are not limited to natural phenomena but also include the symbolic constructs advanced by science to explain the material world:

> ... knowledge and understandings ... are constructed when individuals engage socially in talk and activity about shared problems or tasks. Meaning-making is thus a dialogic process involving persons-in-conversation, and learning is seen as the process by which individuals are introduced to a culture by more skillful members. As this happens they "appropriate" the cultural tools through involvement in the activities of this culture. (Driver et al., 1994, p. 7)

When Driver and associates refer to "more skillful members" of a culture, such as members of the scientific community, they allude to Vygotskian notions of mediation and internalization, akin to Brown and colleagues' (1989) notion of cognitive apprenticeship. Theorists such as Paul Cobb (1994a, 1994b) also have argued for the compatibility of cognitive views:

> Currently, considerable debate focuses on whether mind is located in the head or in the individual-in-social-action, and whether development is cognitive self-organization or enculturation into established practices. . . . I question assumptions that initiate this apparent forced choice between constructivist [symbol-processing] and sociocultural perspectives. I contend that the two perspectives are complementary. Also, claims that either perspective captures the essence of people and communities should be rejected for pragmatic justifications that consider the contextual relevance and usefulness of a perspective. I argue that the sociocultural perspective informs theories of the conditions for the possibility of learning, whereas theories developed from the constructivist [symbol-processing] perspective focus on what students learn and the processes by which they do so. (Cobb, 1994b, p. 13)

The arguments offered by Cobb and Driver and associates are important in laying the groundwork for an integrated theory of cognition, but there are problems with current definitions of constructivism that need to be worked on before an adequate theory can be advanced.

First, definitions of constructivism are so broad and varied in the educational practices they encompass as to be essentially meaningless. These include everything from the discovery learning of the early 1960s, with its emphasis on the learner as a lone individual, to teacher-centered views of conceptual change, where the right concept, known in advance by the teacher, is promoted, usually at the expense of the individual's prior knowledge with its reliance on the commonsense assumptions of the everyday social world. In effect, the methods of inducing conceptual change are not unlike those advocated by behaviorists, where teachers control environmental stimuli to shape the desired response of the learner. The individual is permitted to construct meanings but only to the extent that they accord with the right answers known by the teacher. Of course, one might argue that teachers are supposed to extend the knowledge of the right answers to their pupils.

However, a second and more troublesome difficulty is revealed in the passage below by Driver and associates, who take pains to distinguish scientific knowledge from the commonsense knowledge of the everyday world:

"Commonsense" ways of explaining phenomena . . . represent knowledge of the world portrayed within everyday culture. They differ from the knowledge of the scientific community in a number of ways. Most obviously, common sense and science differ in the ontological entities they contain. . . . Secondly, commonsense reasoning, although it can be complex, also tends to be tacit or without specific rules. Scientific reasoning, by contrast, is characterized by the explicit formulation of theories that can be inspected in the light of evidence. . . . Thirdly, everyday reasoning is characterized by pragmatism. Ideas are judged in terms of being useful for specific purposes or in specific situations, and as such they guide people's actions. . . . The scientific commitment, therefore is not satisfied by situationally specific models, but strives for models with the greatest generality and scope. (p. 8)

In distinguishing their approach from practices associated with conceptual change, Driver and associates encourage students to retain their commonsense knowledge and informal ideas as a reasonable basis to guide their actions in the everyday world. They reject the usual tendency of science educators to devalue such knowledge. At the same time, they ask learners to separate their everyday understandings, what I call *lifeworld knowledge*, from knowledge as characterized within the scientific community. Lifeworld knowledge is the taken-for-granted reality that the child possesses prior to schooling—the commonsense, symbolic backdrop against which school subjects are presented and that serves students as a reality check about what they are being taught. Driver and associates would encourage students to hold their knowledge of science apart from the concerns of the everyday world.

In my view, this defeats the purpose of teaching science in the first place. The purpose of teaching science is to enable the learner to construct meaningful connections between the domains of science and life in the everyday world. And the problem with science teaching within general education is that too many students do exactly as they say. They keep science at arm's length from the commonsense world, and thus fail to understand its relevance for their lives.

By extension, a similar argument fits learning in the arts. The concerns of the everyday world and the world of the professional fine arts community are often isolated from each other. Members of the fine arts community work in various art media, and artists talk about the problems they confront in working with media. Art critics speak or write about these works in terms that are arcane, written for other members of the art world, and about issues that hardly concern most individuals in the everyday world. Indeed, it has been argued by adherents of the symbol-processing view that learning in art is the ability to think within the specific media used by members of the artistic community.

However, a work of art is not merely about itself; it is also a representation of the world outside of art—often the everyday social world. If it were only about itself, an analysis of its subject matter and formal qualities, like color and line, as elements that give rise to aesthetic experiences, would encompass the totality of its content. Moreover, audiences respond by talking or writing about the content of the work, using verbal language, that is, the language of the lifeworld, the world of everyday social interactions. And this is especially the case when works of art are not easy to understand. Therefore, within general education, the purpose of art education is *not* to induct individuals into the world of the professional fine arts community. Rather, its purpose is to enable individuals to find meaning in the world of art for life in the everyday world.

An integrated cognitive theory would harmonize the major features of the theories described above. Each orientation in isolation has both positive and negative features. Theories emphasizing symbol processing direct attention to the internal processes occurring in the mind of the learner (i.e., formal operations), but, at the same time, they are burdened by a computational model of symbol processing, by an objectivism that restricts the range of meanings to things that symbol systems can convey efficiently within the limits set by the logic that governs their operation. In particular, it places limits on imagination, a topic to be stressed in Chapter 6.

Sociocultural theorists represent knowledge acquisition as occurring within a social context through which the knowledge undergoing construction acquires meaning, but their theories have difficulty in describing the emergence of abstract thinking such as categorization or generalization. In their emphasis on the social construction of reality, sociocultural theorists run the risk of minimizing or denying the possibility of independent thinking at variance with the norms of the culture.

Sociocultural theories are unclear about what is meant by context. Does the term *context* refer to a cultural milieu such as American culture or White middle-class suburban culture? Can it also refer to the culture of a particular ethnic group, or to the culture of the professional fine arts community, or the scientific community? Does the concept of context apply to a domain of knowledge? Driver and associates have applied this latter definition of context to the sciences, and one might entertain this possibility for other domains of knowledge as well.

It is also clear that each of the cognitive learning theories reviewed above is by itself insufficient to favor the various forms of learning that human beings possess. However, some combination of desirable features may provide a useful basis for educational practice in all subject fields. In what follows, I list some features that are needed to account for learning as it occurs in the arts.

REQUIREMENTS OF AN INTEGRATED COGNITIVE THEORY
FOR EDUCATION IN THE ARTS

A cognitive theory that can explain learning in the arts will need to meet the following conditions: It will need to transcend the computational analogy, which restricts thinking to literal representations of what is real, as opposed to metaphorical constructions that enable one to devise alternative conceptions of what is real. Among the things that it should explain are the following:

- The symbolic character of thinking—how symbols develop and change in artistic activities, how artists find ideas, how ideas undergo modification, and how works of art are interpreted by viewers
- The range and variety of symbolic entities, including both propositional (verbal or numerical) and nonpropositional (gestures, images, metaphors) entities
- How learners acquire new knowledge and skills by constructive processes (assimilation and accommodation) or enculturation into knowledge communities
- How prior knowledge conditions the structure of new knowledge
- How students monitor their own learning (i.e., metacognition) and how metacognitive strategies are learned
- The cognitive functions of emotions
- How knowledge becomes meaningful when linked to its social context
- How meaning is transacted from the situations where it occurs, as, for example, in cognitive apprenticeship, where one learns from more knowledgeable members of specific knowledge communities, or scaffolding
- The conditions of transfer, that is, ways that knowledge from one domain finds applicability in other domains
- Domain specificity—the idea that proficiency in one domain may not guarantee proficiency in another
- The role played by the individual's motives, interests, and purposes in activating learning, that is, the role of human agency in learning
- How differences in the structures of knowledge require that learners adapt their knowledge-seeking strategies
- The role played by imagination in the creation of works of art and in their interpretation

Table 3.1 compares and summarizes the leading ideas of the symbol-processing view with those of the sociocultural view. The integrated view that appears in the right-hand column is a compilation of ideas from the symbol-processing and sociocultural perspectives integrated into the view that individuals construct their own understandings.

IMPLICATIONS FOR EDUCATION IN THE ARTS

An integrated approach to cognition shows promise for harmonizing a number of conflicting tendencies in the policies and practices of art educators. If the symbol-processing view could extend beyond the computational metaphor and the objectivist theory of meaning, it could preserve the idea that the arts are symbol systems in their own right, in effect asserting the cognitive character of the arts. An integrated theory would have to adopt meaning making and understanding as organizing principles, as opposed to computational competence or information processing. The principal effect of this would be seen in educational activities where the symbolic forms of the arts would be more closely linked to everyday life, and where the meanings one grasped about art would be seen and felt to be linked to the lifeworld. It would likely entail a greater reliance on the arts experienced in popular culture as sources of content.

Sociocultural theory places art learning in a socially bound situation and identifies the role of teacher as cultural mediator, but learning then is constrained by the limits of the culture itself. If the culture is large and complex like our own, this may not be a problem since there is more knowledge available in the existing milieu than can be learned in several lifetimes, and that knowledge is expanding at a phenomenal rate (Koroscik, 1996b).

Yet somehow, the notion that art is a domain where the knowledge, techniques, and possibilities for new works are already known, is logically odd, for new works of art are being created and new scholarship about older and widely known works of art is occurring in many fields, such as art history, at an ever-increasing rate. Years ago, Morris Weitz (1963) described "art" as an "open concept." He wrote:

> "Art," itself, is an open concept. New conditions (cases) have constantly arisen and will undoubtedly constantly arise; new art forms, new movements will emerge, which will demand decisions on the part of those interested, usually professional critics, as to whether the concept should be extended or not. . . . What I am arguing, then, is that the very expansive, adventurous character of art, its ever-present changes and novel creations, makes it logically impossible to ensure any set of defining properties. We can, of course choose to close the concept. But to do this with "art" . . . is ludicrous since it forecloses on the very conditions of creativity in the arts. (p. 152)

Table 3.1. Emergence of an Integrated Theory of Cognition

	Symbol Processing	Sociocultural	Integrated
Research basis	Research on learners in knowledge-rich areas at higher education levels, e.g., physics, mathematics, computer science (Perkins & Simmons, 1988)	Research on learners in everyday situations, e.g., groups of dieters, apprentice tailors (Lave & Wenger, 1991)	Research on learners in K–12 classroom situations (Driver et al., 1994; Cobb, 1994b)
Nature of reality	Objectivism: There is an objective reality that exists independent of the knower and is represented mentally in symbolic structures in the mind.	Social relativism or social determinism: Reality emerges as a social construction that occurs largely in and through transactions in language and communication.	Experiential realism: Reality is neither objective nor wholly a social construction. It is an individual construction of one's own making and is guided by individual needs, interests, and the internalization of social norms and purposes.
Nature of mind	The mind is in the head and is that symbolizing activity that enables individuals to know the world that lies outside.	The mind is *not* in the head, but emerges in the individual's interactions within a social world, and through the acquisition of cultural tools.	The mind is a symbolic function in the head but actualizes its potential through the acquisition of cultural tools. Language, number, and works of art are such tools.
Nature of learning	Learning is knowledge construction. Structures coincide with the domains of knowledge, the disciplines, that have the organized character of knowledge as possessed by professional scholars.	Learning is organized around social purposes, e.g., work and occupations, or problems facing society, rather than by abstract domains of knowledge. Learning is enculturation.	Learning is knowledge construction but is organized around the purposes of the learner, including social purposes. Emphasis is placed on human agency and meaning making.

(Continued)

Table 3.1. (*Cont.*)

	Symbol Processing	*Sociocultural*	*Integrated*
Strategies for learning	Learning is guided by metacognitive strategies: the mindful self-management of learning. Early learning sets the stage for later learning.	Learning is enculturation, facilitated by scaffolding provided by parents, peers, and knowledgeable adults, which opens zones of proximal development.	Learning is both guided by metacognitive strategies and facilitated by interventions of knowledgeable adults providing the prompts that form effective forms of scaffolding.
Nature of knowledge	Knowledge is constructed by the lone individual.	Knowledge is located in a social environment and consists of the tools of the culture.	Knowledge construction is not undertaken in isolation; rather, the learner works within a cultural context with cultural tools.
Organization of knowledge	Knowledge is domain-specific, as disciplines organized by domain scholars.	Knowledge is organized around social occupations and activities, the rituals and ceremonies of the social world.	Knowledge is organized around the motives and purposes of the learner. It can include the formal disciplines but is not limited to them.
Nature of meaning	Meaning is found in the internal coherence of symbolic structures, or by predictions of events in nature.	Meaning is not found in objects per se, but in the ways they are used in the social world.	Meaning is found when learners integrate knowledge into their lifeworlds.

The chapter that follows discusses the structures of knowledge given to the student by the curriculum. In general, it asks how differences in the structures of these domains bear upon the tasks the learner must face when confronted with unfamiliar areas of knowledge, and into which type of domains do the arts fit? It is here that the domain-specific character of knowledge is recognized as a cognitive problem.

4

Cognitive Flexibility Theory and
Learning in the Arts

MANY STUDENTS CAN SUCCESSFULLY COMPLETE their studies and obtain high scores on exams of factual information, yet have difficulty interpreting, adapting, or applying that knowledge in contexts different from those where the learning first occurred. Cognitive flexibility is a quality of mind that enables learners to use their knowledge in relevant ways in real-world situations. It involves a capacity on the part of the learner to represent knowledge (concepts, ideas) in multiple ways. Cognitively flexible students take learning to be multidirectional, involving the formation of multiple perspectives.

The concept of cognitive flexibility is based on work by a group of psychologists including Rand Spiro, Paul Feltovich, Richard Coulson, Daniel K. Anderson, and their colleagues. Their theoretical orientation was derived from the study of particular learning difficulties experienced by medical students in the introductory phases of their education. These difficulties are sufficiently similar to problems faced by art students to warrant the present discussion. Indeed, individuals in many complexly structured domains encounter similar learning difficulties.

For example, Georgianna Short (1993, 1995) found that comparable difficulties were encountered by preservice art education majors. Typically, they could pass courses and exams of factual knowledge with high marks, but could not readily apply such knowledge in student teaching situations involving the preparation of lessons calling for the interpretation of works of art. The knowledge was there, but they could not utilize it in instruction.

Similarly, premedical students typically acquire vast amounts of knowledge early in their training, but cannot always recognize its relevance in clinical situations encountered later in their training. In addition, these students frequently develop systematic misunderstandings that potentially can result in serious diagnostic errors. Frequently, these begin in the form of oversimplified representations of knowledge. For example, when medical students believe that the body's cardiovascular system can be analogized to plumbing in a building, they may not rightly understand the basis for the medical conditions that cause high blood pressure.

Thus, the first part of this chapter concentrates on problems of learning and knowledge transfer in what Spiro and his colleagues describe as "complex and ill-structured domains." Their research explains what makes some domains complex and ill-structured, while others are "well-structured," and why attention to these differences is necessary for the successful utilization of knowledge in real-world situations. They also explain why the learning that is characteristic of the introductory phases of knowledge acquisition, which usually entails large amounts of rote memorization, often fails to provide the foundation for such higher-order cognitive activities as transfer (Spiro, Vispoel, Schmitz, Samarpungavan, & Boerger, 1987).

Spiro and his colleagues also made use of a computer hypertext program called *Cardioworld Explorer* to enable medical students to handle greater levels of complexity in their studies of the cardiovascular system. This program was built upon the metaphor that a knowledge domain is a landscape undergoing exploration through traversal over crisscrossed pathways. Since it enabled students to deal with relatively small features of a complex domain in single traversals, they were able to construct accurate representations of the cardiovascular system without being unduly burdened by the intrinsic difficulty of this subject. The landscape metaphor provided these researchers with an approach to instruction likely to succeed when the complexity of the knowledge could overwhelm students who were otherwise highly capable.

The second portion of this chapter introduces additional metaphors that might be applied to instruction to help generate cognitive representations of knowledge in ways that capture real-world complexities. For example, I describe the learner's knowledge base as a cognitive lattice and introduce the idea of "overlapping sets," two concepts derived from urban planning (Alexander, 1988), and the strategic role these might play in the organization of curriculum content in ways to facilitate transfer. Overlapping sets are places where knowledge in separate domains can be shown to overlap, leading to the possibility of intellectual travel from one domain to another. These sets enable the learner to handle more complexity by identifying points of convergence within and between domains of knowledge. As more linkages are identified, and integrated, the learner is equipped to apply this knowledge in new ways. In other words, the learner understands more than the answers on a final examination might indicate, but is enabled to understand how the knowledge might apply in situations that differ from where it was acquired initially.

When a domain is complexly structured, its knowledge needs to be encountered through the study of individual cases. Cases in medicine might include individual patients or a particular disease or medical condition, whereas cases in art may involve interpreting individual works of art or forming judgments of taste or beauty. Spiro and his colleagues do not specifically address learning in the arts, although their depiction of ill-structuredness as involving the study of complex objects or cases fits the typical learning situation found in art.

In my view, complex or ill-structured knowledge is not only found in fields like medicine and art criticism but is also applicable to fields like law, literary criticism, history, and philosophy, to name a few. In short, ill-structuredness is likely to be evident in most one-of-a-kind learning situations, that is, whenever judgments must be made in the absence of rules or generalizations that apply to numerous cases, and this includes most situations in life. The capacity for making effective judgments, given the ill-structured character of life itself, is a major intellectual accomplishment.

Of course, there are differences in the learning problems confronted by medical students and art students. In medical education there is the expectation that ultimately the student will "get it right," that is, understand things like how the cardiovascular system works. A typical task confronting art learners is how to devise credible interpretations of works of art, historical movements, and the like, in the absence of an absolute set of rules for determining whether a given interpretation is warranted.

That art is a complexly structured domain is supported by the fact that different art viewers will interpret a given work of art from various alternative perspectives. Such interpretations will likely differ from each other. When one deals with broader concepts like the evolution of style over time, one assembles an argument from several cases or examples, each enlarging one's understanding of the style and its development. In addition, learners often draw upon knowledge from differing domains outside of art to support the interpretation of a given work of art. Examples of such content includes the social, cultural, political, or historical circumstances surrounding the work, including the artist's biography, all of which provides the context of the work. As more ways of connecting with the work are established, the more likely interpretations are to become complex, overlapping, or multilayered.

To illustrate, an architecture student may look at the Palace at Versailles as an exemplar of Baroque architecture, placing it in a stylistic category where it is compared with other exemplars of Baroque and with works done before its construction and after. That student also may regard it as a political statement asserting the absolute power of the French monarchy as it existed under Louis XIV, where grandeur[1] was a strategy asserting his political dominance. This work can be represented in a variety of contexts, including its location in architectural history, as well as in social and political histories. Since the study of artworks typically engages more than formal or stylistic factors, there is need to seek knowledge from other domains at some remove from architecture. Moreover, the converse is also true—that through study in other domains, one frequently encounters works of art. This implies that works of art cannot be fully understood apart from these embedding contexts and that, lacking a knowledge of the arts, one's understanding of these contexts is correspondingly diminished.

DIFFERENCES BETWEEN INTRODUCTORY AND ADVANCED KNOWLEDGE ACQUISITION

Feltovich, Spiro, and Coulson (1993) identify at least two levels in the learning process, which they refer to as "introductory knowledge acquisition" and "advanced knowledge acquisition." They distinguish these by noting key differences in the purposes of instruction at each level:

> In introductory learning the primary educational goal is often exposure to large areas of curricular content ("coverage" of content), without much emphasis on conceptual mastery of knowledge. . . . In particular students may not be expected to understand concepts too deeply or be able to apply them because it is presumed that following exposure, heightened understanding and knowledge applicability will be incrementally achieved sometime later. (Feltovich et al., 1993, p. 184)

For example, a beginning art history student will dedicate much time to memorizing names, dates, formal and stylistic characteristics of images, and the like. By contrast, professional art historians, working at advanced levels, rarely if ever engage in memorization, not only because they already possess quantities of relevant factual information, but because they are more likely to focus on specific problems such as attribution or chronology as these bear on the interpretation of an individual work or a given art movement. They are more likely to recognize gaps in knowledge or inconsistencies or inadequacies in the ways specific facts were interpreted in the past. In Feltovich and colleagues' (1993) words, these professional scholars have superseded the "restrictive goals of introductory learning":

At some point in the educational process the restrictive goals of introductory learning must be superseded; at some point students must be expected to attain an accurate and deeper understanding of content material, be able to reason with it, and be able to apply it flexibly in diverse, ill-structured, and sometimes novel contexts. (p. 184)

People at the introductory stages of learning in a domain not only have less knowledge but are limited in the array of strategies used to procure knowledge. These are likely to be limited to rote memorization or to rely on the use of analogies that misrepresent the complexity of knowledge in a domain. Rarely do introductory learners have occasion to apply the knowledge in new or everyday situations. They are assessed on this knowledge by simple tests of recall such as true-or-false or multiple-choice forms.

People with high levels of expertise differ from introductory learners not only in the amount they know but in the strategies available to them to advance their knowledge (Koroscik, 1993). The problem is that strategies like rote memorization, which work well in the early stages of instruction, are less useful at the advanced stages of instruction, yet students are often ill-equipped to make this transition. In addition, the assessment of learning at the advanced stages generally does not involve tests of recall but rather is evaluated by the ability to apply the knowledge in a relevant way.

COMPLEX DOMAINS AND LEARNING

What Makes Certain Domains Complex and Ill-Structured?

A central feature of cognitive flexibility theory is the realization both that domains of knowledge differ fundamentally in their structural attributes, and that these differences demand differing approaches to instruction. Spiro and his colleagues discuss ill-structured knowledge and well-structured knowledge in the following ways.

Ill-structuredness. A knowledge domain is "ill-structured when the combination of its breadth, complexity, and irregularity of its content make the prescription of its full range of uses impossible" (Spiro et al., 1987, pp. 1–2). There are no broad generalizations that apply to most cases—nothing like the law of gravity in physics. The learning of new knowledge is made difficult by the lack of broad generalizations that might classify and explain the new content. Cognitive science thus far has produced a better understanding of the processes that apply in well-structured domains, which rely heavily on broad generalizations, computational algorithms, or rules that apply to many cases. By contrast, in ill-structured domains learners must organize study by assembling knowledge from individual cases (Spiro et al., 1987).

Well-structuredness. According to Spiro and colleagues (1987), knowledge transfer in well-structured domains occurs through the ability to retrieve generalizations or principles that apply to multiple cases of phenomena undergoing study. Such knowledge structures are encountered in authoritative sources such as textbooks and lectures. These structures (schemata) are referred to by these researchers as "pre-compiled" since they are prepared or selected in advance of formal instruction. Knowledge acquisition in well-structured domains is defined as the taking in of these schemata rather than by their construction or assembly on one's own. Knowledge encountered in textbooks and lectures "tend[s] to stress generalizations, commonalities, and abstractions over cases" (Spiro et al., 1987, p. 2). Such approaches are clearly effective in situations where the cases or examples tend to be similar or alike in how they are approached for analysis and judgment.

The Problem of Instructional Misrepresentations

In theory, it should be easier both to teach and to learn when domains are well-structured. Indeed, one sees attempts to impose a degree of well-structuredness in domains where it is not native, such as the teaching of art. Examples include the organization of instruction around such pre-compiled constructs as the elements of design or linear accounts of art history, the so-called "line of progress" from the cave dwellers to industrial societies. These approaches organize and simplify the structure of the content to be learned, making the overall learning task easier. However, there is a price to pay for this simplification in that it reduces the flexibility of the knowledge being acquired, limiting its potential for transfer to new situations and the formation of new understandings. New situations in art learning include the possibility of advancing new or differing interpretations of a work of art, an art movement, or a view of history.

When a work of art is misrepresented as well-structured, it likely will end up with a "right" interpretation, foreclosing the possibility of alternative interpretations. These right answers may reflect the opinion of the textbook writer or the teacher. If authors organize texts around the elements of design, for example, they imply that the formal elements are the most important features of the work to be studied, and that the work's exemplary qualities can be fully encountered in formal analyses of these elements. While such analyses are sometimes useful in helping students attend to the details of a work of art, they can prompt the learner away from other aspects of the work, such as its expressive content or social context. Imposing a well-structured misrepresentation on such artworks exacts a toll in that it forecloses opportunities to devise fresh interpretations.

Another example is the evolutionary view of art history implied by the linear approaches characteristic of most art history survey texts. Earlier art is seen as the precursor of later art, with the latent assumption that the later forms in the chronology are better.[2] In accepting the easier choices provided by well-structured representations, the learner's power to construct independent understandings and interpretations of art is necessarily abridged. One sacrifices cognitive flexibility for ease of knowledge acquisition, but doing so sets limits on the potential for original thinking.

Learning and Transfer in Ill-Structured Domains

Since knowledge transfer in ill-structured domains is more complex, instructional emphasis must shift from the learning of large generalizations (pre-compiled schemata) to the assembling of knowledge encountered through exposure to numerous cases. The learner must do more than take in knowledge; he or she must engage in a constructive process involving experience with large numbers of cases (Spiro et al., 1987).

By seeing multiple cases, the learner comes to understand the relative influence of various contexts in which each case is embedded. Spiro and colleagues (1987) state:

> In ill-structured domains, crucial information tends to be uniquely contained in individual cases—examples are not just nice, they are necessary. (p. 7)

Instruction in such instances should promote the utilization of such metacognitive strategies as searching for family resemblance among cases, that is, ways works of art in a particular style might be similar, although not exactly alike; or searching for differentiating factors, for example, "How is this example of French Impressionism different from that example?" With such strategic approaches, the individual constructs an interpretation of a specific case or situation. Such knowledge structures are assembled from elements taken from many cases. The capacity to piece together such elements serves in large part as an operational definition of cognitive flexibility.

"Monolithic prepackaged knowledge structures constraining an individual to apply knowledge in a fixed and limited manner" give way to learning situations where the individual controls the knowledge and attempts to apply it in new tasks and situations (Spiro et al., 1987, p. 3).

Cognitive flexibility is one of the principal qualities of mind for which education should strive. Moreover, it is likely to grow in importance as cognitive demands increase with the steady expansion of new information from various sources (Koroscik, 1996b). This plethora of new knowledge will come in many forms, some well-structured and others ill-structured. At present, most school learning is represented as being well-structured, whether or not this is relevant for the domain in question. Hence, recognizing the difference between learning in complexly structured and in more conventional well-structured domains is an essential component in the reform of general education, especially if the purpose of reform is to fully activate the learner's cognitive potential.

The arts in education should be represented as complexly structured domains. As noted earlier, other domains of knowledge are also complexly structured, including the humanities and most other subjects that operate on a case-by-case basis. The arts are not unique in this regard. But since works of art reflect their social environment, they have a built-in potential to connect domains of knowledge that otherwise would be isolated from each other. Potentially they offer a means to integrate knowledge in the curriculum.

INSTRUCTION THAT PROMOTES COGNITIVE FLEXIBILITY— HYPERTEXT TECHNOLOGIES IN INSTRUCTION

Cognitive flexibility in complexly structured domains is promoted through exposure to cases, but how is this to be done in formal instruction? In other words, how does one preserve the intrinsic complexity of a domain without overwhelming learners with more detail than they can comfortably handle at their educational level? Instruction in well-structured domains organizes content around general principles, propositions, or theories. Learning in the sciences usually occurs this way, especially at the introductory level, but when such methods are applied to complexly structured situations, they can set the stage for comprehension failure at later phases of learning.

Spiro and his colleagues (1987) have devised a method that enables learners to encounter numerous cases by treating the content domain as a "landscape" to be explored. It is explored in detail by paths of travel that crisscross it in many directions, "re-examining each case 'site' in varying contexts of differing neighboring cases, and by using a variety of abstract dimensions for comparing cases" (p. 2). The landscape and path metaphors enable students to encounter multiple cases while exploring the domain in all its complexity with minimal cognitive strain. Spiro and colleagues

(1988) offer the following description of learning as characterized in their landscape metaphor:

> Deep understanding of a complex landscape will not be obtained in a single traversal. Similarly for a *conceptual* landscape. Rather, the landscape must be crisscrossed in many directions to master its complexity and to avoid having the fullness of the domain attenuated. The same sites in a landscape (the same cases or concepts in a knowledge domain) should be revisited from different directions, thought about from different perspectives, and so on. There is a limit to how much understanding of a complex entity can be achieved in a single treatment, in a single context, for a single purpose. By repeating the presentation of the same complex case or concept information in new contexts, additional aspects of the multifacetedness of these "landscape sites" are brought out. . . . Thus cognitive flexibility is fostered by a flexible approach to learning and instruction. (p. 6; emphasis in original)

Their landscape metaphor made use of a hypertext technological representation of knowledge pertaining to the heart and circulatory system to enable learners to explore this domain in a nonlinear fashion. Such systems of learning and instruction help offset the constraints imposed by traditional schemes of instruction that typify much schooling practice. Well-structured representations of knowledge tend to portray knowledge domains as "top-down" structures starting with broad generalizations that group cases together. Once the general principle is understood, it is found to apply equally to each case. However, when the knowledge of a particular domain is not well-structured, but is misrepresented in instruction as being well-structured, this creates knowledge structures that are more rigid and compartmentalized than they need to be:

> The simplifying assumptions of cognitive science apply as well to dominant modes of education. Simplification of complex subject matter makes it easier for teachers to teach, for students to take notes and prepare for their tests, for test-givers to construct and grade tests, and for authors to write texts. The result is a massive *"conspiracy of convenience."* . . .
>
> [T]he overall effect of the simplifying features of knowledge representation systems and instructional strategies . . . is a leveling tendency, a tendency towards *monolithic* approaches. Understanding is seen as proceeding in essentially the same way across instances of the same topic. Our view is different: The conditions for applying old knowledge are subject to considerable *variability*, and that variability in turn requires *flexibility* of response. Monolithic representations of knowledge will too often leave their holders facing situations for which their rigid "plaster casts" simply do not fit. The result is the often heard complaint of students: "We weren't taught that." By this, they mean that they weren't taught *exactly* that. They lack the abil-

ity to use their knowledge in new ways, the ability to think for themselves. (Spiro et al., 1987, p. 4; emphasis in original)

Spiro and colleagues contrast the flexible approach as typified by knowledge in ill-structured learning situations with the more traditional approaches found in well-structured situations (see Table 4.1).

MISCONCEPTIONS RESULTING FROM REDUCTIONS OF COMPLEXITY: THE REDUCTIVE BIAS

Spiro, Coulson, Feltovich, and Anderson (1988) introduce the term "reductive bias" to refer to several potential difficulties that arise when complex domains are represented in instruction as though they were simpler, well-structured domains. These biases lessen the student's ability to develop flexible knowledge needed for application in new situations. They result from a cognitive inclination (a disposition in thinking) to simplify complex material—an inclination that sometimes is reinforced by similar simplificational practices within educational practice (Feltovich, Spiro, & Coulson, 1993; Spiro et al., 1988).

An example of the tendency to simplify can be seen in Gombrich's *Art and Illusion* (1960). In particular, I refer to an engraving of Chartres Cathedral reproduced in the text (p. 72). Gombrich explains that it was made by an English engraver who had not seen the building and who held the belief that all Gothic buildings had pointed arches. In copying a lithographic image of Chartres, he deliberately added pointed arches to the rounded Romanesque windows of the west façade. As Gombrich noted, in this engraver's "universe of form," the Gothic, by definition and rule, meant having pointed arches and no other kinds. This simplification of the facts is the consequence of the reductive bias, in this case one that reduced the complex world of Gothic form. Hence, his stereotyped understanding registered in his rendition.

We don't know how the engraver acquired this faulty concept, but many reductive ideas are the result of particular instructional practices that reduce the complexity of difficult subject matter. Feltovich and colleagues (1993) list three such practices:

- teaching topics in isolation from related ones (compartmentalizing knowledge);
- presenting only clear instances of a phenomenon (and not the many pertinent exceptions);
- requiring only reproductive memory in assessment. (p. 184)

Table 4.1. Knowledge Representations in Well-Structured and
Ill-Structured Domains

	Well-Structured	*Ill-Structured*
Nature of representation	Prepackaged knowledge, such as textbooks or lectures, is characteristic. Knowledge is likely to be cumulative, sequential, and usually organized by grade level, as in math and basal readers.	Knowledge is characterized by flexibility. Fragments of knowledge are assembled to fit the needs of a given context.
Main task in learning	Learners must select relevant schemata from preassembled texts.	Learners must construct schemata by assembling cases and segments of knowledge.
Evaluation of learning	Evaluation of students involves reproduction of knowledge supplied by text or lectures, with paper-and-pencil tests of recall and standardized assessment tests.	Evaluation of students involves knowledge application in new situations, as with transfer; assessment is likely to be at the local level.
Major features	1. Knowledge representations tend to be rigid, depending on authoritative prepackaged sources, such as texts.	1. Knowledge representations are more complex. Learners may need aid to manage difficulties (e.g., Spiro's landscape metaphor).
	2. Knowledge representations tend to compartmentalize knowledge that in use may need to be connected.	2. Cases or examples must be studied as they occur, without the convenience of textbook examples.
	3. Complex knowledge often is represented as being simpler than it actually is (i.e., knowledge is "artificially neatened").	3. Cases or examples differ from one another, requiring learners to find commonalities among them.
	4. Knowledge domains are represented as possessing more regularity and consistency across specific cases than is actually the case.	4. Knowledge domains can be messy and inconsistent, lacking the regularity of clear boundaries or categories.
	5. Top-down knowledge systems run into combinations of events not covered by the text. Learners may get stuck when unanticipated problems are encountered.	5. Bottom-up knowledge systems are able to adapt to unanticipated problems through the assemblage of situation-sensitive schemata.

Reductive biases are likely to get established at the introductory phases of learning when novice students may be overwhelmed by the complexity of the domain they are attempting to master, especially when teachers artificially simplify the learning task by either eliminating hard cases or glossing over troublesome details. The resulting conceptual impairment may not appear until the knowledge is to be called upon by problems confronted at advanced levels of knowledge acquisition.

The reductive bias can take several forms:

- Oversimplification of complex and irregular structures
- Overreliance on single analogies[3]
- Overreliance on precompiled knowledge structures
- Compartmentalization[4]

Oversimplification of Complex and Irregular Structures

One form of the reductive bias is the tendency to treat superficial similarities among related phenomena as unifying characteristics. This might be seen when students mistake one style for another, such as Impressionism for post-Impressionism. In fact, the two styles are closely related, with some artists exhibiting some attributes of each. They share common characteristics, for example, the tendency to use the same palette and to depict similar subjects, such as outdoor cafes, people in contemporary dress (in contrast to the use of classical drapery by academic artists of the same period), harbor scenes, and people enjoying their leisure. When emphasis is placed on these similarities, students may tend to ignore or minimize important differences between the two styles, and thus miss opportunities to deepen their understanding of the historical issues that impelled post-Impressionist artists to modify their style. Missing out on this difference would make it difficult for students to understand the onset of Modernism, the leading impulse in Western art of the late nineteenth and early twentieth centuries.

One Modernist attribute was seen in the tendency of avant-garde artists to set themselves apart from middle-class life, and to act as outside observers commenting on its contradictions and ironies. This attitude tended to influence post-Impressionist artists like Georges Seurat, whose expressive content has been interpreted by such art historians as Linda Nochlin (1990) as including a critique of Impressionism itself, especially its tendency to express the positive features of bourgeois life while excluding its darker side. When students are prompted to focus on subject-matter similarities between Seurat and an Impressionist artist like Pierre Auguste Renoir, they could miss out on the subtler differences.

Avoiding oversimplification. How can teachers avoid the tendency to oversimplify? Spiro and colleagues (1988) write that "the remedy is to take special measures to demonstrate complexities and irregularities" and to "lay bare the limitations of first pass understandings, to highlight exceptions, to show how the superficially similar is dissimilar" (pp. 4–5).

The following example might serve as a strategy to surmount oversimplification: A middle school teacher introduces a unit on French Impressionism and post-Impressionism by pointing out several characteristics of the Impressionist style, what I have called a "recognition rule" (Efland, 1995).[5] These include the following:

- These painters loved the effects of vibrant color.
- They sought to create the effects of outdoor lighting (*plein air*).
- They painted with expressive brush strokes rather than producing the slick finished surfaces of traditional academic painting.
- They frequently showed middle-class people enjoying their leisure in outdoor settings, such as garden restaurants and boating scenes.

These four attributes do, in fact, apply to many works by Impressionist artists, and together they provide a "first pass" understanding of the stylistic attributes of Impressionism suitable at the introductory phases of instruction. As such, they work like a rule or generalization in a well-structured domain. Moreover, they are easy to teach and learn. Children recognize these characteristics with a handful of examples. The rule in this instance also exemplifies Spiro's notion of a "conspiracy of convenience," in which the desire for simple instructional procedures reduces complexity. The problem for this teacher is how to transcend the rule, one commonly found in textbook representations of the Impressionist style.

The teacher recognizes that the list of generic attributes fails to differentiate all types of Impressionist paintings[6] and that the same rule would allow certain post-Impressionist works by Seurat to be categorized as Impressionist works. Using that observation, she displayed Seurat's *Sunday Afternoon on the Isle of Grande Jatte* with other paintings of people enjoying their leisure, in particular, Renoir's *La Moulin de la Galette*. In comparison to the Renoir, the figures in the *Grande Jatte* appear to be stiff, almost frozen. It is hard to see the subject of both paintings as people enjoying their leisure. Yet, when asking students questions about which picture shows the *most* enjoyment, the teacher found that opinion was divided evenly between the two scenes. At this point students were asked to view the image of a nineteenth-century corset.[7] When this was placed alongside the *Grande Jatte*, it triggered such observations as, "The ladies in *Grande Jatte* are probably wearing corsets like these, so it is hard to imagine that they could be relaxed and having a good time."

Assessment of oversimplification. Feltovich, Spiro, and Coulson (1993) suggest that assessment items "should be crafted to reflect known misconceptions" (p. 206). In the lesson discussed above, the evaluation items could include items that identify knowledge of the recognition rule, which can be demonstrated when students point to works where it applies, such as the Renoir. Other items could deal with "hard cases," which are exceptions to the rule. For example, Edgar Degas's *Absinthe Drinker* hardly can be said to show people enjoying their leisure.

Overreliance on Single Analogies

Among the examples that Spiro and colleagues (1988) use to describe this bias is the tendency to use single analogies to explain a complex process or phenomenon. The tendency of medical students to conceive of the cardiovascular system through the analogy of plumbing in a building exemplifies this. Like all other analogies, this one is partially relevant, but by reducing the conceptual complexity of this system to mere plumbing, these students potentially miss critical understandings, setting the stage for later comprehension failure. Other examples of partial analogies can be found in biology texts, such as where the eye is likened to a camera. Human vision, unlike the camera, is selective and is guided by the interests of the viewer. Closer to home, researchers in artificial intelligence liken the brain to a computer.

In art, analogies may be found in the idea that art is a *mirror*, that art is good when it is as real as a photograph, and that photographs don't lie. Extending students' aesthetic horizons would require alternatives to the mirror analogy (Abrams, 1953). For example, viewing the work of art as an object that illuminates, such as a *lamp*, an object that can project the emotions and feelings of the artist, might be an alternative. Still another might be to regard the work as a doorway or window into other cultures or time periods. Students bound to the first view will have difficulty understanding artworks not based on natural appearances, such as African sculpture, Japanese paintings influenced by Zen Buddhism, and, certainly, twentieth-century abstract art. Students having one or more of the latter views may realize that creativity involves more than mere reflection, while students capable of using several analogies have a more flexible basis for understanding how beliefs about art can bring into play different intellectual issues and aesthetic criteria. In justifying their aesthetic judgments, they also become mindful of the views about art they are using. And the more views of art they possess in their cognitive repertoire, the more kinds of art they can understand and enjoy.

Use of multiple analogies in instruction. When the reductive bias is caused by the use of a single analogy, a way to overcome this deficit is to replace single representations with multiple representations. Complex concepts can rarely be represented with a single schema, or analogy (Spiro et al., 1988). Single representations miss important facets of complex concepts. "Cognitive flexibility is dependent upon having a diversified repertoire of ways of thinking about a conceptual topic" (Spiro et al., 1988, p. 5).

In the following example, a teacher uses a series of Cindy Sherman's photographic self-portraits to challenge the "mirror of nature" analogy. This photographic artist projects differing gender roles into her self-portraits, roles imposed on women by specific cultural norms or social expectations. One question students could confront is whether the real Cindy Sherman is embodied in any single representation; another question would be to explain why she created such different images of herself. Since photographs supposedly don't lie, the learner could be challenged to determine whether the artist is not reflecting just herself in these portraits, but is projecting specific meanings about women in American society. Does her art mirror life as it is, or does it illuminate the viewer through her exaggerated poses?

Evaluation of analogies. Students could be given two dissimilar Sherman photographic portraits for interpretation. Student responses to the photographs should show awareness of the artist's strategy of altering self-representations to make a particular feminist statement. Cognitive flexibility would be demonstrated when students were able to expand the number of views of art they could use to account for the underlying basis of the work.

Spiro and colleagues (1988) also stress the point that in working with multiple representations it is important to revisit and rearrange these as new cases of representations are encountered. This enables one to reconstruct older understandings. The hypertext curricular approaches used by Spiro and his colleagues enable students to revisit case sites, each time from a differing perspective, thus enabling students to deepen their understanding in ways that are cognitively flexible. If a similar process were used with an artist like Sherman, teachers would have a way of seeing how their interpretations of these photographs might change as more cases are visited and revisited.

Overreliance on Pre-Compiled Knowledge Structures

In art a form of the reductive bias can be seen when students with some prior knowledge sometimes adopt rigid, formulaic strategies to interpret works of art. For example, a student schooled in formal analysis to identify and analyze the elements and principles of design, sometimes will apply this strategy to interpret works of art, although the conceptual task may require interpretation of the social context of the work, where formal analytic approaches would likely not be meaningful.

Instruction based on contrary cases. To remedy this tendency the teacher might demonstrate the limitations of formal analysis as an exclusive means for interpreting works of art. This could be demonstrated with works of art like Warhol's *Campbell's Soup Cans*. From a formal standpoint, the image of the soup can would not differ in any significant way from the actual object in the supermarket, and no amount of formal analysis would enable the art viewer to distinguish the Warhol from the supermarket commodity.

A teacher could stage an incident in which students are asked to describe, analyze, interpret, and judge one of Warhol's *Brillo Box* compositions. The teacher might then ask the students to repeat the exercise with real Brillo boxes from the supermarket, and explain why one is art and the other mere merchandise. Attention to this problem might be prompted by questions like, "Why do the usual approaches to interpretation falter in this instance?" Similar approaches also might apply in dealing with Marcel Duchamp's "ready-mades." What makes these works of art is not any particular set of formal qualities, but the social context in which they are placed for viewing, namely, the museum or art gallery.

The typical art history survey course abounds with pre-compiled knowledge structures. Among these are the "grand narratives" that usually organize texts built upon a chronology that suggests that art is part of the progress of civilization from the cave man to modern industrial civilization, and that later developments in art are likely to be better than early developments. Donald Presiosi (1989) describes the typical art history survey text, such as Helen Gardner's *Art Through the Ages* (1948) or H. W. Janson's *History of Art* (1962); the slide collection; the college survey course; and museums as conceptual apparatuses that impose and mutually reinforce each other to produce a certain structure of belief. This structure also tends to include such ideas as that most great artists were male geniuses and that genius itself is an attribute conferred on a few White Europeans to the exclusion of most women artists and people from non-Western cultures. The progress narrative also tends to assert the hegemony of

Western art. Once these structures of belief are in place, it is hard to dis-
place them with alternative interpretations of history.

In *Postmodern Art Education: An Approach to Curriculum*, Efland, Freedman, and Stuhr (1996) suggest approaches that replace "grand narratives"
with "little narratives."[8] These would be the stories about the art of the
less well known, or the art of disenfranchised or oppressed minorities who
are excluded from the canon of establishment art history. Such inclusion
is made difficult because there are few texts available, nor is there the depth
of conventional scholarly resources. Such knowledge literally has to be
constructed from its indigenous sources. In lessening its dependence on
pre-compiled structures, the domain of art history perforce becomes more
complexly structured. It is also clear that for more advanced students, the
learning process also may need to include the active disassembly or
"deconstruction" of some pre-existing, pre-compiled schemata.[9]

Assessment by change in pre-compiled structures. The midterm or final
examination has become the standard evaluation device used in art history courses, and perhaps there is no better way to be sure that students
recognize the *great looks* in the canon of art masterpieces. But survey courses
tend to be organized around hidden assumptions like the grand narratives
mentioned above.[10] Evaluation items might be constructed to reveal the
presence of such pre-compiled structures, and whether the learner is capable of devising alternative knowledge structures that either contest the
progress notion or identify criteria of excellence other than the work's
placement on a timeline. In the latter case, evaluation items might assess
the student's ability to compare or contrast works of art when taken out
of the chronological context in which they were presented in the text or
classroom discussion.

Compartmentalization

This form of the reductive bias sometimes impels students to isolate concepts and categories from one another when, in fact, they may overlap
and interact with one another.[11] For example, students may have organized their understanding of art into specific categories, such as fine art,
contemporary art, serious art, popular art, or folk art. Art also can be organized around cultural classifications, such as Asian art, African art, or
European art. In addition, students may organize the arts by functions,
such as religious art, advertising art, or industrial design, or into functional
or nonfunctional categories.

However, many of these groupings actually overlap with one another.
For example, artists like Andy Warhol and Roy Lichtenstein are identified

with the fine arts, yet the content of their art is drawn largely from the popular culture and makes use of techniques derived from commercial illustration. The problem, of course, is that there are overlaps among the several compartments that potentially exist to categorize the arts. A simple assessment procedure may show a student to have extensive categories of art concepts, but not show how, or if, these concepts are organized or linked together. A more lucrative form of assessment might entail some form of mapping of the domain of the arts. In the chapter that follows, the concept of cognitive mapping is explored as a means for the assessment of student understandings.

A second form of compartmentalization is seen in the tendency to teach art as though it were an autonomous subject unrelated to the other subjects in the school curriculum. Here, the remedy is more radical and will require a curriculum that intentionally seeks ways to integrate the arts into other subject areas, such as literature, history, and social studies. I discuss this problem later in this chapter. When such a curriculum is in place, it will be possible to design an evaluation that shows how students construct their understandings of art in terms of concepts derived from domains at some remove from art. Assessment efforts will need to do more than determine the presence or absence of concepts, but will need to determine how they are combined, organized, and related to other concepts in the learner's understanding.

THE COMPLEXITY RIDDLE AND THE APPLICATION OF CURRICULUM MODELS

Until now I have dealt with the problem of identifying misconceptions that might develop when complexly structured content has been artificially simplified to facilitate ease of instruction and learning. I have described some ways in which such content might be presented to offset the deleterious effects of oversimplification. Flexibility is facilitated when knowledge is represented in ways that acknowledge the deep-seated, innate complexity in a particular domain of knowledge, but when such domains are laden with an abundance of detail, with many cases that are exceptions to rules and other sources of irregularities, the learner may well experience difficulty and potential failure. He or she will experience the subject as hard to learn.

In anticipation of such problems, well-intentioned educators have tried to minimize potential failure by simplifying the presentation of curriculum content. From Pestalozzi's time early in the nineteenth century, educators have attempted to solve the riddle of complexity. His method consisted in first learning things in their simplest terms, the ABCs, and then increasing the element of complexity by gradual increments that would scarcely be noticed by learners (Efland, 1990). However, when reading was reduced to its simplest elements, like the sounding out of abstract syllables, the exercise frequently ceased to have meaning. Phonics instruction is a vestigial reminder of this approach.

Educators also have tried to simplify knowledge by eliminating ambiguity. The recognition rule for Impressionism, described earlier, could be seen as a way to highlight the important features of the style to make it clear. But the problem with works of art is twofold. First, an art object can belong to more than a single set at the same time. The same work of art can exemplify attributes from differing disciplines. Versailles exemplifies the French Baroque style but is also emblematic of the political power of the French monarchy. Also, transitional works of art sometimes can exhibit qualities that enable them to be classified as belonging to more than one style or period. Robert Rauschenberg sometimes is listed as an Abstract Expressionist artist but is identified with Pop art as well.

Second, works of art might link up with elements of knowledge that are widely separated. Versailles as a symbol of royal authority might be compared with other architectural symbols of centralized authority, such as St. Peter's Cathedral in Rome, the Kremlin in Moscow, or the palace of a Mandarin emperor in dynastic China. Is it possible to organize instruction in ways that preserve the complexity of a domain, yet do not overwhelm the learner with excessive detail? This was the problem that Spiro and his colleagues addressed in their curriculum landscape model.

In dealing with this problem, I have both devised models of curriculum content and studied the advantages and disadvantages of various models (Efland, 1995, 2000). Earlier, I discussed Bruner's notion of the spiral curriculum as his solution to the problem, but saw difficulties with its tendency to organize knowledge in a top-down fashion starting with the key ideas provided by disciplinary scholars. The spiral curriculum was based on curriculum development work in math and science in the late 1950s and 1960s, a time when many researchers assumed that the learning process was the same for all areas of knowledge.

I proposed a model based on the idea that learners' knowledge structures are a cognitive latticework of interwoven concepts. It also was my attempt to overcome the top-down feature of the spiral curriculum (Efland, 1995). The lattice is akin to Spiro's landscape metaphor, although it differs in that his was a domain awaiting discovery by intellectual exploration, whereas the lattice was conceived as a structure actively undergoing construction as learning progressed.[12] The lattice and the landscape are similar metaphoric representations that attempt to capture the complexity of the knowledge undergoing instruction without overwhelming the capabilities of students. Each of these metaphors involves three interrelated factors:

- The way knowledge is organized in an individual's knowledge base
- The way domains of knowledge are organized by domain scholars
- The way content is organized in its instructional representations

I assume that certain arrangements of curriculum content will enhance learning if, in some approximate way, they are patterned after the structures of the knowledge being taught, and that ultimately these structures should enable learners to represent domain knowledge to themselves in flexible ways for effective application in relevant situations. Theoretical models are important when they suggest optimal representational patterns that the content might take to facilitate success in comprehension.

The City as Metaphor for the Curriculum

An analogy related to the cognitive lattice equates the planning of a curriculum to the planning of a city (Efland, 2000). Urban planners use the practice of zoning to simplify the design of cities by designating land-use zones for residential, recreational, commercial, and industrial purposes. Placing these functions in separate zones gives cities a simpler and more rational structure, although critics of the built environment like Jane Jacobs (1961) and planners like Christopher Alexander (1988) began noting that simplification per se does not necessarily make cities more livable. Too much simplification reduces the quality of life, as is evident in many urban renewal projects or in the sprawling suburbs. Simplification, or more accurately, oversimplification, is a problem in the planning of both a city and a curriculum.

The zones of a city are like the subjects in a curriculum, and when such zones are rigidly enforced without the possibility of variances, the city is made simpler and more rational, yet loses flexibility in ways it can accommodate the built environment to the life purposes of its inhabitants. In this regard, it is akin to the artificial imposition of well-structured representations on a domain of knowledge that is inherently complex and irregular. On the other hand, if there is a total absence of constraints on land use, there would be chaos. Plans for land use should exist, yet must be flexible enough to accommodate changing needs.

Conversely, complexity for the sake of complexity—complexity in and of itself—will not make cities and towns easier, better, or more stimulating places for living. Complexity can add richness, variety, interest, and uniqueness that can enhance community life, but it also can lead to confusion and disorder. The analogy between the planning of cities and the planning of curricula is clear in that simple albeit well-structured arrangements of knowledge or the built environment cannot be ends in themselves but should serve to enhance the quality of understanding in the one case and the viability of the community in the other.

Overlapping Sets

In contemporary planning practices, cities often try to make their land-use schemes more flexible and livable by assigning multiple functions to the same land parcel. This is done both to lessen urban sprawl and for practical convenience. A business such as a bakery located in a commercial zone may have its proprietor living in a second-floor residence above the shop, or a high-rise parking structure might have shops on the street level. A second example of overlapping sets might be a town's business district, which may contain buildings having historical value worthy of preservation. Thus, a given parcel of land could be zoned both for business and for historical preservation. Such overlaps are subject to different zoning criteria, but of importance is that these overlapping districts often play a significant role in defining the character of the community as a place with a history, where historical attractions give it a uniqueness that makes the community more desirable and satisfying as a place to live and work.

A parallel situation exists in plans for the curriculum. When domains of knowledge are rigidly compartmentalized, the potential for seeing connections within and between domains is minimized, limiting their potential for the formation of higher-order understandings. Such boundaries limit the potential for transfer. Yet without boundaries the curriculum would become a disorganized, amorphous mass. A balance has to be struck between a too rigid configuration of domains and a situation with too few or even no boundaries at all.

For example, with the onset of Modernism in the late nineteenth and early twentieth centuries, boundaries became established that began separating high culture from popular culture. With the start of the present century, it is becoming evident that this separation between high and low culture was a condition of the past that has changed. As mentioned earlier, the principal content of the art of artists like Warhol and Lichtenstein was the imagery of commercial illustration and the icons of popular culture. In this case, a former cultural boundary has become a zone of contention.

The Hub Metaphor

Although tremendously influential in guiding curriculum development initiatives in math and science, Bruner's spiral curriculum was less applicable in ill-structured domains. My proposed lattice metaphor accommodated a greater degree of ill-structuredness, but I have concluded that it could lead to too much complexity at the introductory phases of learning. An alternative to the lattice metaphor is the "hub metaphor" proposed and utilized by Yang (2000), where knowledge is organized like the hub system of a major airline. If airlines scheduled direct flights between all of the cities they served, they would soon be overwhelmed by the sheer complexity of the flight schedule they would have to maintain. If certain cities were instituted as hubs or transfer points, the scheduling system could be simplified and made less cumbersome by having several planes, flying relatively short distances, meet at the same terminal to exchange passengers.

In curriculum work, a hub might consist of a broad theme through which one might reach a variety of related destinations. Yang, for example, used the dragon motif as a hub through which students could study Chinese culture. Like Spiro and his colleagues, she also utilized hypertext technology. As students journeyed from the hub to visit various sites (images of the dragon selected from the artwork of three time periods), their knowledge of the dragon motif could develop and become more elaborate, along with their knowledge of its changing significance in Chinese culture. Curriculum planners might adapt these metaphoric notions to both integrate areas of study and help students construct possible linkages among ideas often isolated by arbitrary subject boundaries. At the same time, they should be mindful of the limitations of each metaphor.

THE INTEGRATED CURRICULUM

Current school curricula tend to be tightly compartmentalized into subjects. This is evident in the typical block schedule of the secondary school student, but is equally evident at elementary levels. If the aim of education is to fully activate the cognitive potential of the learner, ways have to be found to integrate knowledge from many subjects to achieve a fuller understanding than would be provided by content treated in isolation. Integrated approaches to instruction rely heavily on the transfer of knowledge from one domain to another. Integration of subjects in education is not new. It was widely advocated during the progressive education movement of the 1930s, and it characterized the curriculum initiated by Waldorf schools in Germany and Switzerland in the 1920s, which were based on the educational ideas of Rudolf Steiner. In art education one of the stronger promoters of an integrated approach was Leon Winslow (1939), who believed that art teachers should attempt to relate instruction in art to such fields as history, geography, social studies, language arts, and industrial arts. The unified school experience was favored over subject matter divided by arbitrary boundaries. In the 1930s, arguments favoring integrated approaches were grounded in the need for social cohesion brought on by the Great Depression,[13] whereas current arguments are stated in terms of cognitive benefits likely to arise when subject matter is made meaningful by pointing out its interconnections and potential applications. Since the interpretation of a work of art frequently draws upon knowledge from differing domains, studies of artwork can lie at the core of an integrated conception of general education.

IMPLICATIONS OF COGNITIVE FLEXIBILITY THEORY FOR ART EDUCATION

Cognitive flexibility theory holds several important lessons for art teaching. First, it offers a cognitive explanation of how domains of knowledge differ from one another and the cognitive consequences that the neglect of these differences might have for learning. At one time, the dividing line between the disciplines separated them into cognitive and noncognitive categories, with all the arts placed in the latter. Now, the distinguishing features among disciplines (aside from their content) are differences in their overall structure—between those that are well-structured and those that are ill-structured. Both types of domains are cognitive, but it is essential to grasp fully the character of these differences if we are to succeed in harnessing the cognitive benefits each type of domain has to offer. What I am saying is that the activation of the learner's cognitive potential requires the ability to function in a variety of domains, both well-structured and ill-structured. Moreover, if it is important for students to have experiences with both types of learning situations, and if art is complex and ill-structured, then instruction should honestly represent this state of affairs.[14]

Second, recognition of the structural differences among domains is needed by designers of curriculum materials in order to faithfully represent each domain. The use of various metaphors like the spiral, the landscape, the lattice, or the city were attempts to capture aspects of complexity without overwhelming the learner at the introductory phases of instruction. In addition, hypertext instructional technologies can be helpful in designing instructional materials to handle complexity. However, it is also important to recognize that no single metaphor or analogy is likely to be applicable to all domains. The spiral was shown to work well in math and science, but served less well in the arts and humanities.

Third, it is important for learners to recognize differences in the structures of domain knowledge and to have opportunities to acquire the appropriate strategies for mastery in various domains. A curriculum that provides only well-structured representations of knowledge (principles, laws, concepts) and that fails to alert the student to the need to interpret the individual case, may fail to fully activate his or her cognitive potential.

Fourth, differences in the structures of domains will require different forms of assessment. In particular, the evaluation of instruction in complexly structured domains should show evidence of knowledge assembly from many cases or examples and require looking for knowledge application in new situations, that is, transfer. The recall of information by standardized testing is an insufficient indicator of understanding.

Fifth, art might serve as an integrating vehicle within the curriculum, since the interpretation of art requires that it be situated in its social and cultural contexts. Works of art are more than formal designs that arouse interest. They enable the learner to integrate knowledge from many domains because they are about the life and death issues that affect people where they live, that is, issues affecting their social and personal worlds like war and peace, the need to belong, equity, justice, morality, and the like.

This latter claim is not without caveats, namely, that the connections or relationships among domains would need to be emphasized in instruction. Indeed, establishing these relationships becomes the point and purpose of instruction and provides indications that students are forming understandings. A second caveat is that in an integrated curriculum no domain should be subservient to other domains.

In Chapter 1 I asked whether there is any truth to the claim that the arts are intellectually undemanding occupations, suitable for amusement and diversion but not well suited as places to cultivate the mind. Research in cognitive flexibility does not directly answer this question. What it does suggest is that each domain makes particular demands on thinking and cultivates different strategies for learning, and that the arts are places in the cognitive landscape where the power to devise interpretations becomes uppermost. Is there a cognitive hierarchy? Do some cognitive abilities demand more brain power or intelligence? For those questions there are no certain answers. Are some abilities more important than others? Probably so, but such judgments are social determinations. The arts are educationally important if and to the extent that they enable individuals to integrate their understanding of the world.

The chapter that follows deals with the problem of assessing learning in the visual arts.

5

Obstacles to Art Learning
and Their Assessment

IN THIS CHAPTER I SKETCH OUT two possible approaches to the assessment of art learning. The first devotes attention to work by Judith Koroscik and her colleagues who classified types of errors and common misconceptions possessed by students in the early stages of art learning and those made by more advanced students. A second approach to assessment relies on a procedure known as cognitive mapping. These discussions are not tied to any particular body of knowledge, age group, or set of educational expectations. Rather, they are based on observations of problems that arise when students try to understand works of art.

MISCONCEPTIONS IN LEARNING ABOUT ART—
THE KOROSCIK ANALYSIS

Koroscik's account of learning is derived in large part from the symbol-processing view of cognition described in Chapter 3. Her work was influenced by educational research with students in such knowledge-rich areas as physics, mathematics, computer programming, and the like (see Perkins & Simmons, 1988; Prawat, 1989; Rohwer & Sloane, 1994). She describes learning as knowledge construction and assumes that the resulting structures of knowledge coincide with the structures of knowledge found in the disciplines.

Differences Between the Knowledge Bases of Novices and Experts

Koroscik's work was influenced by studies into differences between novice and expert learners studying in a specific domain of knowledge (Perkins

& Simmons, 1988; Prawat, 1989). From the time of Piaget and the advent of his cognitive developmental theory, ideas about expertise frequently were tied to cognitive developmental stages. The professional scientist would be one whose work made use of formal operations and their symbolic manipulation. Novices would be those learners working at the earlier stages of development using the operations of the sensimotor or concrete operations stage. For Piaget, it would have been inconceivable for one to become a professional scientist or mathematician without reaching the stage of formal operations.

However, developmental stages per se never explained adequately how one could become a high achiever in one area of knowledge, making use of formal operations, while remaining quite naive in other domains, using the same or similar operations. To explain this it is necessary to uncouple ideas about novices and experts from developmental considerations. For example, although I am an adult, I am a novice with respect to speaking Mandarin. By contrast, a 10-year-old Chinese student would have nearly total mastery of the language.

If stages don't explain advanced abilities, what else might account for them? A more lucrative research direction was found by identifying the differences between the cognitive operations used by novices and those used by students who had achieved a greater degree of mastery. Our commonsense way of thinking about the differences between advanced learners (having expertise) and novice learners is in terms of the size of their knowledge base. However, other differences are at least as important as the extent of the knowledge base.

In particular, expertise shows up in the organization of the knowledge base. Access to prior knowledge is an important factor in determining the ways that new learning is acquired. Knowledge that is clearly organized and categorized is easier to retrieve than knowledge organized in a haphazard way. Prawat (1989) cites Polya's assertion that "good organization is even more important than the extent of one's knowledge" (p. 5).

Commonsense Knowledge

There is also the possibility that specific schemata possessed by the learner are naive or even factually wrong. This can delay, constrain, and distort the reliability of new understandings. In a discussion of the possible constraints that children's commonsense knowledge might place on learning in a science classroom, Rosalind Driver and her associates (1994) provided a series of examples to illustrate this point. One was the idea that "objects in motion require a constant force to keep moving." They explain that it is perfectly true that if one wants to keep a piano moving across the floor, one needs to apply a constant push. This commonsense view is acquired from the everyday world of experience, but the presence of this realization may set the stage for difficulties later when the students attempt to understand Newton's laws of motion. Teachers who can anticipate which types of naive concepts are likely to be present in the learner's knowledge base are better able to anticipate and perhaps forestall later comprehension failure.

Examples of children's naive concepts in art also were described by Dennie Wolf (1987),[1] who found that many 5-year-old children believed that paintings were made in factories by machinery. "They make few distinctions between aesthetic and non-aesthetic objects. . . . Although they may be able to identify one object as a map and another as a drawing, they do not see the two as different types or classes of images" (p. 5). Most had not encountered the idea that an image could be the original work of an artist. They also had little idea of differences between reproductions and originals. If children lack the notion of originality, the idea would hardly make sense that an artist like Van Gogh made pictures in a way that intentionally differed from his predecessors. More likely, they would perceive the attributes of his style as an aberration of some sort. Also, if they lack the awareness that there is an original work and that reproductions in textbooks are mass-produced replicas of that original, they will not form a basic understanding of the nature of artistic activity itself.

Moreover, such misconceptions are not limited to young children, as in Wolf's studies. In a class of graduate students, I encountered a student who was puzzled by the question: "Why did Picasso paint *Guernica* in black, grays, and white?" He had assumed that the original painting was in color and that the image, as encountered in the text, was a black and white reproduction. As a result, he could not understand the question. Naivete is not limited to school-age children.

Koroscik's Analysis of Misconceptions Summarized

Koroscik's particular formulation of learning was built upon several studies in cognition (e.g., Bransford, Sherwood, Vye, & Rieser, 1986; Covington, 1992; Feltovich, Spiro, & Coulson, 1993; Glaser, 1988; Perkins & Simmons, 1988; Prawat, 1989). Although the studies she cited rarely if ever dealt with learning in the arts, they provided indicators of where potential problems are likely to develop as individuals attempt to form understandings within a domain of knowledge. She applied these insights to the study of learning in the arts (Koroscik, 1982, 1990a, 1990b, 1992a, 1992b, 1993, 1996a; Koroscik et al., 1994). These studies involved school-age children as well as undergraduate students in courses of art criticism.

In particular, Koroscik's work addressed the identification of road-blocks to intellectual development, with the objective of uncovering factors that may cause novice learners' understandings to remain undeveloped. In Koroscik's view, these difficulties fall into one of three groups:

- They can be caused by inadequacies in the learner's knowledge base.
- They can be the result of weak or inappropriate knowledge-seeking strategies.
- They can be a function of a poor disposition to learn. (Koroscik, 1996b, pp. 8–11)

Learning difficulties also can assume some combination of all three. For example, Perkins (1994) stresses the linkage between students' state of willingness or unwillingness to learn and their selection of appropriate knowledge-seeking strategies. Each "roadblock" is discussed in detail below in relation to art-learning situations (see Table 5.1 for an overview).

Problems with an Art Viewer's Knowledge Base

Extensiveness and organization of the knowledge base. The reasons given for differences in understanding between the novice and expert emphasize both quantitative and qualitative characteristics—that is, having more knowledge versus the organization of that knowledge and the ability to transfer knowledge to new learning situations. Prawat (1992) describes the advantages of expertise in the following way: "Experts know more than novices but their real advantage lies in the ability to access . . . what they know—presumably because their knowledge is organized in a more connected or coherent fashion" (p. 375). Prawat and Floden (1994) also suggest that people who are expert at understanding something tend to view domain knowledge differently than do novices. For example, experts seem to recognize that "knowledge evolves through a process of negotiation within discursive communities and that the products of this activity—like those of any other human activity—are influenced by cultural and historical factors" (p. 37). Knowledge claims are understood by experts to be social constructions that are forever under construction as works in progress. "When good reasons for accepting a knowledge claim can no longer be marshaled, the claim is refuted" (Prawat, 1992, p. 360).

Prawat also suggests that naive learners tend to view knowledge as "fixed entities"—as an array of indisputable answers to unknown questions that seemingly have no point of origin. Learning thus is seen by

Table 5.1. Summary of Errors and Misconceptions in Learning the Visual Arts

Misconceptions	Explanations	Examples
Problems with the knowledge base		
Naive concepts	Prior beliefs often impede the acquisition of new understandings.	"*La Grande Jatte* is about people enjoying themselves in the park—no more, no less."
Underdifferentiated concepts	Students may not be able to distinguish closely related concepts, such as realism and naturalism.	"Seurat was concerned with naturalism, as shown in his choice of colors."
Compartmentalized concepts	When concepts are wedded to specific contexts, students may have difficulty applying that knowledge elsewhere.	Students might know color concepts, such as warm and cool colors, but cannot use this knowledge in studio situations or to interpret artworks.
Garbled or wrong knowledge	Newly acquired knowledge gets mixed up in various ways. Novices get facts wrong or make mistakes in remembering what was learned previously.	"Seurat was an Italian Renaissance painter." "Seurat had a long career as a painter."
Problems with knowledge-seeking strategies		
Myopic search patterns (tunnel vision)	Novices may persist with the same strategy although it does not solve the problem or question.	"If I look harder at the dots, I will eventually understand it."
Disoriented search patterns	Novices often glance at a work haphazardly, not knowing where to start their inquiries.	"I am not sure what influenced Seurat to paint this way. It's hard to say for sure."
Ritual patterns	Advanced viewers may resort to rigid, formulaic interpretations, even when their knowledge base is adequate to grasp deeper understandings.	Students sometimes use principles of design to analyze a work's properties without linking the principles to an interpretation of meanings.

(*Continued*)

Table 5.1. (*Cont.*)

Misconceptions	Explanations	Examples
Problems with disposition toward learning		
Perseveration, guessing, or quitting	Although regarded as defective problem-solving strategies, these also may reveal a viewer's level of motivation.	Perseveration may reveal a learner's resistance to solving problems of interpretation. Guessing might reflect a lack of willingness to pursue a more difficult path to knowledge. Quitting may reflect low motivation ("This work is not worth my time").
Conservative tendencies	Novices tend to approach interpretation by confirming their preconceived ideas, personal biases, or ingrained beliefs.	"Modern art is really dumb." "Good art should be pleasant in subject matter." "My little sister can do better than that."
Performance versus mastery orientation	Novices lean toward the performance orientation, where the motive is to obtain a good grade. Experts are more likely to have a genuine interest in the subject.	Indicators of performance orientation: "Is Seurat going to be on the final exam?" "How much extra credit will a report on pointillism earn?" Indicators of mastery orientation: "What will I learn?" "I am curious to find out about Seurat's scientific interests."

novices as the process of accumulating and reproducing those fixed entities (Eisner, 1993; Koroscik, 1994). "Knowledge for the poor student is a basket of facts" (Anderson, 1984, p. 10).

Naive concepts. Differences in understandings possessed by novices and experts are in part due to the depth and breadth of their existing knowledge of art concepts and procedures. When this knowledge is limited, naive preconceptions often impede the acquisition of new understandings

(Perkins & Simmons, 1988). The examples of naive art concepts, mentioned earlier, were obtained from 5-year-olds (Wolf, 1987). By contrast, the examples that follow were obtained by Koroscik and her colleagues from undergraduate student responses to Seurat's *La Grande Jatte* (Koroscik, 1990b). Again, this emphasizes the point that naive concepts are not limited to the very young but can appear wherever and whenever knowledge remains undeveloped. This is often the case with typical undergraduate students who may elect to take an art course as part of their general educational requirements.

A naive understanding of Seurat's *La Grande Jatte* is exemplified by the student who interprets the painting as "a happy scene in a park." This interpretation makes good sense to someone with the preconception that people in a park must be having a good time. However, persons with extensive knowledge of art and Parisian life in 1884–1886 have interpreted the painting differently. They have argued that, upon first viewing the painting, it indeed appears to be a pleasant scene of family life. This exemplifies what Spiro and colleagues (1988) called a "first pass understanding" (pp. 4–5). However, the work also has been interpreted as an "anti-utopian allegory" (Bloch, cited in Nochlin, 1990, pp. 170–171). Koroscik recalls her childhood understanding of *La Grande Jatte*: a work done to show how dotted brushstrokes could be used to paint scenes. When such beliefs become established, they may confound subsequent learning. Yet, textbooks for school-age children repeatedly stress Seurat's pointillism, and, as a result, many individuals grow into adulthood unable to see past the dots to penetrate into the deeper layers of meaning contained by this work. Other examples of naive concepts might include statements like, "This must be an important painting because it is so large and has a gold frame," or, "It is important because it is prominently displayed in a museum."

Underdifferentiated concepts. Another constraint to understanding is the prevalence of underdifferentiated concepts. Underdifferentiation occurs in learning when two or more concepts or objects (works of art) that bear some superficial resemblance to one another are classified as belonging to the same category. The tendency to group Impressionist and post-Impressionist works as being identical or similar in style, described in the previous chapter, exemplifies this problem. Such concepts are easier to grasp than complex ones, but at the same time they keep the learner from grasping essential differences. If students concentrate on the similarities of *La Grande Jatte* with Impressionist paintings, they might fail to observe that Seurat actually rejected the casual, relaxed approach of the Impressionists; that he did not strive to depict the "fleeting moment," but instead wanted to show permanence and exactness (Kielty, 1964). Other differences have been noted by art scholars. For instance, Nochlin (1990) distinguishes the use of dotted brushstrokes in La Grande Jatte from Impressionist paintings. The following statement shows a high degree of differentiation: "With the dot, [Seurat] resolutely and consciously removed himself as a unique being projected by a personal handwriting. He, himself is absent from his stroke" (Nochlin, 1990, pp. 173–174).

Compartmentalized concepts. If underdifferentiated concepts err because subtle distinctions or differences are discounted or considered to be of less importance, the reverse tendency is likely to yield compartmentalized concepts. Compartmentalization results when concepts are isolated from one another in the learner's understanding. When conceptual linkages are lacking between concepts or objects, the potential for transfer and understanding is reduced (Perkins & Simmons, 1988). By contrast, the expert's knowledge base is likely to be organized around a more central set of understandings that enables him or her to see relationships between and among concepts (Chi, Feltovich, & Glaser, 1981; Prawat, 1989). This organizational structure connects key ideas and procedures in meaningful ways. By comparison, a novice's knowledge base typically is organized into rigid and isolated cognitive structures. Organizational structure limits the novice's ability to grasp relationships. The knowledge of each concept possessed by the learner may register in simple tests of recall, yet the learner cannot integrate these to deepen his or her understanding.

In the case of La Grande Jatte, students might have knowledge about the dotted brushstrokes as well as recognition skills to select pointillist paintings from other styles, but may have difficulty explaining how the dots influence the expressive meaning of the work. By comparison, expert understandings reflect an integration of observations about the painting's formal characteristics and its possible meanings, as exemplified in the Nochlin statement cited earlier.

Garbled or wrong knowledge. A final problem also relates to the organization of the learner's knowledge base, namely, that newly acquired knowledge is predictably confused with older knowledge or is mistaken in some way (Perkins & Simmons, 1988). When a novice's knowledge base contains oversimplifications, the resulting loss of detail results in knowledge and understandings that are less complete and hence typically inaccurate and even factually wrong. It is a common occurrence for novices to get the facts wrong and make mistakes in remembering what they previously learned. Most easily detected are blatant mistakes and misconceptions, such as the conclusion that Seurat was an Italian Renaissance painter or that he was a prolific painter throughout his long career.

Subtler forms of garbled knowledge occur with more advanced learners as well. For example, novices with a fairly ample supply of prior knowledge might confuse the stylistic concepts of realism and naturalism. In such instances, they would be unable to dispute the claim that "Seurat was concerned with naturalism as shown by his choice of realistic colors." By comparison, art scholars rarely confuse naturalism with realism. While many agree that *La Grande Jatte* is a realistic painting, they also may argue that it is not naturalistic (House, 1989; Piper, 1981).

To emphasize the antinaturalistic style of *La Grande Jatte*, scholars have compared the painting with Seurat's later work, *The Models* (1888), in which three female nudes are depicted in the artist's studio against the backdrop of *La Grande Jatte*. This juxtaposition is discussed by House (1989):

> Its figures, their lines relaxed and cursive, are juxtaposed with the wooden figures in the *Grande Jatte*, shown on the studio wall next to them. This contrast plays on oppositions between nature and artifice: the *Grande Jatte's* figures assume the artificial guise of fashion in order to appear in the "natural" setting of the island: next to them are three nudes who can only reveal their natural selves in the ultimately artificial circumstances of posing for "art" in a painter's studio. Judging from the opposition Seurat made here, the stiffness in the *Grande Jatte* cannot be treated as an internal stylistic development in Seurat's art, but must be seen as a calculated, expressive device conceived for that particular project. (p. 129)

By developing an awareness of the gaps and organizational inadequacies in the learner's knowledge base, the teacher is better able to anticipate trouble spots before they confound the development of more sophisticated understandings at a later time. Yet problems also can appear when novice students are limited in the array of strategies used to modify prior knowledge or to procure new knowledge. These problems are looked at next.

Problems with Knowledge-Seeking Strategies

Limited array of strategies. Experts differ from novices in having more strategies available for procuring new knowledge or applying prior knowledge to new learning situations. Different strategies are acquired throughout the learning process. At the introductory phases of learning, students are more likely to rely on rote memorization as a strategy for procuring knowledge, but knowledge acquired in this way is likely to be poorly organized for purposes of transfer and is easily forgotten.

During more advanced phases of domain-specific learning, students may encounter higher-order thinking strategies such as the ability to categorize and to form analogies and metaphors. In the arts, where interpretation is a central preoccupation, the use of analogies and metaphors permits individuals to establish connections among objects and ideas. In the next chapter, for example, metaphors will be characterized as ways in which we understand and experience one kind of thing in terms of another. The dove in the flag of the United Nations symbolizes peace. Works of art also embody symbolic content, even including visual metaphors that may provide individuals with the conceptual tools to understand and communicate about matters relevant to life. Lacking such capabilities, individuals are limited in what they can think about and act on.

At higher levels of expertise, one finds instances where strategies learned in one domain may find application in another. This suggests that some aspects of cognition, especially at the high end, actually may move away from domain specificity to domain generality. For example, Waldrop (1992) describes changes in current scientific thinking as shifting away from "the Newtonian metaphor of clockwork predictability . . . [toward] metaphors more closely akin to the growth of a plant" (p. 329). In this instance, knowledge of biological organization finds applicability in a conceptual problem involving physics, exemplifying transfer across domains of knowledge.

Some typical difficulties with knowledge-seeking strategies are discussed next.

Myopic search patterns (tunnel vision). Because of the rigid structure of their knowledge base, novices typically employ search strategies that are unidimensional. Because they lack the flexibility that permits elaboration of a single conceptual theme, their responses to art tend to be relatively short in duration. For example, trying to understand the Seurat painting by "looking harder at the dots" is not likely to further the learner's understanding. By contrast, scholars who have studied *La Grande Jatte* will frequently extend their inquiries beyond the painting. They also examine the literature, criticism, popular imagery, and pictorial traditions of the culture and time period when the work was created to suggest ways in which the painting embodies the aspirations and tensions within the artist's social milieu. By comparison, an adult novice may look at the painting and say, "I see it as a view of a nice sunny day in the park, no more, no less" (Efland, Koroscik, & Parsons, 1992, p. 7).

Disoriented search patterns. When novices approach the task of understanding something, they are often at a loss over where to begin or what to search for. They typically use arbitrary criteria to guide the direction of their search, often the path of least resistance. When one path is perceived as leading to a dead end, the novice frequently will "change his or her mind" and randomly set out in a new direction.

An example of this search pattern can be found in a response to *La Grande Jatte* such as the following: "I am not sure what other artists may have influenced Seurat to paint in this way. It is hard to say for sure" (Efland, Koroscik, & Parsons, 1992, p. 7). The statement suggests that the viewer has some doubts about how one might go about discovering who or what may have influenced Seurat. Such uncertainty is likely to be accompanied by a random choice of search strategies, whereas art scholars have been more deliberate and methodical in seeking new understandings of the painting. For example, a number of historians explain the characteristics of Seurat's style as being a commentary on the assumptions underlying Impressionism. The scope of these expert search patterns is exemplified in the following statement by House (1989):

> First, [historians] have investigated the physical context of the island of the Grand Jatte itself, located on the river Seine in the suburbs northwest of Paris. Second, they have tried to define the painting's social context by determining what types of people are represented in it. Third, they have examined its institutional context as a manifesto for an artistic splinter group that was first presented in the independent forum of the final Impressionist group exhibition. And fourth, they have looked at its critical context, at the ways in which the painting was received when it was first exhibited. (p. 116)

Ritual patterns. The development of deep understandings also can be constrained by the adoption of formulaic strategies that are symptomatic of a learner's lack of sensitivity to deep structures of the discipline (Perkins & Simmons, 1988). Unlike the naive concepts that were described earlier as defects in the knowledge base, ritual patterns are seen more commonly among advanced learners who may have acquired extensive knowledge. Advanced learners may appear to have acquired a level of sophistication, yet actually approach learning in a rigid, ritualistic way. For example, they may adopt strategies for responding to art such as citing principles of design to analyze the formal properties of an artwork, automatically employing this whether or not it is germane to the task of interpretation. Koroscik notes that teaching students to use a four-step art criticism method, for example, description, analysis, interpretation, and judgment (Feldman, 1973), or aesthetic scanning (Broudy, 1987), can impede the development of understandings when these methods are applied in a rote and purposeless manner. In such instances, it is predictable that students will lose track of what they are actually searching for (Koroscik, 1990b).

By contrast, scholars such as art historians are inclined to recognize that interpretations of the same work may change over time as more contextual evidence comes to light and as theoretical paradigms shift within their discipline. Thus, the methods for seeking new interpretations should be subject to change as well. House (1989) explains:

> The historian's task is to seek the range of meanings that can be found in a work at a particular historical moment and to highlight the assumptions that underlie the various ways in which it has been interpreted, both in the past and the present. . . . It is the life of the work, not the life of the artist, that must command our attention. (pp. 130–131)

Disposition Toward Learning: The Will to Learn

A third facet that comes into play in cognition is a student's *disposition* toward learning, in this case, a disposition toward art and the effort involved in understanding it. Dispositions sometimes are referred to as "habits of mind" (Prawat, 1989, p. 3; see also Perkins, 1994). Perkins, in particular, describes thinking dispositions as "the enthusiasm, commitment, or felt tendencies that motivate curiosity and sustain effort on solving an intellectual problem or interpreting a work of art" (p. 4). One might be highly motivated to learn or might go through the motions of learning in a desultory way. Prawat (1989) distinguishes student dispositions as what he calls a *performance* versus a *mastery* disposition. A performance orientation may direct the student to get the job done as quickly and painlessly as possible, whereas a mastery orientation directs the student to increase knowledge because he or she is intrinsically interested in the material.

Perkins (1994) also describes the interaction of specific dispositions with strategies. For example, some learners are disposed to view works of art hastily. They fail to take note of what they are seeing because they don't take the time to look for relevant details. "Hastiness" in this instance is a negative disposition. For success, learners will need to adopt the strategy of "slowing down their looking." If the strategy calls for slowing down, we might be justified in concluding that the disposition to hastiness was set aside or overridden. Thus, when viewing habits change, teachers can use that fact as evidence that students are more favorably disposed to study works of art.

Koroscik identifies some typical problems that are the result of poorly motivated dispositions. They are discussed next.

Perseveration, guessing, or quitting. Novices frequently will continue in their pursuit of knowledge even in the face of evidence that their particular strategic approach will not bear fruit. Koroscik uses the example of the student who tries to reach an understanding of Seurat's pointillism by looking harder at the dots. This dogged persistence is a type of cognitive rigidity brought on by a lack of alternative strategies in the learner's repertoire (Koroscik, 1990b). The willingness to change strategies can be evidence of a strong and positive disposition toward learning. By contrast, negative dispositions become evident when a sense of purpose is lacking or when learners start guessing at interpretations or simply giving up. Some guesses are clearly better than others but tend to reflect a tendency to proceed without confirmation (Perkins & Simmons, 1988). Experts are far more willing to persevere on the basis of contextual information when it can provide a means to inform and confirm their interpretations of an artwork. Experts are also likely to change strategies when it becomes clear that the persistence is driven by an obstinacy that is failing to bring about understanding.

Conservative tendencies. Koroscik used the term *conservative tendencies* to describe the inclination of novices to approach learning by confirming preconceived ideas and personal biases, which sometimes reflect peer-group consensus. At the other extreme, many novices blindly adopt authoritative conclusions without question, operating on the belief that if something is written in a book, it must be true. At the same time, they may be steadfast in their belief that "modern art is really dumb," or assume that "good art should have pleasing subject matter," or that "paintings should be easy to understand with no hidden or obscure meanings." A "spirit of conviction" contrasts with the "spirit of exploration" that typically characterizes expertise (Perkins & Simmons, 1988). For instance, it is quite common for art scholars to continuously challenge the boundaries of the discipline when they revisit such paintings as *La Grande Jatte*.

Performance versus mastery orientation. Dispositions also show up in a novice's tendency to approach learning with a *performance orientation* rather than a *mastery orientation* (Prawat, 1989). A novice is inclined to get the job done as quickly as possible, with learning serving as a means to an end rather than an end in itself. He or she might ask, "Will the final exam contain any items about *La Grande Jatte*?" Students motivated by a desire for mastery are more likely to ask, "What will I learn?"

Limitations of the Koroscik Formulation

Koroscik's work is valuable in helping teachers understand where to look for difficulties confronted by art learners. While it offers a set of diagnostic tools that can alert teachers to possible stumbling blocks, its potential for assessing the progress of individual students remains undeveloped. To extend her work would require detailing a range of positive outcomes by which to mark student progress in the arts. For example, her work exemplifies naive concepts but does not detail what might count as sophisticated responses of learners, either children or adults. Much work would have to be done to devise scales of responses as well as scaling procedures by which student outcomes could be ranked.

Furthermore Koroscik's research, like much of the work based on the comparison of novices and experts, tends to be highly prescriptive. It tends to impose standards of adult expertise upon children. While this might be appropriate in the professional preparation of artists, critics, or art historians, it is doubtful that such criteria are suitable for either schoolchildren or lay adults. Koroscik (1990b) has argued that "looking at differences between novices and experts is useful for suggesting a range of possible learning outcomes within a directional framework differentiating naive understandings from those that are more fully developed" (p. 7).

While it is true that the enhancement of cognitive abilities is likely to register as movement toward professional scholarly behavior, in my view alternative forms of assessment are needed that are tied to the purposes that art education is likely to serve as part of a general education. The attainment of professional knowledge, and methods of inquiry is not likely to be prominently listed. A more likely set of goals are those having the power to integrate knowledge, including knowledge of the arts, into the learner's understanding. What is needed is an approach to assessment that shows how or whether learners can apply the arts to enlarge their understanding of their social and personal worlds. When teachers are able to do that, they will be better able to justify the arts as part of the general education of learners. The section that follows attempts to provide indicators of such learning.

THE LIFEWORLD AND CULTURAL COGNITIVE MAPPING

The mapping approach to assessment is suggested by the integrated model of cognition formulated in Chapter 3. Unlike Koroscik's approach, the use of mapping as an approach to assessment is less likely to be centered on the disciplines. It is concerned with the integration of knowledge into the lifeworld of the learner. However, the knowledge represented in the map may include the formal disciplines of knowledge, although it is not limited to them. It also would include the knowledge conveyed by the mass media and the popular culture, including the influences of family and peers.

In common with Koroscik's approach, the mapping approach takes knowledge to be a construction of the learner.

In what follows, the learner's knowledge base is depicted as a lifeworld. The lifeworld as a concept entails more than the domains of knowledge per se, but embraces the learner's view of the world as a whole. The purpose of mapping, then, is to assess how or whether the learner has found meaning and connectedness between the domains featured in the school curriculum and his or her lifeworld.

This alternative form of assessment is likely to be compatible with an integrated view of cognition. For this purpose, two additional concepts are introduced into this discussion. The first interprets Jürgen Habermas's notion of the lifeworld. The learner's lifeworld as a concept replaces the knowledge base. The second appropriates Kevin Lynch's (1960) procedure of cognitive mapping as a means for assessing the integration of a student's knowledge. Lynch developed this approach for use with adults to see how they orient themselves to the city in which they live. Its use in the assessment of art learning has not as yet been undertaken, although researchers in multiple repertoire theory, discussed in Chapter 2, including Kindler and Darras (1998), have shown that children can represent their experience graphically by maps as early as age 5, a fact that I observed with my son. Whether such maps can be assessed for indications of learning, must still be regarded as a speculative possibility.

Habermas's Concept of the Lifeworld

The contemporary German philosopher Jürgen Habermas conceives of societies as systems and lifeworlds. A lifeworld consists of a "culturally transmitted and linguistically organized stock of interpretive patterns." It is the result of three simultaneously occurring processes, namely, "cultural reproduction, social integration, and socialization." These processes produce "the structural components of the lifeworld: namely culture, society and person" (Outhwaite, 1994, p. 86). Culture, society, and person are socially constructed concepts, acquired by learning. Habermas uses the lifeworld concept to characterize the historical evolution of modernism as a contemporary cultural condition in the West, including the particular tendency of individuals to experience domains of knowledge in relative isolation from one another.

In Habermas's view, the evolution of modernist consciousness involved the differentiation of these three worlds: (1) the social world, (2) the self or subjective world of the individual, and (3) the objective world, that is, the world that exists independent of our knowing (Outhwaite,

1994). In premodern societies, these tended to remain undifferentiated. Since the onset of the modern industrial state, with its highly differentiated divisions of labor and its market economies, people have grown increasingly conscious of the separation of these worlds. This sense of separation is built into the stock of knowledge acquired by the individual from parents and peers, the mass media, the popular culture, and the study of subjects in school. The lifeworld is the taken-for-granted reality experienced prior to formal knowledge seeking. It is the commonsense, symbolic backdrop into which school subjects are projected, regardless of whether the teacher is mindful of it, and that continues to register as a presence while schooling is in progress. Students use their existing lifeworld orientation as a reality check on what they are being taught, while understanding that the knowledge they have acquired is experienced as the integration of the new knowledge into their world picture. The sense of separation experienced in the lifeworld is caused by an inability to integrate its various aspects. This is reinforced by such modern schooling practices as the isolation of curriculum content into subjects and the compartmentalization of concepts within subjects.

Habermas also assumed that the various domains of knowledge (the disciplines) developed autonomy by having differentiated themselves from the individual's lifeworld. In a sense each discipline has become a discursive community in its own right. Each speaks its own language, which differs from the language of the commonsense world. Although these disciplines have greatly benefited humanity,[2] their separation within the learner's lifeworld is experienced either as a loss of meaning or coherence or as an inability to relate new knowledge to what is already known. Alienation thus is inscribed upon these domains, including the arts, and is experienced as a loss of meaning. Evidence for this separation can be seen when well-educated adults, including those who claim to enjoy the arts, report an inability to comprehend contemporary works. Similarly, most lay adults find the physics of quantum mechanics a source of bafflement.

Indeed, to acquire knowledge in the various domains, one must become enculturated into these knowledge communities, each at some distance from the other and from the individual's lifeworld. This may explain why the domains that constitute schooling are experienced by many students as lacking meaning or relevance. Education should enable learners to integrate the domains of knowledge into their lifeworlds. Figure 5.1 is a conceptual map of the lifeworld. The three zones of the lifeworld posited by Habermas are shown as concentric circles, while the domains of knowledge—the arts, humanities, and sciences—are shown orbiting the lifeworld, as knowledge that is detached, without integration. Arrows

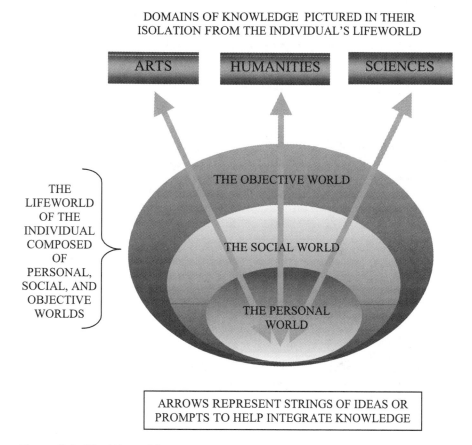

DOMAINS OF KNOWLEDGE PICTURED IN THEIR
ISOLATION FROM THE INDIVIDUAL'S LIFEWORLD

ARTS   HUMANITIES   SCIENCES

THE
LIFEWORLD
OF THE
INDIVIDUAL
COMPOSED
OF
PERSONAL,
SOCIAL, AND
OBJECTIVE
WORLDS

THE OBJECTIVE WORLD

THE SOCIAL WORLD

THE PERSONAL
WORLD

ARROWS REPRESENT STRINGS OF IDEAS OR
PROMPTS TO HELP INTEGRATE KNOWLEDGE

Figure 5.1. The Lifeworld

reaching up to these domains represent the attempt of teachers to help students establish meaningful connections with these domains.

Cultural Cognitive Mapping

In his book *The Image of the City*, Kevin Lynch (1960) noted that people carry internal, mental models of their physical environment. He calls these cognitive maps. Cognitive maps are mental schemata that hold some representation of the spatial arrangement of the physical environment. Psychologists hold different beliefs about their exact nature. They think these schemata are frequently sketchy and incomplete and reflect subjective beliefs about what is important. Lynch was among the first to attempt to understand how people's feelings about the quality of their environment and their perceptions of it can be used to analyze the impact of environmental design with a view to improving it (Bell, Baum, Fisher, & Greene, 1990; Lynch, 1960).

Lynch asked his subjects to draw maps of their city and give detailed descriptions of their typical routes of travel, listing the important landmarks visible along the way. He found that five categories emerged as common features in all maps. These include paths, edges, districts, nodes, and landmarks. Paths are the shared routes of travel, such as streets or walkways. Edges are limiting or enclosing features, such as the freeway that forms the eastern boundary of my neighborhood, or the lakeshore of Chicago. The freeway that is my edge may well be another person's path of travel. Districts are larger spaces that have a common character, the Greenwich Village area in New York, for example. Nodes are the points where paths converge, where behavior is focused, and where potential choices in travel options may occur. Finally, landmarks are distinctive features that people use to orient themselves in space, such as the Washington Monument in the District of Columbia, or the Empire State Building in Manhattan. A person's cognitive map made up of these components represents an individual's personal image of his or her environment. Lynch found that when cities or neighborhoods lack distinctive landmarks, their inhabitants become disoriented and experience difficulty in finding their way.

In adapting Lynch's concept of cognitive mapping, the Marxist literary critic Frederic Jameson (1988, 1992) argued that individuals need some sort of image or map of their society as a whole. Creating this map, in his view, is a task that involves individuals, artists, and theorists, who, in their shared perceptions, develop a sense of place, a model of how society is structured. The incapacity to map socially is as crippling to political and social experience as the incapacity to map spatially is for urban experience. Jameson (1992) explains:

> Kevin Lynch taught us that the alienated city is above all a space in which people are unable to map (in their minds) either their own positions of the urban totality in which they find themselves: grids such as those of Jersey City, in which none of the traditional markers (monuments, nodes, natural boundaries, built perspectives) obtain, are the most obvious examples. Disalienation in the traditional city, then, involves the practical reconquest of a sense of place and the construction or reconstruction of an articulated ensemble which can be retained in memory and which the subject can map and remap along the moments of mobile, alternative trajectories. (p. 51)

Lynch's studies were limited to the individual's representation of actual physical spaces, whereas Jameson was advocating the cognitive mapping of postmodern experience, through which individuals produce subjective representations of their cultural condition, including the social forces that may oppress or constrain them. For Jameson, the work of cultural cognitive mapping is facilitated by the study and exploration of works of literary art.

Since one of the purposes of education is to enable individuals to understand their personal and social worlds, works of visual art might play the role of landmarks in the cognitive mapping of these worlds. Moreover, the mapping of the postmodern condition may include both popular and high culture as orienting points in lifeworld experience. Better yet, popular and high culture might appear as overlapping forms of cultural expression in the subjective maps of individuals, raising questions about the boundaries separating them.

Mapping the postmodern. The title of this section is taken from Andreas Huyssen's (1990) essay of the same name. Like Jameson, he conceived of postmodern culture as a terrain to be explored, with the metaphor of mapping representing understanding. In place of Lynch's subjective map of the city, individuals would be asked to devise a cognitive map to represent metaphorically the organization of a specific domain of knowledge, or an aspect of that domain such as a work of art. In place of the physical landmarks that Lynch asked for, teachers might ask their students to select cultural cognitive landmarks (works of art or objects in the popular culture) as reference points that might reflect important ideas or concerns in their lifeworlds.

The school curriculum should provide paths of intellectual travel (strings of ideas) that would prompt learners to pursue specific questions. These might be posed by the teacher or by the students themselves. The questions of the teacher and those of the students might cross one another in one of the nodal points discussed earlier. Nodal points also might serve as intersections among the domains of knowledge. In the previous chapter, I introduced the concept of overlapping sets as places where knowledge common to two or more domains would enable the learner to travel intellectually in his or her search for understanding. These sets thus can become points of entry for reaching possible understandings located in less familiar domains. Recognition of such common points facilitates travel from one domain to another—to integrate knowledge or to apply knowledge from one domain to problems addressed by another.[3]

The following example illustrates the possibility of a lesson in a high school art class studying American painting after World War II. This art unit also is integrated with American history where students are studying the Cold War era. The art teacher asks students to respond to Jasper Johns's *Target with Four Faces* (see Figure 5.2). The lesson is introduced with an excerpt from the videotape series by Robert Hughes entitled *American Visions*. The students discuss developments in the fine arts after World War II. The teacher also reads aloud the following passage by Hughes (1997):

> The submerged text of Johns's target paintings connects to the stresses of Cold War America. To begin with, the whole nation felt it was a target. Magazines, newspapers, television, and politicians' speeches repeated this theme unceasingly, pounding it into the collective imagination like a ten inch spike. There, over in Russia . . . were countless ICBMs in their silos, pointing their nuclear tips at you, and you, and you. (p. 514)

The art teacher also prompts students to discuss the feeling of paranoia, the feeling that evil forces were plotting against America both from outside and from within. "Was this feeling based on fact?" "How did it reflect American society in the mid-twentieth century?" A student asks the art teacher to explain what Hughes meant by the expression "the McCarthy years." The topic also is pursued in history class, where the history of the Cold War era showed that concern over the Communist conspiracy had reached near hysteria. The history teacher suggests that students might look at some of the major spy scandals of the late 1940s and 1950s. The art teacher asks students to watch old spy movies and TV series made during the era to study the question of how conspiracy and paranoia were thematized in both the press and the popular culture.[4] The teacher prompts the students with questions like, "Why were themes like paranoia and conspiracy found in both the popular culture and the fine arts of that time period?" The teacher also asks students to identify contemporary television series that might deal with similar themes.

Cognitive mapping. These teachers then assessed the learning process by having students devise maps that feature Johns's *Target with Four Faces* (1955) as a reflection of American society during the Cold War era. The assessment task involved having the students prepare a map linking this work of art to the social and cultural conditions of the time period when it was painted. The teachers look for paths that link the work thematically to other works of art done roughly in the same period, such as Adolf Gottlieb's *Blast II* (1952), a painting whose use of abstract forms also refers to the possibility of nuclear destruction. The teachers consider questions such as, How do other paths represent the situational context that prevailed at the time of this work's creation, namely, the Cold War situation? Are there paths that connect the artist's biographical or personal situation with the theme of paranoia? Johns, a gay man, lived at a time when homo-

Figure 5.2. Johns, Jasper. *Target with Four Faces*. 1955. Assemblage: encaustic and collage on canvas with objects, 26 x 26" surmounted by four tinted plaster faces in wood box with hinged front. Box, closed, 3¾ × 26 × 3½". Overall dimensions with box open, 33⅝ × 26 × 3". The Museum of Modern Art, New York. Gift of Mr. and Mrs. Robert C. Scull. Photograph © 2001 The Museum of Modern Art, New York. © Jasper Johns/Licensed by VAGA, New York, NY.

sexuality was believed to have "secret affinities with Communism," a point referred to by Hughes (1997, p. 515). The teachers might ask themselves, Are these ideas seen as separate issues or do they converge at nodal points? Are there references to the work's formal considerations, such as the dark green and yellow colors of the target image? For example, do the paths explored by students lead them to ask why Johns chose these colors instead of the traditional red, white, and blue of the target image, colors he used repeatedly in his American flag paintings?

Assessment by means of mapping might be done to document changes in students' understanding over time. For example, does the map become more elaborate and show more detail, or does it remain essentially the same? Does it indicate that information present in previous versions is now forgotten or omitted? Have errors identified in older versions of the map been replaced in later revisions? The map could take the form of a physical diagram, a drawing showing nodes and paths, but it also could take the form of a written report that would be read to determine the interconnections among ideas.

Cognitive maps documenting the linkage of ideas might look like the map in Figure 5.3, which represents areas of knowledge. In some cases, zones dividing subjects may overlap, as when the popular culture is shown overlapping or sharing the events influencing art world history. The discussion of Johns's target paintings by Robert Hughes in *American Visions* (1997) might resemble this map.

Limitations of Mapping

The mapping method of assessment is highly speculative and far from foolproof. Some students may be better at map making (cartography) than others, which raises the question of whether mapping is a skill in its own right, bearing little resemblance to the structures of knowledge present in the learner's lifeworld or conceptual system. This in turn raises the traditional worries one has about any test situation, namely, its validity and reliability. When Lynch had people map their city, he could compare these subjective reports against the physical locations referred to by the maps; however, he was not evaluating the people making the maps but rather the coherence of the urban setting as registered in these maps. He was judging the qualities of differing urban environments.

If teachers were to use maps as assessment tools, they would need to inventory the highlights of the domain they expected learners to register, as well as some sense of how key elements of this knowledge would link together. In addition, there would have to be a way for the teachers to check on the validity of the maps so that they could develop a degree of

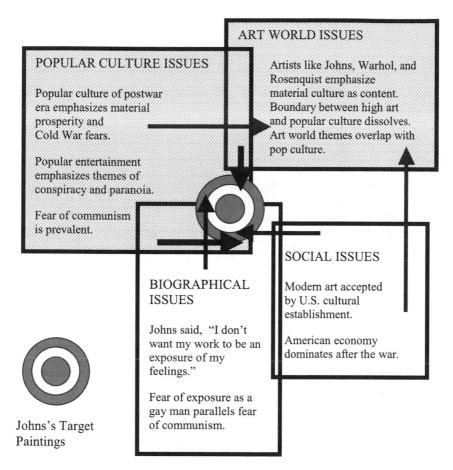

Figure 5.3. Concept Map Linking the History of Art, Cold War History, and the Popular Culture of the 1950s with Jasper Johns's Biography.

certainty that the knowledge, values, and beliefs actually in the possession of the learners registered on the maps. This might be done by having students explain their maps orally or in writing, including what the maps contained; why certain things were connected and made important, while other things were isolated; what things were major landmarks or minor features, and so on. For example, if students were to conceptually link the Johns painting to the American Civil War of the 1860s, that is, to a social context where it did not belong, the map would register the student's misunderstanding of the historical context.

IMPLICATIONS FOR INSTRUCTION AND ASSESSMENT

In Koroscik's view, it is clear there are many ways that one's understandings of the visual arts can be foiled. Moreover, it is possible to use what we know about these problems to anticipate the source of difficulties before they arise. Using her approach, we would have to distinguish between problems that were due primarily to an impoverished or malfunctioning knowledge base, a poor choice of knowledge-seeking strategies, or a poor disposition regarding art, or some combination of these.

The assessment of instruction would need to be built upon selected aspects of the knowledge base and the specific challenges to understanding that the content provided. It is also clear that assessment as structured around Koroscik's categories involves more than merely recording the acquisition and retention of subject matter. In particular, assessment for the more advanced levels of knowledge acquisition requires testing for transfer, and this involves teaching for it as well. Citing Covington (1992), Koroscik (1996b) noted that "transfer is potential, not automatic" (p. 12). However, testing for transfer in the assessment of learning is more difficult than testing for simple recall. One would have to design a test that anticipated in advance a range of novel uses or situations in which existing knowledge might be applied.

INSTRUCTIONAL PROMPTS IN INSTRUCTION AND ASSESSMENT

Bransford and his colleagues (1986) have shown that students make use of previously acquired knowledge to understand something only when prompted to do so. The knowledge base of most individuals is inactive, or inert, especially if there is no reason or motive to energize inquiry. The student actually may have knowledge but not grasp its relevance for a new learning situation. The same is likely to apply in the testing situations. Thus, instructional cues and prompts from teachers can be of importance in activating relevant aspects of prior knowledge, for purposes of learning new knowledge or for assessment.

A number of studies of learning in art (Koroscik, 1982; Koroscik, Short, Stavropoulos, & Fortin, 1992) have shown that contextual variables in the form of verbal cues can significantly influence learning outcomes. At present, it is unclear whether such prompts activate the utilization of the appropriate knowledge-seeking strategy, whether they call attention to relevant structures in the knowledge base, or possibly whether the prompt gives rise to motivations or dispositions for learning. Or, some particular combination of all three facets may be involved. At any rate, it is clear that instruction involves more than merely imparting knowledge, and that the teacher must have subject-matter knowledge to recognize what is important to emphasize in instruction.

When the concept of the knowledge base in Koroscik's sense is supplanted by the lifeworld notion, the use of instructional prompts continues to play a role. In fact, lifeworld features or issues might well become the principal source of instructional prompts. The Johns painting by itself may seem remote to high school students, since it was done generations before they were born and registered concerns that affected their parents' or grandparents' lives rather than their own. Adding this landmark to their lifeworld map means linking it in some way to their life in the present. For example, the sense of conspiracy and paranoia registered in this painting continue to be pervasive themes in the present period. These themes are also evident in television series popular in the 1990s and 2000s, such as the *X-Files* or *La Femme Nikita*. If students can link the feelings aroused by the multilayered narratives of conspiracy with the *Target with Four Faces*, they display evidence of understanding the painting.

To carry out this mapping, students might be engaged in a project where they begin to collate films and television programs with events in the Cold War era. For example, *Mission Impossible* was a popular TV series during the Cold War era when most inimical forces were felt to lie beyond the nation's borders. Then, when the external threat diminished, the *X-Files* became a typical entertainment series in which the evil that besets us is unknown, invisible, and unnamable, the result of covert conspiracies by the CIA or a clandestine shadow government operating with or without the complicity or knowledge of elected officials. Throughout the 1990s, conspiracy theories also abounded in documentary accounts of the Branch Dravidian incident in Waco, Texas, or the Ruby Ridge incident in Idaho. Thus, the arts, including those in the popular media, can be shown to provide representations of the landscape of postmodern social and cultural reality, as found in the cultural products of society—its literature, music, history, and philosophy—both serious objects created for aesthetic enhancement or enjoyment and objects in the popular culture.

DESIGNING CURRICULUM CONTEXTS FOR IMPROVING ART UNDERSTANDING

The study of artworks provides occasions for the acquisition of cognitive strategies to carry out interpretive forms of inquiry. And since acts of interpretation frequently require that connections be established between knowledge in differing domains, it lays the groundwork for an integrated conception of general education. Moreover, works of art are almost always about something else other than art. Whether the work in question is a painting or a symphony, it is also a reflection of the times and culture from which it came, and the understanding of such a work means seeing it in relation to the world that gave rise to it.

In the first portion of the chapter, I used the example of Seurat's *La Grande Jatte* as a vista into Parisian society and culture experienced by this artist in the 1880s and 1890s. That work also reflects his social attitudes on progress and science, as seen in his desire to depict the life and activities of his own period rather than employ the classical imagery and themes favored by the academies of art and middle-class taste. His works also reveal an understanding of light and color as these elements were understood in the science of the late nineteenth century. Thus, a strategically chosen work of art can serve as a point of transfer, enabling learners to integrate knowledge from several domains as they fashion their understanding. Knowledge construction in this sense is more than mere acquisition. It involves the construction of an interpretive world, a complex latticework or cognitive map made up of nodal points and interconnecting elements. In the same way, I used a Jasper Johns work to access the theme of paranoia as it was felt in American culture during the Cold War era and as a condition that continues to bear on our lives.

The chapter that follows takes up the topic of imagination and the cognitive processes like metaphor that enable it to take place. It is my belief that a clear understanding of the cognitive basis for imagination will add to our conception of what the arts can teach and ultimately what their purpose in general education should be.

6

Imagination in Cognition

LIKE FEELINGS AND EMOTIONS, imagination is a prickly topic with a history of exclusion from the realm of the cognitive. In this chapter, my first purpose is to portray the cognitive potential of imagination in education and to explore its possibilities for developing knowledge and understanding. My second purpose is to identify the place of the visual arts in education as seen from the perspective of the imagination.

The paucity of psychological studies of imagination is not the result of oversight. Imagination was widely discussed in literary and philosophical circles throughout the eighteenth and nineteenth centuries. Its neglect throughout the twentieth century reflects the constraining influence of positivism, a legacy from which we have yet to shake ourselves free. Behaviorists avoided the study of imagination and the related topic of mental imagery because they did not have access to the internal experiences and sensations of individuals other than through the documentation of subjective impressions (Gardner, 1987).

Imagination is the act or power of forming mental images of what is not actually present to the senses or what has not actually been experienced. It is also the act or power of creating new ideas or images through the combination and reorganization of previous experiences. This latter power "is often regarded as the more seriously and deeply creative faculty which perceives the basic resemblances between things, as distinguished from *fancy*, the lighter and more decorative faculty which perceives superficial resemblances" (*Websters New World Dictionary, College Edition,* 1964, p. 725). This dictionary definition illustrates the legacy of value problems associated with the topic. We have a tendency to dismiss or discount ideas if they exist "only in the imagination," and to mistrust individuals having "an overactive imagination." Cartesian skepticism is embodied in the articulation of such sentiments.

In many contexts, *imagination* is used as a term of praise, as when we discuss the creative talent of an artist or the achievements of scientists. Yet in other contexts, it carries negative connotations, as when we say that someone's imaginary notions or ideas lie "beyond belief."

As used in this chapter, imagination refers to the cognitive processes that enable individuals to organize or reorganize images, to combine or recombine symbols, as in the creation of metaphors or narrative productions. The definition implies that the products of imagination differ from everyday, ordinary thinking by being more innovative and less concerned with typical or conventional communication. The term *imaginative* can refer to innovation in formal arrangement, meaning, or both. It adds novelty to the cultural landscape, and thus one could argue that terms like *imaginative* or *imaginary* are social designations made about particular objects or events, rather than a specific class of cognitive operations. Imagination is not any one specific cognitive operation in its own right but is the result of cognitive acts that enable individuals to construct meanings that are generally less dependent on conventional, rule-governed, or propositional forms of thinking and communication. The creation of a fresh metaphor in spoken or written expression is one example, while the juxtaposition of images in a collage to generate a new image, is another.

The account that follows opens with a historical sketch of the concept of imagination in the history of philosophy, since its study began long before psychology emerged as a science in its own right. This is followed by the study of mental imagery.

IMAGINATION IN PHILOSOPHY

In Plato's view, the imagination of the artist (which he called inspiration) was suspect, since artists were under the control of the muses and hence incapable of willing their own actions.[1] Lacking such control, artists could not be expected to have knowledge of the source of their powers. They were merely instruments of the divine, not even to be regarded as the authors of their creations. Genius was a gift from the gods—extrahuman in origin.

By the seventeenth century, Rene Descartes had established 21 rules for the direction of the mind as a defense against "the blundering constructions of the imagination" (Jones, 1952, pp. 662–663). Truth was not to be found in the poetic allusions of literature or in the fantasies of the visual arts, but in the certainties of logic, mathematics, and geometry. Modern rationalism thus was born. A rationalist believed that the world consisted of physical substances (bodies) and mental substances (minds), and that the rational mind, as a mental, nonphysical substance, was essentially disembodied.

The rationalist would say that what makes us human is our rationality, which is of the mind, not the body. The data provided by the senses do not by themselves provide us with reliable knowledge. Sensations must be ordered by the mind's power of reason, with its innate ideas and categories that are independent of the senses. Once clear and distinct ideas could be formed about objects and events in nature, these likely would reflect the structure of nature itself. Nature is thus a rational world. With the rise of such views, the cognitive status of imagination became suspect, since the images on which it depends have their origin in bodily and sensory encounters where they are subject to distortions and imperfections.

Philosophers writing in the empiricist tradition were also wary of the imaginative, especially as it was employed in figurative speech. John Locke (in Lakoff & Johnson, 1980) said that such devices "are for nothing else but to insinuate wrong ideas, move the passions, and thereby mislead the judgment" (p. 191).

By the end of the eighteenth century, the cognitive status of imagination fared somewhat better. Immanuel Kant (1790/1964) recognized it as a "productive faculty of cognition." Using the faculty of imagination, the mind could create "another nature" from imagery given it by actual nature. Moreover, imagination could entertain. "When experience becomes too commonplace, we remold it." Kant also argued that imagination enables us to "feel our freedom from the laws of association that organize empirical experience, so that the material supplied by nature can be fashioned into something different, something which surpasses nature." Furthermore, imagination is creative; it brings intellectual ideas into movement, "thus enlivening the mind by opening it to the prospect of an illimitable field of kindred representations" (p. 318).[2]

Yet in the Kantian view, the "real work of cognition" still takes place in the formation of concepts. Concepts are products of our understanding, which is formal and governed by rules, whereas our perceptions are bodily, material, and passive[3] (Johnson, 1987). Later, I discuss Johnson's revision of the Kantian account of imagination. By placing imagination on a contemporary epistemological footing grounded in a view he calls "experiential realism," Johnson sets aside the mind–body dualism that Kant inherited from Descartes.

In the late nineteenth and early twentieth centuries, positivism made war upon the artistic imagination, which operated without rules or apparent rational intent. Moreover, there was no way to verify the reliability of artistic insight. Depth psychologists like Freud and Jung, although less constrained by positivism, explored and charted the subconscious regions of the mind, but in delving into the psychological basis for feelings and emotions, they widened the gulf between the cognitive and the affective. Twentieth-century philosophers like Ernst Cassirer (1944) postulated that the recollection of past events and the anticipation of future events made use of symbolic processes that required imagination for their realization. "Symbolic memory is the process by which man not only repeats past experience but also reconstructs it. Imagination becomes a necessary element of true recollection" (p. 75). In John Dewey's (1934) view, imagination is "the generous blending of interests at the point where the mind comes in contact with the world, when old and familiar things are made new in experience" (p. 267). Yet imagination remained a closed book in the psychology of behaviorism, which dominated the first half of the twentieth century.

PSYCHOLOGICAL STUDIES OF MENTAL IMAGERY

With the rise of the cognitive science perspective, the cognitive character of imagery and imagination once again could become a new candidate for investigation, although by the means afforded by psychological research, especially in work by Roger Shephard (1978a, 1978b), Stephen Kosslyn (1980), and others. In opening the issue of how to account for the existence of mental imagery, these psychologists began raising fundamental questions about the adequacy of computational models of mind first advanced in the cognitive sciences, and, as a consequence, their work has been a source of controversy (see Pylyshyn, 1973).

There have been at least three kinds of studies that have dealt with the role of mental imagery in cognition. First, there have been compilations of anecdotal studies, including self-reports of individuals whose significant scientific discoveries or artistic accomplishments were occasioned by strong acts of imaginative creativity. In particular, Shephard (1978a, 1978b) collected accounts of the imaginative activity of scientists. These provide dramatic portrayals of the role that mental imagery played in the thought processes that led these individuals to do their most important work or make key discoveries. Shephard (1978a) cited Albert Einstein, who reported that verbal processes did not seem to play any role in his processes of creative thought. In fact, he maintained that his particular abil-

ity did not lie in mathematical calculation either, "but rather in visualiz-
ing . . . effects, consequences and possibilities." He performed what he
called his *gedanken* (thought) experiment where he imagined himself trav-
eling alongside a beam of light at speeds of 186,000 miles per second. What
he mentally "saw" corresponded neither to anything "that could be experienced perceptually as light nor to anything described by Maxwell's equations, which calculated the relationships between the various forms of
electromagnetic energy. These visualizations prompted him to formulate
his special theory of relativity" (p. 126).

A second approach to the study of mental imagery involved empirical
studies, where mental imagery was compared with ordinary perceptual
activity (Shephard & Metzler, 1971) or was contrasted with information
presented in verbal, linguistic form (Kosslyn, 1983). Results obtained by
Shephard and Metzler indicate that in many instances mental imagery is
remarkably able to substitute for actual perception, with subjects seemingly able to make the same judgments about mental objects such as
geometric shapes as they do about real objects encountered directly in perception. Johnson (1987) suggests that these studies of mental imagery offer
empirical support for the presence of "image-schemata" as a basis for imaginative thought (p. 25). Kosslyn and his colleagues also have devised a
comprehensive theory of what they call a "quasi-pictorial form of mental
representation called imagery" (Kosslyn, 1983). According to Gardner
(1987), "This form of mental representation is as important for an understanding of cognition as is the more usually invoked propositional form"
(p. 327).

Kosslyn's position on the cognitive status of imagery was contested
by Zenon Pylyshyn (1973),[4] who insists that cognition is principally a computational function and denies that there is any independent mental reality to imagery. He claims that "any mental image, schematic structure,
or operation on them can be represented in propositional (e.g., verbal,
numerical) form" (cited in Johnson, 1987, p. 27). Johnson acknowledges
that we can describe images and schemata in propositional form, but for
him the real issue is whether these have reality in the first place. In a similar
vein, Gardner (1987) suggested that "the fact that computers can—and
usually do—transmit information in only one symbolic form (e.g., propositional, language-like representations) is no reason to assume that
human beings do the same" (p. 129). Indeed, his theory of multiple intelligences aggressively denies that limitation.

A third approach to the study of imagination is based on linguistic work
by George Lakoff, who with Mark Johnson (1980) studied the cognitive
foundations of such seemingly abstract mental activities as categorization
and metaphor as observed in empirical studies of linguistic behavior. They

maintain that there is a growing body of evidence for the existence of what they call "an image-schematic level of cognitive operations." Like Piagetian schemata, these exist at a level of generality and abstraction that allows them to serve repeatedly as identifying patterns in a variety of cognitive activities similarly structured in relevant ways (Johnson, 1987).

Lakoff and Johnson's image-schemata are similar to Piagetian schemata in that they are structures based on images derived "naturally"[5] from bodily and perceptual experience. However, Lakoff and Johnson's theoretical orientation differs from that of Piaget in that they see a continuing role for image-schemata in cognition and the types of mental representations they make possible. Piaget's cognitive developmental theory, by contrast, stressed the evolution of schemata from their bodily and perceptual origins at the sensimotor stage of development to the formal operations stage, where they ultimately evolve into the abstract, symbolic, language-like representations characteristic of adult cognitive operations. Cognitive abilities at the formal operations stage were seen by Piaget as the pinnacle of human cognitive development, and his research project was principally the study of how formal operations come into full flower. Once the earlier stages of development were superseded, their continued existence was less likely to be the object of study. Lakoff and Johnson, by contrast, concentrated their research on the role image-schemata play in laying the groundwork for nonpropositional forms of thought such as imagery and metaphor.

CATEGORIZATION IN COGNITION

To establish the groundwork for a cognitive explanation of imagination, I begin at some distance from the conventional concerns of imagination by discussing categorization as a cognitive process. Categories in the formal sense are bound up with rules that define the conditions of membership or nonmembership of objects, events, or persons as things that are organized and classified mentally in like groups. In many ways these rules correspond with those of logical thinking and the operation of propositional forms of thought. Categorization also refers to how people group things in the world of everyday, commonsense experience.

We learn about the natural world through our senses, through the multiple sensations of sights and sounds, warmth and coolness, roughness and smoothness, tastes and smells. We also learn within a social world through interactions with family members, peers, and the community at large. Our understanding emerges through these encounters. With experience, our world picture becomes increasingly diverse, and to control this vast enumeration of things, we organize it by categories, by samenesses and differences, friends and foes—even by likes and dislikes. We organize our world on the basis of common attributes.

A Cartesian rationalist would insist that the mind furnishes the categories with its innate ideas and that these are not found in the world. They are nonempirical. These formal categories can serve to impose order on our perceptions. Without such order, our perceptions could become the breeding ground for error and the excesses of the imagination.

Lakoff and Johnson (1980) take exception to this view.They believe that it is more efficient to learn about groups of things by their shared characteristics than about each thing in isolation. Categorization involves thinking about things in terms of commonalities, not about the uniqueness of individual cases. This action is mostly automatic and unconscious, giving rise to the view that objects and events in the world come in natural kinds.

Piaget also did not accept the idea that categories are innate properties of the mind. In his view, they are cognitive structures that have developed as a result of learning and hence are not properties of the world but cognitive achievements. They emerge from the mind's effort to organize what is given in perception so as to secure meaning. Were it not for the capacity to categorize, we would soon become "slaves to the particular."[6]

Categories also group things and people and serve as a basis for social behavior. Jokes about women drivers or mothers-in-law assume that members of these groups share common (in these cases pejorative) characteristics. Such categories and their affective loadings are built into everyday language where often they can disseminate sexist or racist stereotypes. These are negative aspects of categorization. On the constructive side, the commonsense classification of birds, flowers, and fish into groups with like characteristics provides the basis for organizing knowledge for use in everyday activities and for the school curriculum.

Classical Categories and Their Alternatives

We tend to assume that the category groupings we form in our everyday affairs offer accurate representations of things as they are in the world, leading to a reliable view of reality itself. Lakoff (1987) explains:

> From the time of Aristotle to the later Wittgenstein categories were thought to be well understood and unproblematic. They were assumed to be abstract containers with things either inside or outside the category. Things were assumed to be in the same category if, and only if, they had certain properties in common, and the properties they had in common were taken as defining the category. (p. 6)

Wittgenstein's family resemblance categories. Yet, Ludwig Wittgenstein (1953) realized that people do not necessarily organize experience by classical modes of categorization, but often tend to devise alternative systems to circumvent the constraints imposed by such categories. He exemplified this with the concept of the game. There is no single property or collection of properties that all games share, and thus it is impossible to devise a definition that includes all things called games and simultaneously excludes non-games. What unites games as a category is what Wittgenstein called *family resemblance*. According to Lakoff (1987), "Games like family members are similar to one another in a wide variety of ways. That, and not a single, well-defined collection of common properties is what makes them a category" (p. 16). Moreover, people in everyday life are not troubled by this lack of a definition. Usually, we have no difficulty recognizing the objects and events called games.

Art as a category. In like fashion, Morris Weitz (1963) argued that *art* as a concept also functions as a family-resemblance category, in that none of the existing definitions of art cover all cases of art. Art also has extendable boundaries as new media and styles come into being and as new works are created.[7] When art was defined as formal order, the curriculum featured the study of formal principles stressing elements and principles of design, but when art was defined as the expression of the artist's feelings, creative self-expression was the preeminent practice. When Weitz suggested that these definitions were, at best, recommendations to view art from a particular vantage point, art educators began recognizing the possibility of multiple perspectives in the curriculum. This change from a traditional, classical conception of categorization to a family-resemblance system began surfacing in proposals for eclectic curricula open to various ideas about what can be art.[8]

Prototype-based categories. In classical theory, items in a category share a common property possessed by all category members, where these attributes define the category. Consequently, no member of a set would have any special status (Lakoff, 1987). Yet in the early 1970s Eleanor Rosch began identifying what she called prototype effects within categories like color, birds, or chairs. When people were asked to group colors that seemed to belong together, they would put all the reds together, all the blues together, and so on. But, if asked to select the best or most typical example of red or blue, most people could readily do that as well. These optimal color selections act like specific prototypes often based on family resemblance by which individuals mark their experiences of colors. Since prototypes suggest that some members of a group are more representative of the category than others, the idea of prototypes is at variance with classical theory, where all cases should have the same standing as exemplars of the category.

Basic-level categories. Akin to prototype-based categories, are what Roger Brown (1958, 1965) earlier called "basic level" categories. Like Rosch, he found that there are levels of membership within categories. To exemplify, when children learn about flowers as a category, they may be involved in such actions as planting, picking, and smelling the blossoms. They also learn that the blossoms are called flowers, mentally establishing them as a class of things. Later learning may add knowledge of more kinds of flowers and may come to learn that flowering plants are members of a larger entity, the plant kingdom. But the basic level of the category remains that of flowers. Basic-level categories seem to have the following characteristics, as summarized by Lakoff (1987):

- They are learned in conjunction with distinctive actions, such as smelling flowers.
- They are learned earliest, when things are first named.
- They are at the level at which names are shortest or used most frequently.
- They are "natural" levels of categorization in the sense that physical bodily actions are undertaken while the category is being established mentally.

According to Lakoff, with additional learning, the category becomes more elaborate and proceeds upward to form a "superordinate" level made up of generic categories, as when the plant kingdom becomes the all-encompassing repository that supersedes flowers in the example given earlier. Categorization also can proceed downward from the basic level to form "subordinate" levels of categories, the various varieties of roses, for example. Categorization at the sub- and superlevels is less likely to be learned in conjunction with natural actions, and for this reason these additional levels or extensions are results that Brown called "achievements of the imagination" (Lakoff, 1987, pp. 32–33). Brown's use of the term *imagination* recalls the dictionary definition given earlier, namely, that it is the act or power of forming mental images not actually present to the senses, or that have not actually been experienced. These imaginative achievements are thus extensions or elaborations of the basic level of the category. Figure 6.1 shows the relation of the basic level of a category to its subordinate and superordinate extensions.

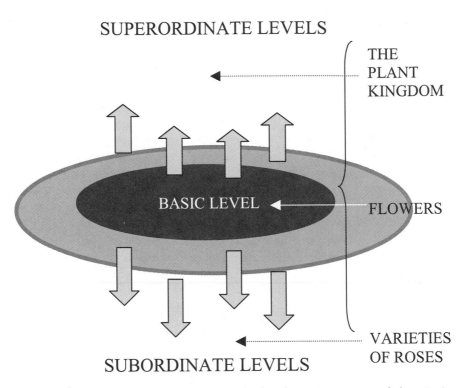

SUPERORDINATE LEVELS

THE
PLANT
KINGDOM

BASIC LEVEL

FLOWERS

SUBORDINATE LEVELS

VARIETIES
OF ROSES

Figure 6.1. Emergence of Superordinate and Subordinate Category Levels from Basic Level Categories

SOME IMPLICATIONS—EXPERIENCE, ABSTRACTION, AND METAPHOR

Work on categorization in philosophy, linguistics, and psychology has challenged the classical conception of categories, where they were thought to operate as innate (a priori) ideas built into the mind. Currently, it is becoming clear that categories are structures of knowledge abstracted from multiple experiences that are largely perceptual in character, and that they are "natural" in the sense that they arise from distinctive actions of the body such as grasping, touching, or seeing. Although categories are cognitive achievements, they are not disembodied. Their elaboration in cognition is, in part, a function of imagination, the ability to discern relevant similarities in a collection of cases that defines these as like things—that is, as a category.

In addition, Lakoff and Johnson (1980) have observed and documented the fact that "the categories of our everyday thought are largely metaphorical and that our everyday reasoning involves metaphorical involvements and inferences. As a consequence ordinary rationality is imaginative by its very nature" (p. 193). They add:

> Metaphor is one of our most important tools for trying to comprehend partially what cannot be comprehended totally: our feelings, aesthetic experiences, moral practices, and spiritual awareness. These endeavors of the imagination are not devoid of rationality; since they use metaphor, they employ an imaginative rationality. (p. 193)

Using classical categorization in some instances and basic level or prototype categorization in other instances, Lakoff and Johnson began to elaborate a theory of knowledge that could account for the mind as a power that develops multiple forms of thought. More than that, they also portrayed mind as a power that could create meaning through such devices as metaphor. In the course of this work, they explored the role of image-schemata as the underlying structure of knowledge that provides the foundation for a conception of cognition that includes categorization, reason, metaphor, as well as propositional and nonpropositional forms of thought.

Learning in all domains utilizes these forms of cognition, although it is likely that propositional reasoning is more likely to be experienced in philosophy, physics, and mathematics than in the arts. It is principally in the arts where one encounters metaphors as ways of establishing meaningful connections between ideas and concepts. As we shall see, metaphor also appears in the language of scientists, where it is likely to remain hidden.

Two illustrations follow, the point of which is to show that metaphors are likely to work passively in scientific discussions, whereas in the arts they become the principal source of meaning. The first illustration uses statements that rely on a metaphor coined by Johnson (1987), *theories-are-buildings*:

> Is that the *foundation* for your theory?
> Quantum theory needs more *support*.
> You'll never *construct a strong* theory on those assumptions.
> I haven't figured out yet what *form* our theory will take.
> Here are some more facts to *shore up* your theory.
> Evolutionary theory won't *stand or fall* on the *strength* of that argument.
> So far we have only put together a *framework* of the theory.
> He *buttressed* the theory with *solid* arguments. (p. 105; emphasis in original)

Each expression is clear and unproblematic, underscoring the point that the theories-are-buildings metaphor is meaningful. In fact, members of the scientific community would not likely recognize the metaphor at work in their daily speech.

The next example discusses metaphor at work in the interpretation of the clock motif in the paintings of Marc Chagall. In several of Chagall's paintings done in the 1930s and 1940s, a recurrent image is the flying clock, sometimes accompanied by images of other objects in flight. In one such work, *Time Is a River Without Banks* (1930–1939), the clock dominates the center of the composition (see Figure 6.2). It is accompanied by a flying fish and a violin. In the lower right-hand corner one sees a pair of lovers. Another work is entitled *Clock with Blue Wing* (1949). We know literally that clocks don't fly, nor do fish, nor do they have wings enabling them to do so. So a question for the viewer becomes, What meaning do the flying clocks have in this artist's work? Do these images refer to the folk metaphor that *time flies*? Does the pair of lovers have any special significance in a painting that seems to comment on the passage of time, perhaps the artist's remembered youth in Russia, or a former love affair. Is the clock emblematic of the beating of the human heart, a symbol of love but one that also suggests the ticking away of life? Numerous critics also refer to Chagall's use of images of people in flight to represent the emotional ecstasy of the pair of lovers, as in his work *The Birthday* (1915).

There is no way to be sure which of these interpretive conjectures is tenable. For this reason, such works of art open what David Perkins (1994) calls a "reflective intelligence." The clock has become an object for thought, for interpretation. The clock metaphor is active and can enliven the cognitive activity of the viewer.

Cognitive Structures in Piaget's Theory of Development

Lakoff and Johnson's concept of image-schemata underlies their theory of metaphor. To understand this concept more fully, I compare it with Jean Piaget's concept of schemata. Schemata are not new in theories of cognitive development and have been a principal object of investigation by Piaget and others. For Piaget, cognitive development begins when infants start to recognize certain regularities in their experience. Increasingly, they come to rely on the memory of prior encounters, the actions that initiated them, and the resulting responses as providing a reasonable guide for future actions. Piaget attributed the development of this ability to the formation of specific cognitive structures called schemata. He used this concept to help explain why individuals develop relatively stable, even predictable

Figure 6.2. Chagall, Marc. *Time Is a River Without* Banks. 1930–1939. Oil on canvas, 100 × 81.3 cm. The Museum of Modern Art, New York. Photograph © 2001 The Museum of Modern Art, New York.

responses to stimuli. Schemata are symbolic structures that organize perceived events. They are abstract structures that summarize information
from many different cases, but tied to these structures is the awareness of
particular operations or actions undertaken by the mind to understand
what is given in perception. Piaget describes the development of these
cognitive structures as becoming increasingly mentalistic, abstract, and less
dependent on the senses. Their cognitive operations become less physical
and more formal (rule governed) as the organism matures. Cognitive development also proceeds through several stages marked by changes in these
structures. In his formal operations stage, Piaget describes the mind's power
to organize symbolic structures in logical and scientific propositions that
describe, explain, and reliably predict events in nature. Schemata as conceived by Piaget evolve into logical, scientific and propositional structures.
His main work consisted of tracking the evolution of these structures from
the first exploratory actions undertaken by the infant, like the grasping of
objects, to the formation of abstract symbolic structures, comprising numbers and letters that, although meaningless in themselves, are understood
as representations of the actual world.

The function of cognitive development, in the Piagetian view, is to
produce more and more powerful logical structures that permit the individual to act upon the world in more flexible and complex ways. Flavell's
(1963) description of Piaget's schemata also describes these structures as
"kinds of concepts, categories, or underlying strategies that group together
a collection of distinct but similar actions" (pp. 54–55). Of importance is
that these structures in their early phases include sequences of actions
undertaken by the infant to explore and understand its environment. The
possibility that some schemata might evolve into classes of imagery rather
than abstract symbolic forms was not discussed by Piaget, although some
descriptions of his concrete operations stage sound like image-schemata
(see Flavell, 1963, pp. 165–168).

Lakoff and Johnson's Image-Schemata

Lakoff and Johnson do not discuss Piaget directly, although their philosophical explorations and work in linguistics attempt to characterize meaning
in terms of *embodiment*, that is, in terms of preconceptual, bodily experiences (Lakoff, 1987). They postulate a type of schema that begins with
images and bodily experiences acquired directly in perception as providing the foundation for categorization, abstract reason, propositional and
nonpropositional forms of thinking, metaphor, and narrative. Image-
schemata should not be confused with the images we recall from prior per-

ceptions. Rather, they are cognitive structures that are derived from a variety of images. Johnson (1987) illustrates his image-schema called "compulsive force" by showing how there are structural similarities between a jet airplane being forced down the runway by the power of its engines and the forces acting upon continental plates. He also finds compulsive force in social pressures that force him to join the PTA. The meaning of compulsive force is embodied directly in the percepts acquired in experience and does not have to await additional actions put forth by the mind to comprehend them.

Johnson illustrates this further with the image-schema of balance as giving rise to a structure that applies to many instances of balanced phenomena. Initially, balance acquires meaning through experiences where we orient ourselves physically within our environment. We live in a gravitational field and resist the pull of gravity as we learn to maintain our equilibrium. He writes:

> It is crucially important that we see that balancing is an *activity that we learn with our bodies* and not by grasping a set of rules or concepts. First and foremost balancing is something we *do*. The baby stands, wobbles, and drops to the floor. It tries again, and again, until a new world opens up—the world of balanced erect posture. (Johnson, 1987, p. 74; emphasis in original)

The image-schema of balance is acquired by activities like learning to stand and walk, experiences that are learned in the course of development often before there are words to name or describe them—hence their nonpropositional character.

Metaphoric projection. Once established, these image-schemata are potentially available for metaphorical elaboration so that balance can extend to such things as a balanced personality, a balanced equation in mathematics, the balance of justice in the machinations of the legal system, and so forth. Johnson (1987) maintains:

> It is the projection of such structure that I am identifying as the creative function of metaphor, for it is one of the chief ways we can generate structure in our experience in a way we can comprehend. (p. 98)

Lakoff and Johnson claim further that higher-order, rational thinking can be accounted for through extensions of these image-schematic structures by metaphoric projection. To underscore the point that these image-schematic structures have a logical basis, I describe the structure of metaphor as posited by Lakoff.

The structure of metaphor. A metaphor has three parts: a source domain, a target domain, and a source to target mapping (Lakoff, 1987). Understanding the metaphor means grasping how these elements are intellectually connected. In many of Lakoff and Johnson's examples, the source domain is grounded in some aspect of preconceptual, or basic level, bodily experience, as in the case of balance given above. Lakoff illustrates this with a family of metaphors he calls "more-is-up, less-is-down." This is seen in expressions like, "The crime rate keeps *rising*," "The number of books published each year keeps *going up*," "That stock has *fallen* again" (Lakoff, 1987, pp. 276–277).[9] In each example, the source domain is verticality, while the target domain is quantity. Verticality is a good source domain since it is directly understood in our bodily experience of gravity. *More* is understood as *up* because "whenever we add more of a substance say water to a glass—the level goes up. When we add more objects to a pile, its level rises. Remove objects from the pile or water from the glass and the level goes down" (Lakoff, 1987, p. 276). Thus, verticality and quantity become linked together through common structural correlations that permit verticality to represent quantity.

What Lakoff (1987) is saying is that the schemata that emerge from our bodily experience have a basic logic that enables them to form connections in at least two ways: first, things that are alike in some way can be grouped together as categories; and second, things that are seemingly unlike can be joined and made meaningful through metaphor. "What has been called abstract reason has a bodily basis in our everyday physical functioning" (p. 278). Indeed, Lakoff and Johnson's theory of meaning and rationality can be rooted in aspects of bodily functioning.

Metaphors establish connections among objects and events that are seemingly unrelated, although, in the "more-is-up" example just cited, the source and target are so close that they act like everyday propositional speech rather than what ordinarily is thought of as being truly metaphoric. Metaphors are encountered in all studies, including the arts. The arts have no monopoly on metaphor but, as we shall see, they do have a particular claim to the subject of metaphor, namely, that the arts are places where the artist and the spectator are conscious of what is metaphoric in a given expression. In other realms, the use of metaphor is likely to remain in the background.

Lakoff and Johnson's main claim is that image-schemata, which emerge from bodily sensations and perceptions, reach the mental, epistemic, or logical domains in cognition, which makes acts of cognition like categorization and metaphor possible. What typically is referred to as higher-order thinking, the larger understandings that are called abstract and disembodied reason, has its beginnings with the formation of image-schemata in bodily experience.

Kantian Antecedents of Image-Schemata

Johnson described image-schemata as nonpropositional structures of imagination, a concept derived from his reading of Kant's *Critique of Pure Reason* (1781/1997). In this seminal work, Kant elaborated a theory of imagination based on four divisions, which he called "reproductive imagination," "productive imagination," "imagination as a schematizing function," and finally "creative imagination" (pp. 273–276). In particular, Johnson (1987) drew upon Kant's notion of imagination as a schematizing function:

> Kant clarifies the irreducible character of imaginative schematic activity by distinguishing the *schema* from the *concept* and also from the specific *image*. The image is a mental picture that can be traced back to sense experience. The concept is an abstract rule specifying the characteristic a thing must have to "fall under that concept." The *schema* is for Kant a procedure of imagination for producing images and ordering representations. . . . It is thus partly abstract and intellectual, while also being a structure of sensation. So it provides the needed bridge between concepts on the one hand and percepts on the other. (pp. 153–155; emphasis in original)

Image-schemata are described further by Johnson (1987) as "embodied patterns of meaningfully organized experience" (p. 156), that is, structures of bodily movements and perceptual interactions. It is here that differences between Johnson and Piaget arise. For Piaget, actions, especially at the higher levels of cognition, are operations of the mind that work on the perceptions it receives. Actions of the body, such as learning to walk, were of lesser interest to Piaget and are discussed in his sensimotor stage of cognitive development. Piaget's research on cognitive development, as noted earlier, was focused on the formation of the propositional structures that support logical-scientific thinking. What Johnson adds to the discussion is an explanation of how this power of mind is bodily in origin. In Johnson's conception, the body and mind are undivided.[10]

Piaget's understanding of the cognitive was more dynamic than the Kantian view with its innate mental structures, but Piaget still tended to portray the course of intellectual development as a journey away from the sensory foundations of knowledge. Despite his early training as a biologist, he, like Kant before him, conceived of the mind's formal operations as being less dependent on, if not entirely separate from, the body. Piaget's project can be thought of as the effort to map the achievement of Kantian categories without the precondition of Kant's metaphysical speculations (Fabricius, 1983).

By contrast, Lakoff and Johnson's intellectual exploration presents the basic level of bodily and perceptual experience as the foundational source of cognition and the origin of meaning. Like Piaget, they sought to provide an alternative to the Kantian view that higher-order logical structures emerge "a priori as the universal essence of rationality" (Johnson, 1987, p. 99), and argue instead that such higher-order cognitive structures emerge from our embodied, concrete experience. Their definition of cognition includes traditional Piagetian propositional schemata, but they also add image-schematic, nonpropositional structures.

The Kantian conception of imagination was problematic because it divided the mind into a physical or material side governed by strict deterministic natural laws, which encompassed our bodily being (including sensations) and feelings, and a formal side consisting of understanding. This gulf separated understanding from perceptual experience, the mind from the body, in a dualism that went back to Descartes, and that survives in Piaget's tendency to separate thinking from feeling. However, schematic imagination as conceived by Kant had the potential to bridge this gap. Johnson (1987) adds:

> I would suggest that though Kant could never admit it, that his remarkable account of imagination actually undermines the rigid dichotomies that define his system, showing very powerfully that they are not absolute metaphysical and epistemological separations. Hence imagination is a pervasive structuring activity by means of which we achieve coherent, patterned, and unified representations. The conclusion ought to be, therefore, that imagination is absolutely essential to rationality, that is, to our rational capacity to find significant connections, to draw inferences, and to solve problems. Kant, of course, pulls back from this conclusion because it would undermine the dichotomies that underlie his system. (p. 168)

Kant's problem disappears when we deny the alleged gap between understanding, imagination, and sensation. Johnson (1987, p. 167) asks, "What if, following the consensus of contemporary analytic philosophy, we deny the strict separation of the formal realm from the material?" If we were to regard these as poles on a continuum, there would be no need to exclude imagination from the cognitive. Kant recognized a vast realm of shared meaning structure in imagination but could not bring himself to grant this dimension cognitive status.

TOWARD A THEORY OF IMAGINATION—CATEGORIZATION, SCHEMATA, AND NARRATIVES

Johnson (1987) suggested that "an adequate account of meaning and rationality (as well as of understanding and communication) awaits a comprehensive theory of imagination. Such a theory would complement and influence our present theories of conceptualization, propositional content, and speech acts. In its broadest sense, it would provide a comprehensive account of structure in human experience and cognition" (p. 171). He then listed several features of what a cognitive account of imagination would entail, three of which are described next.

Categorization

By this Johnson means not the classical view of categorization but a view that describes the way human beings actually "break up their experience into comprehensible kinds" (p. 171). Prototypical categorization is preferred over types that seek sets of necessary and sufficient conditions.

Schemata

Johnson cites the need for a comprehensive theory of schemata, that is, "general knowledge or event structures." He states, "We need to survey the basic kinds of schemata, to see how they can be developed metaphorically, to investigate their complex interrelations, and to explore their connections with propositional structures" (p. 171).

Narrative Structure

When it comes to explaining how humans make sense of their world, wrote Johnson,"there must be a central place for the notion of narrative unity. Not only are we born into complex and communal narratives, we also experience, understand, and order our lives as stories we are living out" (pp. 171–172).

Although Johnson (1987) identifies the structure of narrative as one of the components in a comprehensive theory of imagination, his account does not elaborate how the capacity for narrative is related to other features of imagination, such as metaphor. But narrative structure does share certain common features with metaphoric structure, in that narratives have a source point in human experience where they originate with some kind of problem or situation. Jerome Bruner (1996) uses the term "trouble" to identify the starting points in many narratives. A typical narrative, he wrote, opens with a phrase like

> "I was walking down the street, minding my own business when . . . " The action unfolds leading to a breach, a violation of legitimate expectancy. What follows is either a restitution of initial legitimacy or a revolutionary change of affairs with a new order of legitimacy. (p. 94)

There is also a target point (some kind of resolution, outcome, or moral of the story), and finally there are pathways that map the intervening connections.

Narrative in Bruner's (1996) view is also a disciplined mode of thought for construing the present, past, and possible human conditions. Narratives don't provide explanations, but rather lead to understanding, which is defined as "the outcome of organizing and contextualizing essentially contestable, incompletely verifiable propositions in a disciplined way" (p. 90). The narrative mode of meaning making tells a story of what something is about. "Understanding, unlike explaining, is not preemptive. One way of construing the fall of Rome narratively does not rule out other interpretations." "Some narratives about 'what happened' are simply righter, not just because they are rooted in factuality, but because they are better contextualized, rhetorically more 'fair minded' and so on" (pp. 90–91).

RELEVANCE TO ART EDUCATION

For most people, the term *imagination* "connotes artistic creativity, fantasy, scientific discovery, invention and novelty" (Johnson, 1987, p. 139)—bearing little or no correspondence to the everyday world. Such beliefs are holdovers from nineteenth-century romanticism. Johnson was intent upon explaining how the image-schemata that arise in bodily and perceptual experience give rise to such imaginative operations as metaphor and narrative. Moreover, these processes operate across the whole gamut of human cognition from the day-to-day transactions of ordinary life to abstract conceptualization at the high end. Johnson was intent upon demonstrating that these operations occur in everyday speech, in the language of scientists, and in the arts. And to underscore the point that metaphor and imagination pervade the whole gamut of human cognition, he intentionally postponed any discussion of the arts until the main point of his argument had been made—that imaginative cognitive operations like metaphor emerge at the higher end of the spectrum of human cognitive performance. As noted earlier, Kant (1790/1964) believed that imagination brings intellectual ideas into movement, "thus enlivening the mind by opening it to the prospect of an illimitable field of kindred representations" (p. 318).

And since metaphor is an essential component of imagination in such forms of cognition as abstract reason, this has unmistakable implications for the arts as well. The arts are places where metaphoric leaps of imagination are prized for their power and aesthetic excellence. Moreover, it is in the arts where the experience, nature, and structure of metaphor becomes the principal object of study. This happens in activities where individuals create works of art, but it comes into play in the interpretation of works of art as well. Deepening the wellspring of the imagination and the role it can play in the creation of personal meaning, and in the transmission of culture, becomes the point and purpose for having the arts in education.

Making a place for the arts does not mean giving oneself over to the ornamental fringes of knowledge or to the abandonment of the hard facts of reality. Indeed, quite the reverse is true. Before a metaphor can become active in the learner's mind—*as a metaphor*—he or she must understand the underlying reality or context where the metaphoric nature of the image or expression is active.

Let me emphasize this point once more—the arts are places where the constructions of metaphor can and should become the principal object of study, where it is necessary to understand that the visual images or verbal expressions are not literal facts, but are embodiments of meanings that can be taken in some other light. It is *only in the arts where the processes and products of the imagination are encountered and explored in full consciousness*—where they become objects of inquiry, unlike in the sciences where the metaphors that are used remain hidden.

Having learners understand the imaginative as ornamental devices like metaphor, used mainly by artists and poets, is of secondary importance. I lean more toward activities where the learner comes to an understanding of the world referred to in works of art, and the role that the artist plays in representing that world. Moreover, an art education that fails to recognize the metaphoric character of meanings in the arts is without serious educational purpose.

Having said this, it remains to be seen whether the metaphors that are active in the visual arts add anything to cognition that is not already provided by experience in the everyday world or by arts like music or literature. Are there such things as visual metaphors whose meaning is conveyed directly by images rather than words, and, if so, how do they differ? What would be lost if they were left out of educational practice?

Noel Carroll (2001) raised the first question by asking whether there are such things as visual metaphors. He answered by noting that images differ from words in being recognized "simply by looking" (p. 348). Unlike verbal symbols, the image is read directly, not having to be decoded. Images can be symbolic, like the dove on the flag of the United Nations, although not all images are necessarily visual metaphors. The family photographs I took on my last vacation are not metaphors.

However, a work like Man Ray's photomontage entitled *Violin d'Ingres* (1924) is a visual metaphor, as is the clock motif in the Chagall paintings discussed earlier. In the Man Ray, the bare back of a nude female model is reminiscent of the early nineteenth-century odalisques of Ingres. However, Man Ray placed two black *f*-shaped holes such as those found in violins or cellos on the back of the model. This realization suggests something quite shocking, that this woman is no longer a person but an instrument, that is, something to be played with—perhaps an instrument of sexual desire. This interpretation is reinforced by the turban on the model's head, which brings to mind Ingre's paintings of harem odalisques. The image plus the title give rise to the metaphoric insight that Ingre's odalisques are violins, or conversely that violins are odalisques.

When I first encountered this work, I didn't like it, and even now I find its implied sexism distasteful. Yet, at the same time, my personal displeasure explains why visual metaphors can be persuasive, even powerful, social instruments. Man Ray's works were seen by a relatively small elite in his own day. By contrast, today's students live in a visual culture where they are subjected to the influences of literally thousands of visual images, some as clever as Man Ray's. For example, a public service announcement on the impact of drugs makes its point by showing a brain affected by drugs as an egg being fried. In a powerful way the image dramatizes the dangers of drug abuse. No moral sermon is needed.

But visual images as metaphors are not necessarily beneficial. Laura Chapman (2001) observed that the visual messages that target today's youth are designed by professionals who excel at what visual imagery does well, namely, direct attention, create desire, tap into emotions, all the while suppressing critical thinking. Artful techniques are used for profit and political power. She also noted that advertisers spend about $3,000 a year per child to win hearts and minds, which approximates what we spend per pupil on classroom instruction in the United States.

Not only are there visual metaphors, but we have become a society that literally is inundated by them. Attention to their impact and influence should become part of contemporary education. One should learn to recognize how visual metaphors work and why they can be persuasive. At the same time, political pressures on the schools seem intent upon directing attention away from the visual aspects of the social environment.

IMPLICATIONS FOR GENERAL EDUCATION

It is clear that cognition entails more than the ability to secure the meanings stated in propositional form such as language and number. Meaning is conveyed by nonpropositional forms as well, which rely heavily on metaphor. Yet schooling for most students occurs within a curriculum where knowledge is experienced as a series of isolated, random facts. This compartmentalized curriculum reflects a long tradition in Western philosophy, which in large part is the consequence of a divided mind. On one side is cognition proper, the province of reason, conceptualization, logic, and formal propositional discourse. On the other is the bodily, perceptual, material, emotional, and imaginative side of our nature. "The most significant consequence of this split," says Johnson,

> is that all meaning, logical connection, conceptualization and reasoning are aligned with the mental or rational dimension, while perception, imagination and feeling are aligned with the bodily dimension. As a result both non-propositional and figuratively elaborated structures of experience are regarded as having no place in meaning and the drawing of rational inferences. (1987, p. xxv)

These polarities have reified themselves into structures of consciousness. If thinking is cognitive, then its contrary (feeling) is noncognitive. If cognition involves the use of verbal and mathematical symbols to construct rational or formal propositions, then perceptual imagery is taken to be nonpropositional and hence noncognitive.

Education should have as its ultimate purpose the maximization of learners' cognitive potential. This requires recognition of the realm of imagination and the cognitive tools, like categorization and metaphor, that make its operation possible—in all subjects to be sure, but quintessentially in the visual arts.

7

The Arts and Cognition:
A Cognitive Argument for the Arts

THE END OF THIS EXPLORATION into cognition is nearly at hand. Still remaining are the tasks of describing the educative role of the arts within a cognitive perspective and the consequences for learners when the arts are absent as part of their overall educational experience. I begin by reviewing a series of key observations. The first is that the integrated view of cognition offered at the close of Chapter 3 is an amalgamation of three contending views: (1) that the mind is a computational function using symbols; (2) that cognition is a constructive process used to enable individuals to secure meaning; and (3) that learning includes the acquisition of social reality, the idea that learning becomes meaningful when it occurs in a sociocultural or situational context. An integrated view of cognition is one that accommodates these three factors.

Second, I noted that strong philosophical dualisms in Western culture have worked to separate the mind from the body, the cognitive from the affective, the real from the imaginative, and science from art. The structure of most school curricula reifies this dichotomy, placing the sciences in the cognitive domain while the arts are dispatched to minor-league status, in the realm of the affective. To be sure, the arts are praised as sources of delight, as embellishment or beautification (icing on the cake), but rarely are they taken to be active sources of insight, knowledge, or understanding. Throughout this book I have taken exception to this view.

Third, the change of paradigm from behaviorism to cognitivism has had comparatively little effect on math and science. They were classified as cognitive subjects before and are regarded as cognitive now. With the arts the situation differed. Before they were "in the affective domain which meant they were non-cognitive. Now they are cognitive, which includes the intuitive, the creative, and the emotional" (Parsons, 1992, p. 71). The implications of this change of category have yet to register either in what is taught as art or in how it is taught.

It is also true that placing the arts in the category of the cognitive has done little to change their low standing in the school curriculum. If every domain is cognitive, then being classified as cognitive no longer confers status. What differentiates domains from one another are the types of cognitive operations and knowledge-seeking strategies the various disciplines have to offer. In short, the argument on behalf of the arts no longer turns on the question of whether or not the arts are cognitive. The question becomes, What cognitive abilities do the arts provide that other subjects can neither provide, nor do as well as the arts? In particular, what special capabilities do the visual arts contribute to cognition as a whole?

In the 1980s, efforts to answer the question were offered by Howard Gardner and Elliot Eisner. In his multiple intelligences theory, Gardner suggested that each of the seven intelligences identified by his theory operates with a symbol system that is uniquely its own, with many of these systems involving the arts. He suggested that a wider representation of the various intelligences or symbol systems would widen the range of cognitive abilities exercised, bringing a degree of balance to the curriculum. He criticized the tendency of schools to focus on verbal and mathematical symbol systems while excluding those offered by the arts.

Eisner argued that the mind develops multiple forms of representation through experience gained through the senses, with some grounded in visual perception and others originating in auditory or tactile sources. If it were possible to convey everything that humans wanted to express with one or two forms, the others would be unnecessary or redundant. But since each of the arts offers unique ways of representing ideas and feelings, which cannot be matched by other systems of representation, their presence can be justified in terms of the cognitive abilities they nurture. Eisner's and Gardner's arguments both were built upon the notion of nonredundance, the idea that the arts provide unique opportunities for the development of the mind that are not available in other modalities.

Since these were positions essentially derived from the symbol-processing orientation, they were less congenial to the sociocultural cognitive position. The view of cognition proposed in Chapter 3 attempts to integrate the symbol-processing view with sociocultural views, to establish a position poised between these polarities.

What I take from Eisner's and Gardner's arguments is that different domains of knowledge utilize differing cognitive abilities for their mastery, and that such capacities are not likely to evolve if absent from the life experiences of individuals. The richer the array of subjects experienced, the wider the range of cognitive potentialities that learners are likely to develop.

Schools were created to maximize these potentialities but, of course, they cannot be expected to teach everything. A cognitive argument supporting the arts needs to state why the capabilities they advance provide essential benefits to learners. Let me underscore the point that the cited abilities have to be seen as fundamental to a fully developed intellect, and not merely desirable. Moreover, if these abilities might be acquired through other subjects, the argument must state why they could be better realized through the arts.

Fourth, the argument on behalf of the arts in education should emphasize what they have to offer that is likely to improve the life-chances of individuals preparing for the future, a time that promises to be less certain and predictable than the past. We have no foolproof way to gainsay the future, but it is quite likely that the trends that we have witnessed since the end of the Cold War will likely continue into the twenty-first century. These include a number of concerns:

- The continued globalization of international economies, as characterized by the spread and domination of multinational corporations
- A growing sense of powerlessness at the local level as industries move to other countries where labor costs are lower
- The global integration of monetary systems and social systems
- The homogenization and loss of indigenous cultures—casualties of globalization and market penetration
- The acceleration of technological advance, with new forms of technological play, virtual reality, and the centralization of mass communication media
- The degradation of the natural environment on a global scale, an increase in population, the exhaustion of natural resources, and global warming
- The increased pace, quality, and variety of information exchange by means of popular culture, mass consumerism, travel, and the Internet
- The rising aspirations of oppressed peoples in many places, including demands for social equity and cultural identity
- The mistrust of governments and their role in the personal and social affairs of individuals, which is reflected in the rise of paramilitary and vigilante groups

All these phenomena speak to the need for communication and intelligent action in responsible ways in a more complex world than we have known in the past. These and other phenomena that could be mentioned will raise the cognitive demands made upon individuals now coming of age.

In my opinion the integrated view of cognition discussed earlier avoids the dualisms that have plagued educational practice throughout the modern era. It can set the stage for the widened array of cognitive abilities that are demanded by the challenges of the postmodern world, including those abilities fostered through experiences in the arts.

The argument that follows cites four features provided by the arts:

- *The cognitive flexibility argument*, which takes into account the complex and ill-structured character of learning in the arts, which requires the study of cases and their interpretation. Ill-structuredness becomes evident in one-of-a-kind learning situations, where judgments are made unguided by rules or generalizations that cover multiple cases. This includes most situations in life.
- *The integration of knowledge argument*, where the interpretation of works of art draws strength from knowledge in collateral domains, enabling the learner to understand the context of the work.
- *The imagination argument*, where imagination is identified as a pervasive structuring activity using metaphor and narrative to establish new meanings and achieve coherent, patterned, and unified representations. Imagination is essential to our rational capacity to find significant connections, draw inferences, and solve problems.
- *The aesthetic argument*, which establishes the point that perceptually vivid aesthetic encounters in the arts have educative value.

The first three were the principal subjects of the previous three chapters, while the fourth refers to one of the traditional reasons given for the arts in human experience, namely, that they utilize the imagination to transform mundane experience into aesthetic experience, an experience that Ralph Smith (1986) and others have chararactized as inherently worthwhile. This latter reason tends not to be cited in cognitive justifications for the arts. However, the excellence of the arts in perception helps explain why particular works can arouse and sustain our interest and attention, and hence why they have educative power.

COGNITIVE FLEXIBILITY

The first reason for the arts was the subject of Chapter 4, where it was proposed that what distinguishes domains of knowledge from one another (other than their specific content) are differences in their overall structure. Domains such as the sciences and mathematics, as they are represented in typical schooling practices, are said to have a well-structured character. It is important to emphasize that domains in schooling situations are not disciplines in their own right, but representations of disciplines, and as such might misrepresent the structure of the domain. While the sciences are portrayed as well-structured domains, in actuality they may be less regular, especially when a given case may challenge a long-standing law or general principle. Other domains, including the arts, are represented as being complex and ill-structured. While the arts are complex and rely on the study of cases, they sometimes feature elements, like styles, that cover many cases. Learning within each type of domain employs differing cognitive processes for mastery. It is essential to grasp fully the character of these differences if we are to succeed in harvesting their cognitive potential. Cognitive flexibility is the ability to change strategies as one becomes mindful of the structural demands of each domain, and the ability to activate the appropriate means to secure meaning or understanding. To be flexible one needs a repertoire of strategies from which choices can be made, many of which are learned in the arts.

Well-structured knowledge will likely employ verbal and mathematical symbols, and be governed by a systematic propositional logic that can achieve particular explanations of phenomena. It utilizes key ideas, leading generalizations, or laws that cover most, if not all, cases. By contrast, complex and ill-structured knowledge will likely utilize nonpropositional schemata or symbolic forms governed by a logic that utilizes metaphor and narrative to construct meanings. It is likely to apply to experiences where broad generalizations are unavailable to explain things.

Case-Based Learning in the Arts

Cognitive activity in complex and ill-structured domains emphasizes the individual case in the absence of broad generalizations. It relies on interpretive activity to construct understandings. Since people draw on different background knowledge and have different purposes, they will come to differing, albeit credible, interpretations. I refer again to Bruner's (1996) illustration that "one way of construing the fall of Rome narratively does not rule out other interpretations" (pp. 90–91). A similar logic applies to the interpretation of works of art. One interpretation of a work of art does not rule out others, and indeed the accumulation of alternative interpretations enriches the culture as new insights imbue older works with fresh meaning.

What a work of art might have meant in one generation will likely change when it is interpreted *by* and *for* another. This also applies to individuals, who will construct different meanings about a given work. A case in point might be Paul Ziff's highly formalistic treatment of Poussin's *Rape of the Sabine Women*. When Modernist conceptions of art were prevalent, he wrote a formal analysis of this work from which the following was taken:

> We may attend to its sensuous features, to its "look and feel." Thus we attend to the play of light and color, to dissonances, contrasts, and harmonies of hues, values, and intensities. We notice patterns and pigmentation, textures, decorations, and embellishments. We may also attend to the structure, design, composition, and organization for balance and movement. We attend to the formal interrelations and cross connections in the work, to its underlying structure. We are concerned with both two and three-dimensional movements, the balance and opposition, thrust and recoil, of spaces, line, form and color. (Ziff, quoted in Smith, 1986, p. 50)

A critic informed by a feminist perspective might argue that Ziff's concentration on the formal aspects of this work blinded him to the subject at hand—a rape. The same critic might ask, Who was this painting's intended viewer? And, Why is a rape a subject for someone's aesthetic contemplation and pleasure? Feminist critical interrogation raises new and different questions and opens the work to new interpretations and understandings. In turn, these new meanings not only reflect the changing consciousness of the culture but help bring about such changes through the spread and sharing of ideas.[1]

Therefore, one answer to the question of why the arts are cognitively significant is that they provide encounters that foster the capacity to construct interpretations. The need to interpret is necessary in life, since reliable knowledge is often unavailable or filled with ambiguous and conflicting data. The interpretation of works of art not only enables one to construct understandings about them but enables individuals to interpret other situations where life's circumstances are uncertain or unclear.

It may be argued that the capacity for interpretation and the cognitive activities that nurture it might be acquired through study in other fields, like law, medicine, and history, and this is true. Where the arts have a decided advantage is that interpretive activity can be introduced at a relatively tender age, whereas medical interpretation (diagnosis) would have to await years of training and the acquisition of a considerable base of information. Moreover, in a field like medicine, interpretation is limited to existing medical conditions that should result in a single and hopefully "right" diagnosis. Works of art are likely to give rise to multiple interpretations, and indeed the accumulation of alternative interpretations contributes to the culture-building process. Moreover, the arts are doubly engaged in interpretive acts: first, in the actual creation of such works, and second, in efforts on the part of the viewer, listener, or reader to elucidate the possible meanings of such works.

What I have said up to now would apply to all the arts—literature, poetry, music, and the like. The case for the support of the visual arts would be made by reference to the particular nature of the visual image, namely, that it is recognized directly in perception "by looking" without the need to decipher musical notation or the symbol systems of written language to apprehend it.

Interpretation in the Creation of a Work of Art

The first kind of interpretation incorporates personal knowledge as seen from the artist's perspective. A work of art is about something. It is an artist's interpretation of what he or she has seen, felt, or undergone. It is an imaginative reordering of that experience and its embodiment in a medium. This is as true for the school child as it is for the professional artist, although, of course, the professional artist has accumulated a greater fund of experience and has a greater mastery of the media used to bring his or her vision to realization. Artistic productions capture and mirror the artist's interpretive vision.

Interpretation in Art Criticism

The second type of interpretive activity occurs through the critical investigation of a work of art by the viewer. Interpretations about works of art begin with the perception of the work. Some investigations limit themselves to surface features of particular works, while others reach beyond the work, to analyze how it is situated with respect to its cultural context.

The Bias Favoring Well-Structuredness

The distinction between well-structured and ill-structured domains raises a second issue, namely, that there is a bias in education favoring well-structuredness as the ideal model toward which all domains of knowledge should aspire. Even the designation of *well* or *ill* carries this bias. Well-structured representations of domains tend to do less violence to the sciences,[2] but are wholly unsuited for the arts and humanities. The life and death situations portrayed in the arts and humanities, as in the history of nations, movements, and biographies of persons, will more likely possess the thematic structure of a narrative or the life story of an individual. The unique aspects of an individual case are likely to be emphasized, even though such cases at times do echo broad and overarching themes, like "man's inhumanity to man" or, "the rich get richer," but such statements about life and what it means are not experienced through generalizations about it. Instead, they are stated and understood as adages or maxims rather than as scientific principles.

Works of art take the form of nonpropositional structures of imagination, derived from images or percepts that awaken feelings and emotions. The situations presented by life have their comic, tragic, and ironic components, and although one tragedy sometimes may seem like another, each unfolds with its own unique story. *Oedipus Rex* and *Macbeth* are tragedies, but no lawful generalization summarizes all the particulars that classify these dramas as tragedies. Each is a world onto itself—its own case.

To heighten the differences between well-structuredness in the sciences and the ill-structuredness of the arts, I ask the reader to contrast the work of sociologists with that of artists. For example, a sociologist might investigate the causes of homelessness by making a number of observations of urban settings, such as the rise of real estate prices, the loss of affordable housing by the working poor, the loss of employment opportunities as whole industries disappear, the closing of mental institutions, and the like. This social scientist may conduct interviews with the homeless to identify their stories and their personal views of their plight. These observations may be tabulated in statistical reports for dissemination to government agencies and city councils. Such well-documented reports serve city officials by providing reliable data on the extent of problems and potential solutions.

Contrast such reports with works by the Polish artist Krzysztof Wodiczko that are part of the *Homeless Vehicle Project* (reproduced in Gablik, 1991, pp. 100–101). Gablik described this show by noting that the homeless vehicle itself was based on the supermarket shopping cart and was designed to deal with the conflicting needs of the homeless. These needs, she explained, include visibility and protection, and she noted further that the shopping cart was also a metaphoric reference to the shopping mall:

> The Homeless Vehicle serves, thus, both as a practical object and as a symbol of the right of the poor not to be excluded from social life. Instead of shunting the homeless out of view, it heightens their visibility and legitimizes their otherwise unrecognized status as members of the urban community. . . . One of the features of the cart, besides transportation and shelter, is that it compels us to acknowledge the homeless as more than wrapped up objects in the street that we ignore and step over. (pp. 100–101)

The data provided by the social scientist may be important for coming to terms with social problems, and I don't belittle its importance. However, Wodiczko's exhibition offers viewers a qualitative encounter that

engages the viewer's thinking and feeling about the plight of the homeless in ways that objective, sociological treatises with statistical compilations do not. The work of Wodiczko appeals to our conscience, and we
may come away from such shows feeling a moral sense of obligation.

What I am saying is that the work of this artist and that of the social
scientist exemplify differences between well-structured knowledge and
complex and ill-structured knowledge. They serve differing, albeit legitimate, social purposes, and, in this instance, the work of the artist helps
build the culture through its power to arouse social and moral concerns
that may result in remedial action.

INTEGRATION OF KNOWLEDGE THROUGH THE ARTS

The second reason for the arts from a cognitive perspective is closely linked
to the first. A work of art is an expression of the artist's vision made possible by the actions of his or her imagination. Moreover, the expressive
content of a work of art reflects the larger situation surrounding the work,
namely, the social and cultural influences and sources of motifs initially
perceived and felt by the artist. Acts of interpretation enable individuals
to discern the work in relation to the cultural and social worlds it mirrors.
Moreover, the relation between artwork and culture is reciprocal. That is,
the work of art becomes meaningful when it is seen in the context of the
culture, and the culture becomes understandable as read through its arts.
For this reason I suggest that the places where the integration of knowledge is maximized lay in works of art as keys to understanding. This also
suggests that the arts should be centrally located within the curriculum as
an overlapping domain (see Figure 7.1).

The Work of Art as Cognitive Landmark

I also suggest that key works of art might serve as cognitive landmarks to
orient learners as they weave their maps of knowledge and understanding. Such works can serve as places in the web of knowledge where paths
of inquiry may cross, and where connecting links between domains might
become established. The maps of knowledge that individual learners develop for themselves should resemble the hypothetical map of the curriculum. Wisely used, the arts can play a pivotal role in establishing links
with other domains of knowledge. The map metaphor also suggests multiple pathways to learning.

The Palace at Versailles, discussed in Chapter 4, was an exemplar of
French Baroque architecture, but it is also a landmark marking the politi-

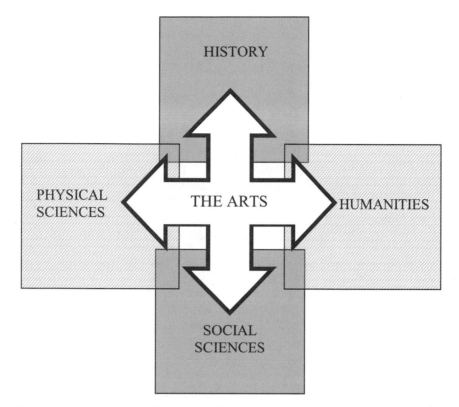

Figure 7.1. Integration of Knowledge Through the Arts

cal history of Europe by asserting the absolute power of the French monarchy under Louis XIV. As a landmark it could be located in the history of the Baroque architectural style, in a story of what preceded this style and what followed, but it also could fit into the history of political absolutism. Without knowledge of the absolutist rule of the French monarchy and Louis XIV in particular, we cannot understand why Versailles was built in the first place. Art cannot be fully understood apart from these embedding contexts. And when one lacks a knowledge of the arts of a particular time and place, one's understanding of these contexts is correspondingly diminished.

This does not mean that works of art are places where all meaningful insights will suddenly become clear. In fact, they might serve to reveal sites of conflict, especially when they violate our expectations of what art should be about, or even whether or not the object is art at all. Arthur Danto (1990), for example, refers to such works of art as "disturbatory," since they are often the instigators of problematic encounters that stimulate thinking about the works' possible meanings. The viewer is likely to ask, What is it? What is happening here? Viewers may struggle to orient themselves to the work, to make sense of it, and this effort, when successful, both results in understanding and often rewards the viewer with the pleasure of an aesthetic encounter. Hans and Shulamith Kreitler (1972) have called this the "cognitive orientation" process.

In Chapter 5 I noted Frederic Jameson's (1992) point that individuals need some sort of image or map to orient themselves within their society, with literary works serving as landmarks in the postmodern landscape. When Jameson illustrated this premise, he used two paintings of shoes, Van Gogh's *Peasant Shoes* and Warhol's *Diamond Dust Shoes*. I wondered why he chose the visual arts to make his point about the literary arts. Why not illustrate his opening arguments with literary works themselves? The answer was suggested by Noel Carroll's (2001) observation that "works of visual art are cognitive structures whose meaning is comprehended perceptually that is, without recourse to any subtending code" (p. 348). They are experienced directly through distinctive actions of the body, such as "looking." The understandings, feelings, and emotions they give rise to are part and parcel of that experience and have an immediacy and directness by virtue of the sensory origins of the encounter.

Location of the Arts in the Cognitive Landscape

The understanding of a work of art requires it to be grasped in relation to the social and cultural realms where it took form, and, reciprocally, the understanding of the work also helps the learner comprehend the social and cultural worlds it mirrors. This suggests that key works of art could well serve as points of integration among the various domains of knowledge, since a strategically chosen work could serve as the common ground upon which different domains of knowledge overlap and coalesce as learners construct their understanding of the work.

In the individual's mapping of a particular work of art, the work as landmark might be thought of as that point where paths of inquiry converge, crisscross, or join each other. These paths may meet at the work of art and be regarded as the learner's destination, or it could work in reverse. For example, one might start with a work like the target paintings of Jasper Johns, as exemplified in Chapter 5. With further inquiry these works became linked to their social context, where the viewer might acquire an understanding of the Cold War situation as lived through by this artist. Indeed, to understand anything, we must find out how it mirrors the cognitive landscape where it first came into being.

Integration of Knowledge into the Learner's Lifeworld

There is a second way to consider knowledge integration, namely, as the union of domain knowledge with the everyday knowledge of the individual's lifeworld. In Chapter 5 the lifeworld was described as the individual's construction of reality, the commonsense, symbolic matrix into which school subjects are placed in the effort to make them meaningful. It is also the individual's grasp of his or her culture, society, and the world of personal ties. Culture, society, and person are socially constructed concepts acquired by learning. The learner's lifeworld orientation serves as a reality check on what individuals have been taught. Integration of new knowledge into one's world picture is experienced as understanding, but quite often the subjects encountered in schooling remain detached and lifeless. The knowledge acquired may register as being present in a test of recall, but is dead thought.

What do the arts have that enlivens thought? The answer points to the third cognitive component that comes into play in the arts, namely, that they are imaginative undertakings.

Before proceeding, let me summarize what has been said thus far: The cognitive flexibility argument offered in Chapter 4 led to an exploration of domain differences, with attention directed to the arts as complexly structured domains. Inquiry in these domains is based on the study of cases, with understandings taking the form of interpretations. Two forms of interpretation occur in the arts: first, in artistic expression in the various media of the arts, and second, in interpretive actions undertaken during the critical apprehension of the work. Chapter 5 studied the possibility of integrating knowledge through the arts, since their interpretations utilize knowledge about the social and cultural landscape from which they came. Integration of knowledge also was used in a second sense, where it is more than finding connecting links among the various subjects in the curriculum but also refers to the integration of knowledge into the learner's lifeworld. Finally, attention was given to mapping as a mode of assessment.

THE IMAGINATIVE IN COGNITION

As noted in Chapter 6, the role of metaphor and narrative was shown to provide the basis for "an imaginative rationality . . . [that] is one of our most important tools for trying to understand what cannot be fully comprehended: our feelings, aesthetic experiences, moral practices, and spiritual awareness" (Lakoff &Johnson, 1980, p. 193). Lakoff and Johnson characterized mind as a power that creates meaning in multiple ways, such as categorization, reason guided by propositional logic, and metaphor guided by nonpropositional logic. Although their studies were limited to language, their work explored the structures formed by image-schemata as the bodily foundation of knowledge. These structures take form from images and bodily experiences acquired in perception.

Many such physical experiences, like that of balance, are acquired before the names for them are learned, as when the child first learns to walk. Such nonpropositional knowledge provides a foundation built of basic level categories, furnishing a basis for metaphoric elaboration. The experience of balance thus can be extended beyond the physical act of walking, as when an adult considers such things as balanced personalities, balanced chemical equations, or the balance of justice. We understand such abstract entities as equations not only because we have developed a capacity for formal operations, as Piaget described it, but also because such abstractions are elaborations of metaphoric knowledge initially experienced at a basic level in such actions as learning to walk.

Metaphors also have a logic of their own, which usually originates in bodily experiences like balance. Consider the following example, which illustrates a metaphor based on the bodily experience of nourishment as in the expression, "Michael's ideas provide much food for thought." Here, the experience of eating originates in bodily experiences, while the taking in of Michael's ideas feeds the mind. Ideas are understood in terms of food, and the mapping that links the two is a leap of imagination.

In the previous chapter, I concluded that metaphor can and should become the principal object of study within the arts, that only in the arts is the imaginative nature of metaphor explored in full consciousness. And it is this aspect that bestows fresh perceptions and insights as it enlivens thinking.

THE AESTHETIC EXPERIENCE

A number of individuals have attempted to justify the arts in education by citing the role that aesthetic experience might play in learning.[3] Often they stress the aesthetic as a distinctive qualitative category of experience had in the presence of great artworks. The proponents of such theories often hedge away from such pragmatic considerations as the possibility that one might gain knowledge or understanding through such encounters. Yet it is their aesthetic aspect that gives works of art the properties enabling them to become cognitive landmarks. It seems appropriate to touch upon some established views of aesthetic experience.

Beardsley's View of the Aesthetic

Monroe Beardsley identified five features of aesthetic experience as follows: "(a) it is directed toward an object; (b) what comes has the air of being freely chosen; (c) the object is emotionally distanced; (d) there is active discovery of connections, etc.; (e) there is a sense of integration between oneself as a person and the object of interest" (cited in Davies, 1991, p. 53). These ideas of the aesthetic experience suggest a potential role in cognition. For example, Beardsley identifies the quality of object directedness as an attribute of aesthetic experience, and this is a direct reference to the perceptual nature of artworks. Artworks do, in fact, engage the senses. Without such qualities the work will not register as an experience. Still another quality of aesthetic experience emphasizes the discovery of connections, while also speaking of wholeness and integration. Earlier I dealt with notions of curriculum integration that also arise from a desire for wholeness instead of the compartmentalized curriculum common in schooling.

Ralph Smith (1986) also paints a compelling cognitive portrait of the aesthetic based on Beardsley:

> Now if it is reasonable to hold that human powers become animated during our experience of art in the ways just described, if, that is, perception, reason, and feeling are energized in the manner indicated, and if vision becomes uncommonly synoptic and comprehensive, then it seems acceptable to suppose that our experience of art, unlike our experience of most other things, contributes to a sense of personal wholeness or integration. We experience a state of well-being noteworthy for its being unmarred by the discontinuities and frustrations of everyday living. (pp. 25–26)

What I find problematic in Beardsley and Smith is their tendency to single out the heightened aesthetic character of great artworks as a reason to set them apart as exemplars, in isolation from the rest of experience. That one might learn from such works is not denied by these writers, although knowledge acquisition is likely to be regarded as a secondary benefit and not the central point of education in the arts. Both Beardsley and Smith see the aesthetic experience as the point of art, to enable students to enter a realm removed from the world of politics and commerce, a world that they otherwise might never come to know.

While I can fully appreciate their desire to make such high-level aesthetic experiences available through educational activity, I find it somewhat odd that they would permit the pursuit of knowledge to end there. The purpose of education in the arts should certainly involve having aesthetic experiences, but it should include learning from them as well.

Goodman's Cognitive View

An alternative view that stressed the cognitive status of art was developed and elaborated by Nelson Goodman (1978a, 1978b). Goodman believed that each of the arts is a symbol system in its own right and hence is cognitive in character. Music is a symbol system based on the medium of sound, whereas oil painting is based on the medium of paint and canvas. Each medium communicates aspects of human experience not conveyed by other media. Goodman maintained that all the arts had an essentially cognitive function in human life, no less than the sciences. Both endeavors, for example, require active engagement rather than passive perception. He also argued that perception, cognition, and the emotions are involved in all domains of knowledge, and that emotion itself has a cognitive component, an argument echoed in Scheffler (1986) as well. The symbol systems of art, like those of science, are used in constructing different versions of the world, and these systems each capture aspects of experience that otherwise would be lost (Geahigan, 1992, p. 15).

Goodman justifies the arts in education, since each provides specific media of communication that would, in turn, enable specific meanings to be transacted. Each provides a unique form of literacy. If educators are intent upon expanding the cognitive abilities of youth, they can do so by increasing the number of symbol systems offered by the curriculum. The views of Goodman influenced Gardner's multiple intelligence theory.

The problem of aesthetic experience probably would not arise if Goodman's view of the cognitive nature of the arts had prevailed, although other curriculum difficulties would have arisen. To implement Goodman's idea, each form of art would have to be regarded as an independent medium in its own right—each a different way of thinking. With thinking channeled into specific media, there would be no way to integrate knowledge across such divisions.

The Aesthetic as Cognitive Mapping

To circumvent this problem I drew upon an observation made by Frederic Jameson (1988) who characterizes the study of contemporary artworks as the cognitive mapping of postmodern space. Individuals become aware of their cultural condition through their encounters with artworks as cultural landmarks. Moreover, this mapping is an aesthetic process since the artwork is both experienced individually and encountered by the senses. It is not something that "conceptualizes the real in a more abstract way" (p. 358).[4] It is cognitive because cognition begins with the images given in perception. I am not saying that the aesthetic is integrated into the cognitive, but that that the aesthetic is cognitive from the start.

IN SUMMARY: THE PURPOSE OF THE ARTS

The function of the arts throughout human cultural history has been and continues to be the task of "reality construction." The arts construct representations of the world, which may be about the world that is really there or about imagined worlds that are not present, but that might inspire human beings to create an alternative future for themselves. Much of what constitutes reality is socially constructed, including such things as money, property, marriage, gender roles, economic systems, governments, and such evils as racial discrimination. The social constructions found in the arts contain representations of these social realities.

Therefore, the purpose for teaching the arts is to contribute to the understanding of the social and cultural landscape that each individual inhabits. The arts can contribute to this understanding, since the work of art mirrors this world through metaphoric elaboration. The ability to interpret this world is learned through the interpretation of the arts, providing a foundation for intelligent, morally responsive actions. The understandings achieved through the arts can take several forms. They can embody the myths that bind human social systems together. They can reflect dreams, nightmares, illusions, aspirations, as well as disappointments and fears.

We have multiple forms of cognition (propositional and nonpropositional) but in my view these do not stand in opposition to each other. Rather, both emerge from the same common source, the basic level of experience originating in bodily and perceptual encounters with the environment, including culture. The reason why the hunches of the scientist or the imagination of the artist can be intuitive is that they reach an undivided world, the world that the physicist David Bohm calls "the implicate order," a world beyond dualisms that divide the body from the mind, thinking from feeling, or individuals from their social world. The construction of lifeworlds requires access to such sources as represented and extended symbolically in thinking, feeling, and willed action. Such building is, in the final analysis "an achievement of the imagination."

Notes

CHAPTER 1

1. For Plato, ultimate reality was found in the ideal forms, which are eternal and can be apprehended only by training the power of reason. In Book X of *The Republic* he illustrates this belief by using the example of the three beds: the idea of the bed, which is eternal, made by God, and hence most true; the bed of the carpenter that we see in the world of appearances; and, finally, the bed as it appears in a painting. The carpenter's bed has actuality but is an imitation of the ideal we cannot see. Images of beds are imitations of imitations, and being two removes from the ideal are less reliable as knowledge. The painting presents the bed as it appears, not as it is in actuality, and such appearances are deceptive because the pictorial image lacks many attributes of the archetype it imitates. All pictures hence are unreliable sources of knowledge because they do not tell the whole truth, and by extension all art is prone to error, even that of the great poets like Homer.

2. Scientific psychology began with Wilhelm Wundt's laboratory experiments in 1879.

3. Science also is grounded in sensory observation, whereas Platonic notions of thinking are tied to the ideal forms, which are sense-free. While science begins with observations, scientific understanding of such observations is based on the Cartesian premise that the ultimate laws governing nature are rational and can be accessed through the power of reason. Although grounded in observation, the creation of a scientific theory is akin to finding the archetypal form undergirding observations.

CHAPTER 2

1. European psychologists like Sigmund Freud and Karl Jung were less constrained by positivism. See also Amedo Giorgi's essay entitled "Phenomenologi-

cal Psychology," in *Rethinking psychology*, Ed. J. A. Smith, R. Harré, & L. Van Langenhove (London: Sage, 1995), pp. 24–42.

2. Perkins's (1994) description of reflective intelligence also describes what some cognitive psychologists call metacognition and what he calls the "mental self management" of learning (p. 34).

3. The previous discussion is indebted to Rudolf Steiner, *The Philosophy of Freedom*, Trans. M. Wilson (London: Rudolf Steiner Press, 1964), Chapters 4 & 5.

4. The taxonomy is not represented here as a theory of learning. Rather it was a planning document written to enable curriculum developers and evaluators to plan instruction around objectives, indicating appropriate outcomes.

5. In the late 1960s Eisner developed a category of objectives known as expressive objectives to account for the kinds of learning that occur in the affective domain. This represented an early effort on his part to account for the cognitive vs. noncognitive division among subjects.

6. There is another implication that comes from dissolving the boundaries between cognitive and affective subjects, namely, that subjects like math and social studies also have their feeling and emotional qualities.

7. I recall an incident where a school principal excluded the art and music teachers from a committee charged with developing standards for subjects as part of the school's curriculum reform effort. She felt that the reform effort applied only to cognitive or academic subjects.

8. When we organize cases under key generalizations and principles, we are creating knowledge hierarchies.

9. The separation of thinking from feeling can be traced back to the mind-body dualism that began with Cartesian rationalism. Thinking is mental whereas feeling is bodily.

10. Arnheim's work is an exception. Throughout a long and distinguished career, he has steadfastly maintained that we should regard the arts as cognitive endeavors. He believed that cognition begins with perception.

11. In his recent writing Parsons has abandoned the stage notion.

12. Adult influence also was likened to the psychoanalytic concept of repression, which was thought to be the source of neurosis and other forms of mental illness.

13. The idea of society as corrupter can be traced to Rousseau's political ideas that arose during the Enlightenment. In his novel *Emile* Rousseau sought to devise a form of education where the child would learn directly from nature without social mediation. The Rousseauean stream within progressive education was at variance with Deweyan progressivism, which saw social learning in a positive light.

14. Lukacs also maintained that a similar logical structure can be found in the industrial cultures of the socialist world.

15. Gardner observed that Freudian developmentalism was largely a study of affect, whereas Piagetian developmentalism was a study of cognition. He felt that the study of artistic development might show how the two become intertwined. Gardner did not continue to pursue this question.

16. Visual-minded adolescents are stimulated by visual perception, with the appearance of the natural world, whereas haptic-minded art is stimulated by tactile sensations, feelings, and emotions.

17. Chomsky noted that it would be impossible to explain the acquisition of language by processes like imitation, where speech is acquired solely by repeating the sounds one hears from others. The reason for this is that every sentence or string of words is a new combination. As Steven Pinker explains in *The Language Instinct* (New York: Harper Perennial Books, 1994), "Language cannot be a repertoire of responses; the brain must contain a recipe or program that can build an unlimited set of sentences out of a finite list of words" (p. 22). Chomsky calls this program a "universal grammar," and argues that children must be innately equipped with it, since it enables them to decode patterns of speech.

18. B. Wilson in his paper entitled "The Superheros of J. C. Holtz Plus an Outline of a Theory of Child Art," *Art Education: Journal of the NAEA, 27*(8) (1974), 2–9, distinguished child art from school art. My paper "The School Art Style: A Functional Analysis," *Studies in Art Education, 17*(3) (1976), 37–44, was inspired by this distinction. Wilson and I were challenging the prevalent belief that what happens in schools is child art. He showed that child art was an untutored art that was largely acquired by self-teaching. This led me to ask: "What then is school art?"

19. Although Herbert Read's classification of children's art is roughly contemporaneous with Lowenfeld's account, I have chosen to discuss Read's work in the context of Kindler and Darras's views to point out that the idea of multiple repertoires was anticipated by Read when he introduced the idea of alternative art styles in children's art.

20. Daniel Berlyne's arousal theory could be cited as one of the more successful attempts that developed late within the behavioral tradition. Berlyne (1960) attempted to explain arousal as a response to the novel aspects of a stimulus situation or to such conditions as the degree of complexity. A cognitive view of artistic response that utilizes aspects of Berlyne's arousal theory can be found in Kreitler and Kreitler (1972).

21. Behaviorists have sometimes used the term *cognitive* as a synonym for thinking.

CHAPTER 3

1. To be sure, Piaget also observed behavior, but his observations were used to draw inferences about the learner's ways of constructing knowledge.

2. The theories in Kellner's (1995) discussion involve the approaches to cultural studies of the media comprising popular culture, but in the absence of empirical evidence to lend support to any given theory of cognition, it is my view that it makes sense to apply his approach to cognitive theories of learning and development as well.

3. Bereiter makes it clear that this forced choice between Piagetian or Vygotskian notions is not wholly desirable. He suggests a third choice based on Popper's World Three.

4. Bereiter uses the term *constructivist cognition* to identify the Piagetian tradition, whereas the term *sociocultural cognition* identifies the Vygotskian tradition. My term *integrated* refers to the effort to combine these two cognitive traditions.

5. Gestalt psychologists often use the expression "the whole is greater than the sum of its parts," but in saying that the sum of the parts exceeds the whole, could be a way of claiming that the quality of the whole is not computational, or better yet that it cannot be measured or understood by counting the parts.

6. Davis and Gardner do not make the separation between knowing and feeling, and cite Scheffler's essay "In Praise of the Cognitive Emotions" (1986) to argue that symbols can convey emotions as well as knowledge.

7. The term *cognitive revolution* was coined by protagonists of the revolution such as Bruner to differentiate themselves from the prevailing behaviorism. I am persuaded by Rom Harré that the shift from behaviorism was an evolutionary process.

8. Of course, the content does change as well, since with the mastery of symbolic forms one is able to categorize and generalize on a more inclusive level.

9. Goodman was this project's first principal investigator. Gardner, who was formerly a student of Goodman, directed the project after Goodman.

10. Gardner handles this by identifying one of the intelligences as a social or interpersonal intelligence.

11. Bredo gets the idea of climbing out of our minds to be sure that our knowledge is reliable from Richard Rorty.

12. Although Brown and colleagues do not credit Vygotsky directly with regard to the notion of tool use, the many writers they cite do acknowledge the origin of the concept with him.

13. I am indebted to Judith Koroscik for this term.

14. Thomas Kuhn's idea of paradigm shifts in the sciences is a related idea here.

15. These writers dealt primarily with problems of learning in science, but their discussion is sufficiently broad in its implications to apply to other disciplines.

CHAPTER 4

1. Ralph Fleming in his book *Arts and Ideas* (New York: Holt Rinehart and Winston, 1968) uses the expression "cult of majesty" to characterize the strategy.

2. For example, many art history surveys tend to place non-Western art in the back of the book, which projects an attitude that the art of the Western world has evolved to a higher state of excellence.

3. I altered the language used by Spiro et al. (1988), to emphasize analogies.

4. Spiro et al. (1988) list seven forms of the reductive bias. Those included in this chapter were chosen since I was able to find suitable examples of learning problems in art that illustrate these learning difficulties.

5. My recognition rule is a compilation based on several textbooks, many written for school-age children.

6. My rule actually does not apply to all Impressionist paintings, since some painters, such as Pissarro in his *Poultry Market at Gisors*, dealt with the world of work, while Degas's *Absinthe Drinker* hardly portrays the individual in a state of enjoyment.

7. This was suggested by Koroscik to heighten awareness of the portrayal of human figures in Seurat's *La Grande Jatte*.

8. The notion of little narratives comes from Lyotard, *The Postmodern Condition* (Minneapolis: University of Minnesota Press, 1989). See also Efland, Freedman, and Stuhr (1996).

9. Efland, Freedman, and Stuhr (1996) exemplify knowledge construction without pre-compiled schemata in a lesson on the Native American powwow, where students literally are engaged in ethnography to construct their knowledge of the arts as witnessed during such an event.

10. The progress narrative is only one possibility of a grand narrative. There are also narratives like the golden age narratives, as exemplified by John Ruskin's *The Stones of Venice*. He and other nineteenth-century writers saw medieval architecture as a golden age with subsequent history marked by moral and artistic decline.

11. Spiro et al. (1988) list this with "oversimplification of complex and irregular structure," but it also fits with their notion of compartmentalization.

12. The idea of the lattice was taken from a theory on city planning by Christopher Alexander (1988). See Efland (1995) for an account of Alexander's theory and for an argument that applies his scheme to the planning of a curriculum.

13. While the rhetoric was in terms of social cohesion, integrated approaches also were advocated as a way to reduce costs by eliminating special teachers for music and art. See my paper, "Art Education During the Great Depression," *Art Education, Journal of the NAEA, 36*(6) (1983), 38–42.

14. This should not be confused with the issue of learning styles. It is true that learners may have an easier time in one type of domain over another.

CHAPTER 5

1. The examples cited by Wolf were not characterized by her as misconceptions but as indicators of children's developmental readiness to undertake art-learning tasks.

2. Habermas does not take Michel Foucault's position that the disciplines developed to provide forms of social domination.

3. The postmodern concept of intertextuality might well be characterized as overlapping sets or as nodes.

4. Jameson (1988) also discusses paranoia as a general attribute of postmodern culture, "as it expresses itself in a seemingly inexhaustible production of conspiracy plots of the most elaborate kinds. Conspiracy, one is tempted to say is the poor person's cognitive mapping of the postmodern age" (p. 356).

CHAPTER 6

1. Plato's attack of the doctrine of inspiration appeared in the dialogue known as *The Ion*. In *The Republic*, he also opposed the reliability of art as a source of knowledge, because a work of art is a double imitation, that is, an imitation of an imitation. There was also a third argument against the arts, namely, that such works violate public decorum by arousing socially unacceptable passions.

2. These statements on imagination were taken from Kant's later work, *The Critique of Judgment*. The structure of imagination was given in his *Critique of Pure Reason*.

3. The senses were thought to be passive since they are receivers of impressions, whereas the mind was thought to be active in its knowledge seeking.

4. A detailed account of this controversy can be found in Gardner (1987).

5. The term *natural* was coined by Lakoff to refer to images derived directly from the senses as opposed to experiences mediated by verbal or other forms of symbolic representation. See Johnson (1987), p. 27.

6. I attribute the expression to Jerome Bruner.

7. Answers to the question, What is art? traditionally were thought to be true definitions, in the sense that they were advanced to cover all cases of art. Weitz argued that What is art? is the wrong question, that a more appropriate one would ask, What sort of concept is art? or How is it being applied in a given context?

8. For example, Laura Chapman's widely used text *Approaches to Art Education* (New York: Harcourt, Brace and Jovanovich, 1978) employed an eclectic stance.

9. Lakoff's examples of metaphors often don't sound like metaphors since they refer to obvious facts. The reader should bear in mind that his objective was to show that our conceptual system plays a central role in defining our everyday realities and that much of what we think and do is a matter of metaphor.

10. Lakoff and Johnson reject what they term the myths of objectivism and subjectivism in favor a metaphysics they call experiential realism. See Chapter 11 in Lakoff (1987) and Chapters 25–28 in Lakoff and Johnson (1980).

CHAPTER 7

1. See also Jonathan Culler's book *On Deconstruction* (London: Routledge, 1989). The chapter "Reading as a Woman" cites the importance of the reader's personal context as a factor in the interpretation of a literary work.

2. In recent decades, interest in chaos and complexity in the sciences can be seen as an effort to break away from the deterministic tendencies that are characteristic of well-structured domains.

3. This section is based on my essay "Ralph Smith's Concept of Aesthetic Experience and Its Curriculum Implications." *Studies in Art Education, 33*(4) (1992), 201–209.

4. The statement appeared in the questions and answers section following the chapter.

References

Abrams, M. H. (1953). *The mirror and the lamp: Romantic theory and the critical tradition.* New York: Norton.

Alexander, C. (1988). A city is not a tree. In J. Thackara (Ed.), *Design after modernism* (pp. 67–84). New York: Thames & Hudson.

Anderson, R. C. (1984). Some reflections on the acquisition of knowledge. *Educational Researcher, 13*(3), 5–10.

Arnheim, R. (1954). *Art and visual perception.* Berkeley: University of California Press.

Barnes, E. (Ed.). (1896–1897). *Studies in education: A series of ten numbers devoted to child-study and the history of education.* Palo Alto, CA: Stanford University.

Barnes, E. (Ed.). (1902). *Studies in education: A series of ten numbers devoted to child-study* (Vol. 2). Philadelphia.

Beardsley, M. (1966). *Aesthetics from classical Greece to the present.* New York: Macmillan.

Belenky, M., Clinchy, B., Goldberger, N., & Tarule, J. (1986). *Women's ways of knowing: The development of self, voice and mind.* New York: Basic Books.

Bell, P. A., Baum, A., Fisher, J. D., & Greene, T. C. (1990). *Environmental psychology.* New York: Harcourt Brace Jovanovich.

Bereiter, C. (1994). Constructivism, socioculturalism, and Popper's world 3. *Educational Researcher, 23*(7), 21–23.

Berlyne, D. (1960). *Conflict, arousal and curiosity.* New York: McGraw-Hill.

Blanck, G. (1990). Vygotsky: The man and his cause. In L. C. Moll (Ed.), *Vygotsky and education: Instructional implications and applications of sociohistorical psychology* (pp. 31–58). New York: Cambridge University Press.

Bloom, B. S. (Ed.). (1956). *Taxonomy of educational objectives: Cognitive domain.* New York: McCay.

Bohm, D. (1980). *Wholeness and the implicate order*. London: Routledge & Kegan Paul.

Bohm, D., & Peat, F. D. (1987). *Science, order and creativity*. New York: Bantam Books.

Bransford, J., Sherwood, R., Vye, N., & Rieser, J. (1986). Teaching thinking and problem solving: Research foundations. *American Psychologist, 41*(10), 1078–1089.

Bredo, E. (1994). Reconstructing educational psychology: Situated cognition and Deweyan pragmatism. *Educational Psychologist, 29*(1), 23–35.

Broudy, H. (1987). *The role of imagery in learning*. Los Angeles: Getty Center for Education in the Arts.

Brown, J. S., Collins, A., & Duguid, P. (1989). Situated cognition and the culture of learning. *Educational Researcher, 18*, 32–42.

Brown, R. (1958). How shall a thing be called? *Psychological Review, 65*,14–21.

Brown, R. (1965). *Social psychology*. New York: Free Press.

Bruner, J. (1957). On perceptual readiness. *Psychological Review, 64*(123), 152.

Bruner, J. (1960). *The process of education*. Cambridge, MA: Harvard University Press.

Bruner, J. (1973). *Beyond the information given: Studies in the psychology of knowing*. New York: Norton.

Bruner, J. (1985). Vygotsky: A historical and conceptual perspective. In J. Wertsch (Ed.), *Culture, communication and cognition: Vygotskian perspectives* (pp. 21–34). New York: Cambridge University Press.

Bruner, J. (1986). *Actual minds, possible worlds*. Cambridge, MA: Harvard University Press.

Bruner, J. (1990). *Acts of meaning*. Cambridge, MA: Harvard Univeristy Press.

Bruner, J. (1992). Another look at New Look I. *American Psychologist, 47*, 780–783.

Bruner, J. (1996). *The culture of education*. Cambridge, MA: Harvard University Press.

Bruner, J., Goodnow, J., & Austin, G. (1956). *A study of thinking*. New York: Wiley.

Bruner, J., Oliver, R., & Greenfield, P. (1966). *Studies in cognitive growth*. New York: Wiley.

Buck-Morss, S. (1975). Socio-economic bias in Piaget's theory and its implications for cross-culture studies. *Human Development, 18*, 35–49.

Carroll, N. (2001). *Beyond aesthetics: Philosophical essays*. New York: Cambridge University Press.

Cassirer, E. (1944). *An essay on man: Introduction to a philosophy of human culture*. Garden City, NY: Doubleday.

Chapman, L. (2001, March 28). *The mass arts in contemporary life* (slide talk). Visual Culture Panel, NAEA Conference, New York.

Chi, M., Feltovich, P., & Glaser, R. (1981). Categorization and representation of physics problems by experts and novices. *Cognitive Science, 5*(2), 121–152.

Cobb, P. (1994a). Constructivism in mathematics and science education. *Educational Researcher, 23*(7), 4.

Cobb, P. (1994b). Where is the mind? Constructivist and sociocultural perspectives on mathematical development. *Educational Researcher, 23*(7), 13–20.

Cole, M., & Scribner, S. (1978). Introduction. In L. S. Vygotsky (Ed.), *Mind in society: The development of higher psychological processes* (pp. 1–15). Cambridge, MA: Harvard University Press.

Covington, M. V. (1992). *Making the grade: A self-worth perspective on motivation and school reform.* Cambridge: Cambridge University Press.

Damasio, A. R. (1994). *Descartes' error: Emotion, reason, and the human brain.* New York: Avon Books.

Danto, A. (1990). Bad aesthetic times. In A. Danto (Ed.), *Encounters and reflections: Art in the historical present* (pp. 297–312). New York: Farrar, Straus & Giroux.

Davies, S. (1991). *Definitions of art.* Ithaca, NY: Cornell University Press.

Davis, D. J. (1969). *Behavioral emphasis in art education.* Reston, VA: National Art Education Association.

Davis, J., & Gardner, H. (1992). The cognitive revolution: Consequences for the understanding and education of the child as artist. In B. Reimer & R. A. Smith (Eds.), *The arts, education, and aesthetic knowing: Ninety-first yearbook of the National Society for the Study of Education* (Part II, pp. 92–123). Chicago: University of Chicago Press.

Dewey, J. (1934). *Art as experience.* New York: Minton Balch.

Driver, R., Asoko, H., Leach, J., Mortimer, E., & Scott, P. (1994). Constructing scientific knowledge in the classroom. *Educational Researcher, 23*(7), 5–12.

Efland, A. (1990). *A history of art education: Intellectual and social currents in teaching the visual arts.* New York: Teachers College Press.

Efland, A. (1995). The spiral and the lattice: Changes in cognitive learning theory with implications for art education. *Studies in Art Education, 36*(3), 134–153.

Efland, A. (2000). The city as metaphor for integrated learning through the arts. *Studies in Art Education, 41*(3), 276–295.

Efland, A., Freedman, K., & Stuhr, P. (1996). *Postmodern art education: An approach to curriculum.* Reston, VA: National Art Education Association.

Efland, A., Koroscik, J., & Parsons, M. (1992, August). *Assessing understandings of art: A cognitive perspective.* Workshop presentation to Ohio State University and Ohio Partnership for the Visual Arts.

Eisner, E. (1976). *The arts, human development and education.* Berkeley: McCutchan.

Eisner, E. (1982). *Cognition and curriculum: A basis for deciding what to teach.* New York: Longman.

Eisner, E. W. (1993). Forms of understanding and the future of educational research. *Educational Researcher, 22*(7), 5–11.

Eng, H. (1954). *The psychology of children's drawings* (2nd ed.). London: Routledge & Kegan Paul. (Original work published 1931)

Fabricius, W. (1983). Piaget's theory of knowledge: Its philosophical context. *Human Development, 26,* 325–333.

Feldman, E. B. (1973). The teacher as model critic. *Journal of Aesthetic Education, 7*(1), 50–57.

Feltovich, P., Spiro, R., & Coulson, R. (1993). Learning, teaching, and testing for complex conceptual understanding. In N. Freedericksen, R. Mislevy, & I. Bejar (Eds.), *Test theory for a generation of new tests* (pp. 181–217). Hillsdale, NJ: Lawrence Erlbaum.

Flavell, J. (1963). *The developmental psychology of Jean Piaget.* Princeton, NJ: Van Nostrand.

Gablik, S. (1991). *The reenchantment of art.* New York: Thames & Hudson.

Gallimore, R., & Tharp, R. (1990). Teaching mind in society: Teaching, schooling and literate discourse. In L. C. Moll (Ed.), *Vygotsky and education: Instructional implications and applications of sociohistorical psychology* (pp. 175–205). New York: Cambridge University Press.

Gagné, R. (1977). *The conditions of learning* (rev. ed.). New York: Holt, Rinehart & Winston.

Gardner, Helen. (1948). *Art through the ages* (3rd ed.). New York: Harcourt Brace.

Gardner, Howard. (1973). *The arts and human development.* New York: Wiley.

Gardner, Howard. (1980). *Artful scribbles: The significance of children's drawings.* New York: Basic Books.

Gardner, Howard. (1983). *Frames of mind: The theory of multiple intelligences.* New York: Basic Books.

Gardner, Howard. (1987). *The mind's new science: A history of the cognitive revolution.* New York: Basic Books.

Geahigan, G. (1992). The arts in education: A historical perspective. In B. Reimer & R. A. Smith (Eds.), *The arts, education, and aesthetic knowing: Ninety-first yearbook of the National Society for the Study of Education* (Part II, pp. 1–19). Chicago: University of Chicago Press.

Glaser, R. (1988). Cognitive science and education. *International Social Science Journal, 115,* 21–44.

Golomb, C. (1992). *The child's creation of a pictorial world.* Berkeley: University of California Press.

Gombrich, E. H. (1960). *Art and illusion.* New York: Pantheon Books.

Goodman, N. (1978a). *Languages of art* (2nd ed). Indianapolis: Hackett.

Goodman, N. (1978b). *Ways of worldmaking.* Indianapolis: Hackett.

Goodman, N. (1984). *Of mind and other matters.* Cambridge, MA: Harvard University Press.

Goodman, Y., & Goodman, K. (1990). Vygotsky in a whole language perspective. In L. C. Moll (Ed.), *Vygotsky and education: Instructional implications and applications of sociohistorical psychology* (pp. 223–250). New York: Cambridge University Press.

Greenfield, P. (1990). Jerome Bruner: The Harvard years. *Human Development, 33,* 327–333.

Gruber, H., & Voneche, J. J. (Eds.). (1981). *The essential Piaget.* London: Routledge & Kegan Paul.

Harré, R. (1995). Discursive psychology. In J. A. Smith, R. Harré, & L. Van Langenhove (Eds.), *Rethinking psychology.* London: Sage.

House, J. (1989). Reading the Grande Jatte. *Art Institute of Chicago Museum Studies, 14*(2), 115–131.

Hughes, R. (1997). *American visions: The epic history of art in America.* New York: Knopf.

Hunt, J. M. (1961). *Intelligence and experience.* New York: Ronald Press.

Huyssen, A. (1990). Mapping the postmodern. in L. Nicholson (Ed.), *Feminism & postmodernism* (pp. 234–277). New York: Routledge.

Jacobs, J. (1961). *The death and life of great American cities.* New York: Random House.

Jameson, F. (1988). Cognitive mapping. In C. Nelson & L. Grossberg (Eds.), *Marxism and the interpretation of culture* (pp. 347–357). Urbana & Chicago: University of Illinois Press.

Jameson, F. (1992). *Postmodernism, or the cultural logic of late capitalism.* Chapel Hill, NC: Duke University Press.

Janson, H. W. (1962). *History of art.* New York: Abrams

Johnson, M. (1987). *The body in the mind: The bodily basis of meaning, imagination and reason.* Chicago: University of Chicago Press.

Jones, W. T. (1952). *A history of western philosophy* (Vols. I & II). New York: Harcourt Brace.

Kant, I. (1964). Selections from *The critique of judgment.* In A. Hofstadter & R. Kuhns (Eds.), *Philosophies of art and beauty* (pp. 280–343). New York: Modern Library. (Original work published 1790)

Kant, I. (1997). *Critique of pure reason* (P. Guyer & A. Wood, Trans.). New York: Cambridge University Press. (Original work published 1781)

Kellner, D. (1995). *Media culture.* London: Routledge.

Kershensteiner, G. (1905). *Die entwicklung der zeichnerischen begabung* [Development of the graphic gift]. Munich: Carl Gerber.

Kielty, B. (1964). *Masters of painting: Their works, their lives, their times.* Garden City, NY: Doubleday.

Kincheloe, J., & Steinberg, S. (1993). A tentative description of post-formal thinking: The critical confrontation with cognitive theory. *Harvard Educational Review, 63*(3), 296–319.

Kindler, A. (Ed.). (1997). *Child development in art.* Reston, VA: National Art Education Association.

Kindler, A., & Darras, B. (1998). Culture and development of pictorial repertoires. *Studies in Art Education, 39*(2), 147–167.

Koroscik, J. (1982). The effects of prior knowledge, presentation time and task demands on visual art processing. *Studies in Art Education, 23*(3), 13–22.

Koroscik, J. S. (1990a). The function of domain specific knowledge in understanding works of art. In *Inheriting the theory: New voices and multiple perspectives on DBAE.* Los Angeles: J. Paul Getty Trust.

Koroscik, J. (1990b, April). *Novice–expert differences in understanding and misunderstanding art and their implications for student assessment in art education.* Paper presented at symposium, Novice–Expert Paradigms for Student Assessment of Art Learning, Boston.

Koroscik, J. S. (1992a). A comparative framework for designing visual arts curricula. *Arts Education Policy Review, 94*(1), 17–22.

Koroscik, J. S. (1992b). Research on understanding works of art: Some considerations for structuring art viewing experiences for students. *Kasvatus: Finnish Journal of Education, 23*(5), 20–25.

Koroscik, J. S. (1993). Learning in the visual arts: Implications for preparing art teachers. *Arts Education Policy Review, 94*(5), 20–25.

Koroscik, J. S. (1994). Blurring the line between teaching and research: Some future challenges for arts education policymakers. *Arts Education Policy Review, 96*(1), 2–10.

Koroscik, J. S. (1996a). What potential do young people have for understanding works of art? In A. Kindler (Ed.), *Child development in art* (pp. 143–164). Reston, VA: National Art Education Association.

Koroscik, J. S. (1996b). Who ever said studying art would be easy? The growing cognitive demands of understanding works of art in the information age. *Studies in Art Education, 38*(1), 4–20.

Koroscik, J. S., Efland, A., Arabi, A., Beaumont, H., Homan, H., Miller, P., & Robbins, M. (1994, April). *Assessing higher order understanding of Matisse's "The Dance" in interdisciplinary contexts.* Presentation at conference of the National Art Education Association, Baltimore.

Koroscik, J., Short, G., Stavropoulos, C., & Fortin, S. (1992). Frameworks for understanding art: The function of comparative art contexts and verbal cues. *Studies in Art Education, 33*(3), 154–164.

Kosslyn, S. (1980). *Image and mind.* Cambridge, MA: Harvard University Press.

Kosslyn, S. (1983). *Ghosts in the mind's machine: Creating and using images in the brain.* New York: Norton.

Kreitler, H., & Kreitler, S. (1972). *Psychology of the arts.* Chapel Hill, NC: Duke University Press.

Lakoff, G. (1987). *Women, fire and dangerous things: What categories reveal about the mind.* Chicago: University of Chicago Press.

Lakoff, G., & Johnson, M. (1980). *Metaphors we live by.* Chicago: University of Chicago Press.

Lave, J. (1977). Tailor-made experiments and evaluating the intellectual consequences of apprenticeship training. *Quarterly Newsletter of the Institute for Comparative Human Development, 1,* 1–3.

Lave, J. (1988). *Cognition in practice.* Cambridge: Cambridge University Press.

Lave, J., & Wenger, E. (1991). *Situated learning: Legitimate peripheral participation.* New York: Cambridge University Press.

Lowenfeld, V. (1952). *Creative and mental growth* (Rev. ed.). New York: Macmillan.

Luquet, G. (1913). *Les dessins d'un enfant* [The drawings of a child]. Paris: F. Alcan.

Lynch, K. (1960). *The image of the city.* Cambridge, MA: MIT Press.

Miller, G. A., & Gildea, P. M. (1987). How children learn words. *Scientific American, 257*(3), 94–99.

Moll, L. C. (Ed.). (1990). *Vygotsky and education: Instructional implications and application of sociohistorical psychology.* New York: Cambridge University Press.

Newell, A., & Simon, H. (1972). *Human problem solving.* Englewood Cliffs, NJ: Prentice-Hall.

Nochlin, L. (1990). Seurat's *La Grande Jatte*: An anti-utopian allegory. In L. Nochlin (Ed.), *The politics of vision: Essays on nineteenth-century art and society* (pp. 170–193). New York: Harper & Row.

Outhwaite, W. (1994). *Habermas: A critical introduction.* Stanford: Stanford University Press.

Parsons, M. (1987). *How we understand art: A cognitive developmental account of aesthetic experience.* New York: Cambridge University Press.

Parsons, M. (1992). Cognition as interpretation in art education. In B. Reimer & R. A. Smith (Eds.), *The arts, education, and aesthetic knowing: Ninety-first yearbook of the National Society for the Study of Education* (Part II, pp. 70–91). Chicago: University of Chicago Press.

Parsons, M. (1998). [Review of *Child development in art*]. *Studies in Art Education, 40*(1), 80–91.

Perkins, D. N. (1994). *The intelligent eye: Learning to think by looking at art* (Occasional Papers, 4). Getty Center for Education in the Arts, Santa Monica, CA.

Perkins, D., & Simmons, R. (1988). Patterns of misunderstanding: An integrative model for science, math, and programming. *Review of Educational Research, 58*(3), 303–326.

Piaget, J. (1963). *The origins of intelligence in children* (M. Cook, Trans.). New York: Norton. (Original work published 1952)

Piaget, J. (1987). *Possibility and necessity.* Minneapolis: University of Minnesota Press. (Originally published as *Le possible et le necessaire: 1. L'evolution des possibles chez l'enfant,* 1981, by Presses Universitaires de France)

Piaget, J., & Inhelder, B. (1967). *The child's conception of space.* New York: Norton.

Piper, D. (1981). *Looking at art.* New York: Random House.

Prawat, R. S. (1989). Promoting access to knowledge, strategy, and disposition in students: A research synthesis. *Review of Educational Research, 59*(1), 1–41.

Prawat, R. S. (1992). Teachers' beliefs about teaching and learning: A constructivist perspective. *American Journal of Education, 100,* 354–395.

Prawat, R. S., & Floden, R. E. (1994). Philosophical perspectives on constructivist views of learning. *Educational Psychology, 29*(1), 37–48.

Presiosi, D. (1989). *Rethinking art history: Meditations on a coy science.* New Haven, CT: Yale University Press.

Pylyshyn, Z. W. (1973). What the mind's eye tells the mind's brain: A critique of mental imagery. *Psychological Bulletin, 8,* 1–14.

Read, H. (1945). *Education through art.* New York: Pantheon.

Rogoff, B., & Lave, J. (Eds.). (1984). *Everyday cognition: Its development in social context.* Cambridge, MA: Harvard University Press.

Rohwer, W. D., & Sloane, K. (1994). Psychological perspectives. In L. Anderson & L. Sosniak (Eds.), *Bloom's taxonomy: A forty-year retrospective. Ninety-third yearbook of the National Society for the Study of Education* (Part II, pp. 41–63). Chicago: University of Chicago Press.

Schaeffer-Simmern, H. (1948). *The unfolding of artistic activity.* Berkeley: University of California Press.

Scheffler, I. (1986). In praise of the cognitive emotions. In I. Scheffler (Ed.), *Inquiries: Philosophical studies of language, science, and learning* (pp. 347–361). Indianapolis: Hackett.

Schlain, L. (1991). *Art and physics: Parallel visions in space, time and light.* New York: Morrow.

Shephard, R. (1978a). Externalization of mental images and the act of creation. In B. S. Randhawa & W. E. Coffman (Eds.), *Visual learning, thinking and communication* (pp. 133–189). New York: Academic Press.

Shephard, R. (1978b, February). The mental image. *American Psychologist*, pp. 125–137.

Shephard, R., & Metzler, J. (1971). Mental rotation of three dimensional objects. *Science, 171*, 701–703.

Short, G. (1993). Pre-service teachers' understanding of visual arts: The reductive bias. *Arts Education Policy Review, 94*(5), 11–15.

Short, G. (1995). *Problems of advanced learning in the visual arts: The role of reductive bias in pre-service teachers' understanding of domain knowledge.* Unpublished Ph.D. dissertation, Columbus: Ohio State University.

Shuell, T. (1986). Cognitive conceptions of learning. *Review of Educational Research, 56*(4), 411–436.

Smith, R. A. (1986). *Excellence in art education: Ideas and initiatives.* Reston, VA: National Art Education Association.

Snedden, D. (1917). The waning powers of art. *American Journal of Sociology, 23*, 801–821.

Sosnoski, J. J. (1995). *Modern skeletons in postmodern closets: A cultural studies alternative.* Charlottesville: University Press of Virginia.

Spiro, R. J., Coulson, R. L., Feltovich, P. J., & Anderson, D. K. (1988). *Cognitive flexibility theory: Advanced knowledge acquisition in ill-structured domains.* (Tech. Rep. No. 441). University of Illinois at Urbana–Champaign, Center for the Study of Reading.

Spiro, R. J., Vispoel, W. P., Schmitz, J. G., Samarpungavan, A., & Boerger, A. E. (1987). *Knowledge acquisition and application: Cognitive flexibility and transfer in complex content domains* (Tech. Rep. No. 409). University of Illinois at Urbana–Champaign, Center for the Study of Reading.

Sully, J. (1890). The child as artist. In *Studies in childhood* (pp. 298–330). London: Longmans & Green.

Tyler, R. W. (1950). *Basic principles of curriculum and instruction.* Chicago: University of Chicago Press.

Van Langenhove, L. (1995). The theoretical foundations of experimental psychology and its alternatives. In J. A. Smith, R. Harré, & L. Van Langenhove (Eds.), *Rethinking psychology* (pp. 10–23). London: Sage.

Viola, W. (1946). *Child art.* Peoria, IL: Bennett.

Wadsworth, B. (1971). *Piaget's theory of cognitive development: An introduction for students of psychology and education.* New York: David McKay.

Waldrop, M. M. (1992). *Complexity: The emerging science at the edge of order and chaos.* New York: Simon & Schuster.

Watson, J. B. (1914). *Behavior: An introduction to comparative psychology.* New York: Henry Holt.

Weitz, M. (1963). The role of theory in aesthetics. In M. Weitz (Ed.), *Problems in aesthetics* (pp. 145–156). New York: Macmillan.

Wertsch, J. V. (1985). *Vygotsky and the social formation of mind.* Cambridge, MA: Harvard University Press.

White, S. (1989). Foreword. In D. Newman, P. Griffin, & M. Cole (Eds.), *The construction zone: Working for cognitive change in school* (pp. ix–xiv). New York: Cambridge University Press.

Wilson, B. (1999, March). *Grand plans and their subversion: Speculations on the form and formlessness of 21st century art education.* Presentation at conference of the International Symposium on Art Education, Taiwan Museum of Art, Taichung, Taiwan.

Wilson, B., & Wilson, M. (1982). *Teaching children to draw: A guide for teachers and parents.* Englewood Cliffs, NJ: Prentice Hall.

Winslow, L. (1939). *The integrated school art program.* New York: McGraw-Hill.

Wittgenstein, L. (1953). *Philosophical investigations.* New York: Macmillan.

Wolf, D. (1987). Child development and different cognitive styles. In *Seminar proceedings: Issues in discipline-based art education: Strengthening the stance, extending the horizons* (pp. 3–8). Los Angeles: Getty Center for Education in the Arts.

Wolf, D., & Perry, M. (1988). From endpoints to repertoires: Some new conclusions about drawing development. *Journal of Aesthetic Education, 22*(1), 17–34.

Yang, G. (2000). *Exploration of Chinese art using a multimedia CD-ROM: Design, mediated experience, and knowledge construction.* Unpublished Ph.D. dissertation, Columbus, Ohio State University.

Index

Abrams, M. H., 95

Abstraction: and aesthetic experience, 171; and behaviorism, 15; and bias against arts, 1, 2, 4; and cognitive argument for the arts, 168, 171; and cognitive flexibility, 87, 100; and cognitive revolution, 55; and development in children's drawings, 42; and imagination, 138, 142–50, 152, 168; and integrated cognition theory, 77, 80; and learning theory in arts, 12; and objectivism, 5; and obstacles to art learning, 126; and sociocultural cognition, 69, 71, 72, 77, 80; and symbol processing, 38–39, 56, 58–59

Accommodation, 24, 25–26, 30, 40, 65, 73, 78

Acquisition of knowledge: and aesthetic experience, 169; and Bloom's taxonomy, 19; and cognitive argument for the arts, 161, 167, 169; and cognitive flexibility, 85–86, 87, 88, 93, 161; and cognitive revolution, 78; and differences in structure of knowledge domains, 10–11; and integrated cognition theory, 78; and integration of knowledge, 167; and obstacles to art learning, 108, 111, 112–13, 114, 115, 122, 130

Aesthetic experience, 159, 166, 168–71

Affect, 38, 39, 56, 57, 64, 67–68, 136, 139, 156. *See also* Affective domain (Bloom); Emotions

Affective domain (Bloom), 19–20, 21, 22, 48, 156–57

Alexander, Christopher, 83, 101

Analogies, 93, 95–96, 101–2, 105, 116

Anderson, Daniel K., 11, 13, 82

Anderson, Richard, 25, 112

Aristotle, 4, 139

Arnheim, Rudolf, 23, 43–44, 45, 49,

Art/arts: bias against, 1–5, 6, 22–23, 156, 157; as category, 140; cognitive argument for, 156–71; definition of, 140; importance of, 13, 106; as intellectually undemanding, 105–6; isolation from other subjects of, 21–22; for its own sake, 9; location in cognitive landscape of, 166–67; as "open concept," 79; psychology's connection with, 1–13; public perception of, 7; purposes/functions of, 132, 159, 171

Art history/historians, 85–86, 87, 88, 97–98, 117, 118, 120, 128

Artists: sociologists compared with, 163–64

Arts education: and cognitive argument for the arts, 170; implications of cognitive developmental theories for, 48–49, 51; importance of, 7–9;

Arts education (*continued*)
   problem areas affecting, 6–7; purposes
   of, 46, 120, 170; Vygotskian
   implications for, 37–38
Art works: and aesthetic experience, 169,
   170–71; and cognitive argument for the
   arts, 164–66, 168–69, 170–71; and
   cognitive flexibility, 84–85, 100; as
   cognitive landmarks, 164–66; and
   cognitive revolution, 79; creation of,
   13, 78, 153, 161–62, 167; as
   "distributory," 166; importance of, 6;
   and integrated cognition theory, 78, 80;
   and integration of knowledge, 164,
   165–66; original versus reproduction of,
   109; and Parsons's stages in artistic
   development, 27–28, 29, 30. *See also*
   Interpretation; Understanding
Assessment: of analogies, 96; in art history,
   98; of art learning, 12; of change in
   pre-compiled knowledge structures,
   98; and cognitive argument for the
   arts, 167; and cognitive flexibility, 86,
   91, 92, 95, 98, 99, 105; instructional
   prompts in, 130–31; and integration of
   knowledge, 167; and obstacles to arts
   learning, 120, 130–31; of oversimplification, 95; and transfer of
   knowledge, 12; and understanding, 12.
   See also Mapping
Assimilation, 24, 25–26, 30, 33, 40, 54,
   58, 65, 78

Balanced phenomena, 147, 148, 168
Barnes, Earl, 47
Beardsley, Monroe, 4, 169–70
Behaviorism: and cognitive argument for
   the arts, 156–57; and cognitive
   revolution, 52; and definitions of
   constructivism, 75; and development in
   children's drawings, 43; and
   imagination, 133, 136; and integrated
   cognition theory, 75; legacy of, 10, 12,
   14–23, 48; and positivism, 4; and symbol
   processing, 56, 57, 65–66; transition to
   cognitive view from, 12, 18–21, 156–57;
   and Vygotsky's theory, 34
Belenky, M., 38
Bell, P. A., 124
Bereiter, Carl, 54, 69

Blanck, Guillermo, 31, 32, 33
Bloom, Benjamin, 19–20, 22, 48
Bohm, David, 65, 171
Botanical metaphor, 37
Bransford, J., 109, 130
Bredo, Eric, 56, 57, 66–67, 70–71
Broudy, Harry, 7, 117
Brown, J. S., 2, 36, 69–70, 75
Brown, Roger, 141
Bruner, Jerome: and behaviorism, 15,
   16; and case-based learning in arts,
   160; and cognitive argument for the
   arts, 160; and cognitive flexibility,
   160; and cognitive revolution, 64;
   and computer analogy, 68; and
   Enlightenment philosophy, 68; and
   going beyond information given, 13;
   and imagination, 151–52; and
   meaning, 7–8; and mind, 64; and
   narrative structure, 151–52; Piaget
   compared with, 59; spiral curriculum
   of, 58–59, 100, 103; and symbol
   processing, 55–56, 58–59, 64–65, 68;
   and transition from behaviorism to
   cognitive view, 19, 20; and Vygotsky's
   theory, 34, 40
Buck-Morss, Susan, 38–39

Carroll, Noel, 153, 166
Case-based learning, 84, 97–98, 159, 160–
   62, 167
Cassirer, Ernst, 136
Categorization: basic-level, 141, 143, 168;
   classical, 143; and cognitive argument
   for the arts, 168; and cognitive
   flexibility, 92, 94, 99; and cognitive
   revolution, 71, 77; family resemblance,
   140; and imagination, 137–41, 142,
   146, 148, 150–52, 155, 168; and
   integrated cognition theory, 77; and
   obstacles to art learning, 108, 116;
   prototypical, 140–41, 143, 151; and
   sociocultural cognition, 71, 77; sub- and
   superlevels of, 140, 141
Chagall, Marc, 144, 145, 153–54
Chapman, Laura, 154
Chi, M., 114
Chomsky, Noam, 45, 49, 57
City metaphor, 101–2
Clock metaphor, 144, 153–54

Cobb, Paul, 69, 75, 80
Cognition: definitions of, 150; multiple forms of, 171
Cognitive apprenticeships, 69–70, 72, 75, 78
Cognitive developmental theories: basic notion and features of, 23–24; and behaviorism, 14–23; and children's drawings, 41–48, 50; implications for art education of, 48–49, 51; and transition from behaviorism to cognitive view, 12, 18–21, 156–57. *See also specific theorist or theory*
Cognitive domain (Bloom), 19–20, 22, 48
Cognitive flexibility: and acquisition of knowledge, 85–86, 87, 88, 93, 161; and analogies, 93, 95–96, 101–2, 105; and assessment, 86, 91, 95, 98, 99, 105; and case-based learning in arts, 84, 159, 160–62, 167; and categorization, 92, 94, 99; and cognitive argument for the arts, 159–64, 167; and compartmentalization, 90, 91, 92, 93, 98–99, 102, 103; and complexity, 83, 84, 86, 88, 89, 91, 92, 93–95, 96, 98, 99–103, 104–5, 160, 164, 167; curriculum implications of, 13, 83, 99–104, 105; definition of, 82, 88; and domains of knowledge, 13, 82–93, 92, 98–105, 159–60, 162, 167; and hypertext technologies, 83, 89–91, 96, 103, 105; and imagination, 162, 163; implications for arts education of, 104–6; and instruction, 82, 83, 85, 86, 87–88, 89–91, 96, 97–98, 99, 100, 101, 103, 104, 105; and integration of knowledge, 89, 99, 103–4, 105; and interpretation, 82, 84, 85, 87–88, 93–96, 97, 98, 104, 105, 160–62; and metaphors, 83, 89–91, 92, 100–102, 103, 104, 105, 160; and narratives, 97–98, 160, 162; and overlapping sets, 83–84, 102; overview of, 82–85; and reductive bias, 91, 93–99; and simplification, 83, 90, 91, 92, 93, 94–95, 99–100, 101; and structure of knowledge, 13, 81, 84, 87, 88, 92, 93, 97–105, 159–60, 162–64, 167; and understanding, 84, 85, 87, 88, 90, 91, 94–96, 98, 99, 102, 103, 105, 106, 160, 161, 167

Cognitive orientations, 52–55, 166. *See also specific orientation*
Cognitive sciences: and behaviorism, 20, 21; and cognitive flexibility, 86–87, 90; emergence of, 21; and imagination, 136; and symbol processing, 52, 56, 57, 64, 65, 68
Cole, M., 32, 35
Collins, Allan, 69
Compartmentalization: and aesthetic experience, 169; and cognitive argument for the arts, 169; and cognitive flexibility, 90, 91, 92, 93, 98–99, 102, 103; and imagination, 155; and obstacles to art learning, 111, 114, 122; overcoming, 9
Complexity: and cognitive argument for the arts, 158–59, 160, 164, 167; and cognitive flexibility, 83, 84, 86, 88, 89, 91, 92, 93–95, 96, 98, 99–103, 104–5, 160, 164, 167; and obstacles to art learning, 132; and sociocultural cognition, 72; and symbol processing, 65
Computer analogy: and cognitive argument for the arts, 156; and cognitive implications for learning theory in arts, 10; and cognitive revolution, 52, 53, 79; and Eisner's forms of representations, 62; and Enlightenment philosophy, 68; and imagination, 136, 137; and integrated cognition theory, 77, 78; and objectivism, 6; origination of, 65; and symbol processing, 51, 56, 57, 60, 64–66, 68, 77, 79
Concepts: definition of, 135; formation of, 135; naive, 112–13, 117, 120; underdifferentiated, 111, 113–14
Conceptual change, 73–74, 76
Concrete operations stage (Piaget), 27, 108, 146
Content: and cognitive argument for the arts, 164; and cognitive flexibility, 87, 89, 99, 100, 101, 102, 103; and cognitive revolution, 79; and imagination, 151; and integrated cognition theory, 79; and integration of knowledge, 164; and obstacles to art learning, 122, 130; and symbol processing, 58

Context: and assessment, 12; and
cognitive argument for the arts, 159,
162, 164, 165; and cognitive flexibility,
82, 84, 85, 88, 97, 162; and
development in children's drawings,
45; and imagination, 152, 153;
importance of, in learning, 9; and
integrated cognition theory, 75, 77,
78; and integration of knowledge,
159, 164, 165; and obstacles to art
learning, 111, 117, 118, 119, 130;
and sociocultural cognition, 69, 71,
77; and symbol processing, 57, 64,
66–67; and understanding,
131–32
Coulson, Richard, 11, 13, 82, 85, 91, 95,
109
Covington, M. V., 109, 130
Creativity, 40, 88, 95, 133, 135, 136, 147,
152, 157
Criticism, art, 76–77, 84, 117, 120, 144,
161, 162
Curriculum: and aesthetic experience,
169, 170; city as metaphor for,
101–2; and cognitive argument for
the arts, 156, 157, 164, 167, 169,
170; and cognitive flexibility, 83,
99–104, 105; and complexity riddle,
99–103; and contexts for improving
art understanding, 131–32; and
dualisms, 156; and Eisner's forms of
representation, 62; and imagination,
154–55; implications of cognitive views
on, 13; integrated, 103–4; and
integration of knowledge, 164, 167;
landscape model of, 100, 104, 105; and
obstacles to art learning, 121, 122; role
of arts in, 21–22; spiral, 58–59, 100,
103, 104, 105; and symbol processing,
58–59, 62

Damasio, A. R., 66
Danto, Arthur, 166
Darras, Bernard, 47, 48, 49, 49, 121
Davies, S., 169
Davis, Jessica, 22, 52, 55, 56–57, 60–61,
64
Degas, Edgar, 95
Descartes, René, 56, 60, 66, 68, 134–35,
139, 150

Developmental theory: in art education
texts, 22–23; and children's drawings,
41–48; difficulties with Piaget's, 38–39;
and imagination, 144, 146; and
obstacles to art learning, 107–8; and
precognitive theories, 41–43. See also
specific theory
Dewey, John, 70, 73, 136
Domains of knowledge: and aesthetic
experience, 170; and cognitive
argument for the arts, 157–58, 159–60,
162, 164, 166, 167, 170; and cognitive
flexibility, 13, 82–93, 92, 93, 98–105,
159–60, 162, 167; and cognitive
revolution, 53, 55, 59, 60, 74, 77, 78,
79, 80, 81; and development theories in
texts, 24; differences in structure of, 10–
12; and differentiation among domains,
157; and imagination, 143, 148; and
implications of developmental theories
for art education, 49; and integrated
cognition theory, 74, 77, 78, 79, 80, 81;
and integration of knowledge, 159, 164,
166, 167; and interpretation, 10, 11;
and obstacles to art learning, 107–8,
109, 116, 121, 122–23, 125, 128, 131,
132; and Piaget's theory, 24; and
symbols, 53, 59, 60
"Domain specificity," 61, 78, 81, 116
Drawings, children's, 5, 37–38, 41–48, 49
Driver, Rosalind, 72–73, 74–76, 77, 80,
108–9
Dualism: and cognitive argument for the
arts, 156, 159; and cognitive revolution,
66; and Enlightenment philosophy, 68;
and imagination, 135, 149, 150, 155; as
inside-outside problem, 66; and purpose
of arts, 171; and sociocultural cognition,
71; and sociological cognition, 31; and
symbol processing, 56, 64, 66, 68. See
also Descartes, René
Duchamp, Marcel, 97
Duguid, Paul, 69

Education: implications of imagination
for, 154–55; purposes/aims of, 103, 125,
155; reform of, 89. See also Arts
education
Efland, A., 94, 98, 100–101, 116, 117
Einstein, Albert, 136–37

Eisner, Elliot, 19–20, 62–64, 112, 157–58
Emotions: and aesthetic experience, 169, 170; and behaviorism, 48; and Bloom's taxonomy, 22; and cognitive argument for the arts, 163, 166, 169, 170; and cognitive flexibility, 95, 163; and cognitive revolution, 57, 60, 67–68, 78; and imagination, 168; and integrated cognition theory, 78; and integration of knowledge, 166; and purpose of arts, 171; and symbols, 38, 57, 60, 67–68. *See also* Affect; Affective domain
Empiricism, 135
Engels, Friederich, 31, 32
Eng, H., 41
Enlightenment philosophy, 68–69
Equilibration: and Piaget's theory, 24, 26–27
Evaluation. *See* Assessment
Experience: and imagination, 142–50; and symbol processing, 62, 63
"Experiential realism," 135

Fabricius, W., 149
Feelings. *See* Affect; Emotions
Feldman, E. B., 117
Feltovich, Paul, 11, 13, 82, 85, 91, 109, 114
Feminism, 38, 161
Flavell, J., 20, 24, 146
Floden, R. E., 110
Formal operations stage (Piaget), 5, 23, 27, 30, 38, 39, 57, 59, 65, 77, 108, 138, 149, 168
Freud, Sigmund, 23, 41, 136

Gablik, S., 163–64
Gagné, Robert, 10
Gallimore, R., 33
Games, 140
Gardner, Helen, 97
Gardner, Howard: and aesthetic experience, 170; and behaviorism, 20; and cognitive argument for the arts, 157–58; and Eisner's forms of representations, 62–63, 64; and imagination, 133, 137; multiple intelligences concept of, 39, 59–62, 137, 157, 170; and Piaget's theory, 39, 60; and symbol processing, 28, 52, 55, 56–57, 59–63, 64
Geahigan, G., 60, 170

Gildea, P. M., 69–70
Glaser, R., 109, 114
Globalization, 158
Golomb, Claire, 44–45, 46
Gombrich, E. H., 39, 91
Goodman, K., 35–36, 63
Goodman, Nelson, 16, 17, 35–36, 59–60, 61, 64, 66, 68, 170
Goodman, Y., 35–36, 63
Gottlieb, Adolf, 126
Greenfield, Patricia, 15
Gruber, H., 26, 27
Guessing, 112, 118–19

Habermas, Jürgen, 121–23
Harré, Rom, 65, 68
Harvard University: Project Zero at, 20, 49, 59–62
House, J., 115, 117, 118
Hub metaphor, 103
Hughes, Robert, 126, 128
Hull, Clark L., 14–15
Human agency, 53, 63, 64, 68, 72, 78, 80
Hunt, J. M., 20
Huyssen, Andreas, 125
Hypertext technology, 83, 89–91, 96, 103, 105

Imagery: and aesthetic experience, 171; and behaviorism, 16; and cognitive argument for the arts, 163, 166, 168, 171; and cognitive flexibility, 163; and imagination, 133, 136–38, 168; and integration of knowledge, 166; and learning theory in arts, 10; and objectivism, 6
Image-schemata, 137, 138, 146–48, 149, 150, 168
Imagination: and abstraction, 138, 142–50, 152, 168; and aesthetic experience, 168; and behaviorism, 18, 23; and categorization, 137–41, 142, 146, 148, 150–52, 155, 168; and cognitive argument for the arts, 156, 159, 162, 163, 164, 167–68; and cognitive flexibility, 162, 163; connotations of, 133–34, 135, 152; and creativity, 133, 135, 136, 147, 152; and curriculum, 154–55; definitions of, 133, 134, 136, 140;

Imagination (*continued*)
    and dualism, 135, 149, 150, 155, 156;
    and experience, 142–50; implications
    for general education of, 154–55; and
    integrated cognition theory, 77, 78;
    and integration of knowledge, 164;
    Kant's views on, 135, 149–50, 152; and
    mental imagery, 133, 136–38; and
    metaphors, 132, 134, 137–38, 142–50,
    151, 152–54, 155, 159, 167–68; and
    mind, 135, 136, 139, 143; and
    narratives, 134, 146, 150–52, 159,
    167–68; overview on, 133–34; and
    philosophy, 134–36, 142, 143, 155;
    and Piaget's theory, 23, 40, 138, 139,
    144, 146, 149, 150; and psychology,
    133, 136–38, 142; and purpose of arts,
    171; and rationality, 167–68; relevance
    to arts education of, 152–54; and
    representations, 63, 135, 138, 139,
    153, 159; and schemata, 137, 138, 143,
    144, 146–48, 149–52; and structure of
    knowledge, 139, 142, 143, 144, 146,
    147, 168; and symbols, 63, 68, 77, 136,
    137, 153, 155; and understanding, 132,
    133, 138, 148, 150, 152, 153; and
    Vygotsky's theory, 35–36, 40, 63
Impressionism, 93, 94–95, 100, 113–14, 117
Inhelder, B., 5
Instruction: and cognitive flexibility, 82,
    83, 85, 86, 87–88, 89–91, 96, 97–98, 99,
    100, 101, 103, 104, 105; and
    instructional misrepresentations, 87–88;
    and integrated cognition theory, 73;
    and obstacles to arts learning, 130–31;
    prompts in, 130–31; use of multiple
    analogies in, 96
Integrated cognition theory: and
    acquisition of knowledge, 78;
    characteristics of, 156; and cognitive
    argument for the arts, 156, 157, 159,
    164–67, 165, 167; and cognitive
    revolution, 54, 55, 79; and conceptual
    change, 73–74, 76; and domains of
    knowledge, 74, 77, 78, 79, 80, 81;
    implications for arts education of, 51,
    79; and lifeworld, 74, 76, 77, 79, 82,
    167; and obstacles to art learning, 120,
    121; overview of, 72–77; requirements

of, 78–79; and sociocultural cognition,
    78, 80–81, 156; and structure of
    knowledge, 78, 80; and symbols, 78,
    156; table summarizing, 80–81; and
    transfer of knowledge, 78
Integration of knowledge: and
    acquisition of knowledge, 167; and
    aesthetic experience, 166, 169, 170;
    and cognitive argument for the arts,
    159, 164–67, 165, 169, 170; and
    cognitive flexibility, 89, 99, 103–4,
    105; and curriculum, 164, 167; and
    domains of knowledge, 159, 164, 166,
    167; and interpretation, 159, 164; and
    mapping, 120, 164, 166, 167; and
    meaning, 164, 166, 167; and obstacles
    to art learning, 120, 121, 122, 125–26,
    131–32; and structure of knowledge,
    166; and understanding, 164, 165,
    166–67
Intelligence, 17, 26–27, 64, 67, 144. *See
    also* Multiple intelligences
Interpretation: and cognitive argument for
    the arts, 159, 160–62, 164, 167; and
    cognitive flexibility, 82, 84, 85, 87–88,
    93–96, 97, 98, 104, 105, 160–62; and
    cognitive revolution, 55; and domains of
    knowledge, 10, 11; and imagination, 13,
    144, 153; and integrated cognition
    theory, 77, 78; and integration of
    knowledge, 159, 164; and obstacles to
    art learning, 112, 113, 117, 118, 119,
    126, 128, 131–32; and purpose of arts,
    171; right and wrong, 87, 161; and
    structure of knowledge, 10, 11; and
    symbol processing, 67

Jacobs, Jane, 101
Jameson, Frederic, 124–25, 166, 170–71
Janson, H. W., 97
Japanese children, 46
Johns, Jasper, 126, 127, 128, 129, 131,
    132, 166
Johnson, Mark: and Enlightenment
    philosophy, 68, 69; image-schemata of,
    137, 138, 146–48, 149, 150; and
    imagination, 135, 137–38, 139, 143–44,
    146–48, 149–51, 152, 155, 167–68; and
    Kantian antecedents of image-

schemata, 149–50; and metaphors, 5, 69, 143–44, 151; and mind and body, 149; and Piaget's theory, 138, 144, 149, 150; and symbol processing, 68, 69
Jones, W. T., 134
Judgments, making. See Interpretation; Understanding
Jung, Karl, 23, 41, 42, 136

Kant, Immanuel, 56, 60, 135, 149–50, 152
Kekule, F. A., 68
Kellner, Douglas, 54
Kershensteiner, G., 41
Kielty, B., 114
Kincheloe, J., 65
Kindler, Anna, 47, 48, 49, 121
Knowledge: and behaviorism, 48; commonsense, 73–74, 75–76, 108–9; construction of, 58, 71, 74, 80, 81, 87, 98; creation of, 40, 65; garbled or wrong, 111, 114–15; integration of, 89, 164–67, 165, 167; and "knowing how" and "knowing when," 69; new, 78, 89; novice and expert, 39, 72, 93, 107–8, 110, 112–15, 120, 162; and obstacles to art learning, 107–9, 110, 111–12, 112–18; organization of, 53, 81, 101, 108; popular culture, 120; and positivism, 4; prior, 17, 78, 97, 108, 111, 115, 130; procedural, 32; right and wrong, 73; scientific, 4, 5; sensory, 1–2, 4; strategic, 32; and underdifferentiated concepts, 113–14. See also Abstraction; Acquisition of knowledge; Compartmentalization; Complexity; Domains of knowledge; Knowledge base; Lifeworld; Structures of knowledge; Transfer of knowledge
Knowledge base: and obstacles to art learning, 108, 110, 111, 112–15, 121, 130, 131; problems with an art viewer's, 110, 112–15; size and extent of, 108, 110, 112
Koroscik, Judith, 13, 79, 86, 89, 107–20, 121, 130, 131
Kosslyn, Stephen, 136, 137
Kreitler, Hans, 166
Kreitler, Shulamith, 166
Kris, Ernst, 39

Lakoff, George: and Enlightenment philosophy, 68, 69; image-schemata of, 146–48, 149–50; and imagination, 2, 135, 137–38, 139, 140, 141, 143, 144, 146–48, 149–50, 167–68; and metaphor, 5, 69; and Piaget/symbol processing, 68, 69, 138, 144
Landscape metaphor, 83, 89–91, 92, 100–101, 104, 105, 171
Language: and cognitive argument for the arts, 162, 168; and cognitive flexibility, 162; and imagination, 139, 168; and integrated cognition theory, 77, 80; and obstacles to art learning, 122; and Piaget's theory, 33; and sociocultural cognition, 80; and Vygotsky's theory, 31, 32, 33, 36, 49
Lattice metaphor, 100–101, 103, 104, 132
Lave, Jean, 36, 71–72, 80
Learner/learning: and behaviorism, 15, 18, 19, 20, 22, 34; and cognitive argument for the arts, 158; cognitive implications for, 9–10; and cognitive revolution, 52–81; definition of, 53; disposition toward, 110, 112, 118–19, 130; evaluation of, 92; importance of context in, 9; as lone individual, 53; main task of, 92; misconceptions and, 107–20, 111–12; multiple views of, 9–10; obstacles to, 107–32, 111–12; strategies of, 13, 86; and transfer of knowledge, 88–89; and transition from behaviorism to cognitive view, 18, 19, 20. See also specific theoretician, theory, or cognition orientation
Legitimate peripheral participation, 71–72
Lichtenstein, Roy, 98–99, 102
Lifeworld: and cognitive argument for the arts, 167; and cognitive revolution, 55, 79; diagram of, 123; Habermas's concept of, 121–23; and integrated cognition theory, 74, 76, 77, 79, 81, 167; and integration of knowledge, 167; and learning theories, 13; and obstacles to arts learning, 120–29, 131; and purpose of arts, 171
Linguistics, 137–38, 142, 146
Locke, John, 60, 135
Lowenfeld, Viktor, 23, 37, 42–43, 45, 47, 49, 49

Lukacs, Georg, 38–39
Luquet, G., 41
Lynch, Kevin, 121, 123, 124–25, 128

Magritte, René, 2, *3*
Mapping: aesthetic experience as
  cognitive, 170–71; and assessment, 99;
  and cognitive argument for the arts,
  164, 166, 167, 168; and cognitive
  flexibility, 99; and concept linking, 128;
  cultural, 120–29; and development in
  children's drawings, 47; and
  imagination, 148, 168; and integration
  of knowledge, 164, 166, 167;
  limitations of, 128–29; and obstacles to
  arts learning, 107, 120–29, 131, 132
Marxism, 31, 38–39, 124
Marx, Karl, 32
Mathematics, 74–77, 100, 103, 105, 135,
  143, 156, 160
Meaning: and aesthetic experience, 170;
  and cognitive argument for the arts,
  156, 159, 160, 161, 162, 164, 166, 167,
  168, 170; and cognitive flexibility, 104,
  160, 161, 162; and cognitive revolution,
  53, 54, 55, 79; and definitions of
  constructivism, 75; and development in
  children's drawings, 44, 45; and
  Enlightenment philosophy, 68; and
  imagination, 134, 143, 144, 147, 148,
  150, 152, 153, 154, 155, 159, 168; and
  implications for arts education, 51; and
  integrated cognition theory, 53, 72, 73,
  74, 75, 77, 78, 79, 80, 81, 156; and
  integration of knowledge, 164, 166,
  167; and learning theory in arts, 12;
  and mind, 54; nature of, 81; and
  objectivism, 5–6, 79; and obstacles to
  arts learning, 118, 121, 122, 123; and
  reconceptualizing cultural importance
  of arts education, 7–8; and sociocultural
  cognition, 31, 72, 77, 81; and symbol
  processing, 56, 57, 60, 63, 65, 68, 72,
  79, 81
Mediation, 31–36, 39, 45, 49, 52, 75, 79
Medical education, 82–84, 95, 161
Metacognition, 32, 78, 81, 88
Metaphors: and behaviorism, 23; and
  cognitive argument for the arts, 159,
  160, 164, 167–68; and cognitive

flexibility, 83, 89–91, 92, 100–102, 103,
  104, 105, 160; and cognitive revolution,
  54, 55; and imagination, 132, 134, 137–
  38, 142–50, 151, 152–54, 155, 159,
  167–68; and integrated cognition
  theory, 78; and integration of
  knowledge, 164; and learning theory in
  arts, 10; and objectivism, 5–6; and
  obstacles to arts learning, 116, 125; and
  production and interpretation of art
  works, 13; and purpose of arts, 171;
  structure of, 148; and symbol
  processing, 23, 66, 69; visual, 153–54.
  See also specific metaphor
Metzler, J., 137
Miller, G. A., 69–70
Mind: and body problem, 66, 135, 149,
  150, 156, 171; and brain, 66; and
  cognitive argument for the arts, 156,
  168; and cognitive revolution, 54; and
  Eisner's forms of representations, 64;
  and Enlightenment philosophy, 68; and
  imagination, 135, 136, 139, 143, 168;
  and integrated cognition theory, 75, 77,
  80; and meaning, 54; as power that
  develops multiple forms of thought,
  143; rational, 135; and sociocultural
  cognition, 30, 31, 54, 64; and symbol
  processing, 54, 62, 64, 66, 68, 77, 80.
  See also Computer analogy
Mirror analogy, 95, 96, 171
Modern art, 44, 47
Modernism, 93, 102, 121–22, 161
Moll, L. C., 31
Multiple intelligences, 39, 59–62, 137,
  157, 170
Multiple repertoire theory, 47–48, 49, 121

Naive concepts, 112–13, 117, 120
Narratives: and cognitive argument for
  the arts, 159, 160, 162, 167–68; and
  cognitive flexibility, 97–98, 160, 162;
  and cognitive revolution, 55; and
  imagination, 134, 146, 150–52, 159,
  167–68; and learning theory in arts, 10;
  and obstacles to arts learning, 131; and
  production and interpretation of art
  works, 13
Newell, Allen, 52, 55, 56, 65
Nochlin, Linda, 93, 113, 114

Nodal points, 125, 128, 132
Nonredundance, notion of, 157

Objectivism: as biased against the arts, 5–6, 22; and cognitive revolution, 55, 57, 79; and Enlightenment philosophy, 68; and integrated cognition theory, 77, 80; and meaning, 79; in sciences, 5–6; and symbol processing, 57, 64, 65, 68, 77, 80
Olson, David, 64
Outhwaite, W., 121–22
Overlapping sets, 83–84, 102, 125

Parsons, Michael: and cognitive argument for the arts, 157; and developmental theories in children's drawings, 43–44, 45; and obstacles to arts learning, 116, 117; and Piaget's theory of cognitive development, 23–24; stages of artistic development of, 27–28, 29, 30; and structure of knowledge domains, 10; and symbol processing, 61, 62; and transition from behaviorism to cognitive view, 21–22
Path metaphor, 89–91
Peat, F. D., 65
Perception: and aesthetic experience, 159, 169, 170, 171; and behaviorism, 15, 16–18, 23; and cognitive argument for the arts, 157, 159, 162, 163, 164, 166, 168, 169, 170, 171; and cognitive flexibility, 162, 163; and development in children's drawings, 43–44, 46; and imagination, 137, 138, 139, 142, 146–47, 148, 149–50, 152, 155, 168; and integration of knowledge, 164, 166; and obstacles to arts learning, 124; and purpose of arts, 171; and symbol processing, 60, 62, 63, 65, 68, 149; thinking in relation to, 16–18; and Vygotsky's theory, 33
Performance versus mastery orientation, 112, 118, 119
Perkins, David, 11, 17, 67, 80, 107–8, 109, 110, 112–13, 114, 117, 118, 119, 144
Perry, Martha, 47
Perseveration, 112, 118–19
Pestalozzi, Johann, 99–100
Philosophy, 56, 68–69, 134–36, 142, 143, 155

Piaget, Jean: and accommodation and assimilation, 40; Bruner compared with, 59; and children's drawings, 5, 42; and cognitive argument for the arts, 168; and cognitive revolution, 52; contributions of, 12–13, 14; and creativity, 40; developmental theory of, 34, 35, 138, 144, 146; difficulties with theory of, 38–39, 65; dualism in theory of, 150; and environment, 33; Gardner compared with, 60; and imagination, 23, 40, 138, 139, 144, 146, 149, 150, 168; and implications for art education, 48, 49; influence of, 52; influences on, 31; and integrated cognition theory, 72–73, 74; and internalization, 33; Johnson compared with, 138, 149, 150; Kant compared with, 149, 150; and learner, 34; and obstacles to arts learning, 108; overview of theory of, 23–28, 30; and Parsons stages of artistic development, 27–28, 29, 30; and positivism, 5; and possibilities, 40, 65; and precognitive theories, 43; and reality, 40; schemata of, 24–27, 42, 138, 144, 146; stages in theory of, 5, 23, 27, 30, 146; and symbol processing, 40, 56, 57, 59, 60, 61, 65; and transition from behaviorism to cognitive view, 20, 23; Vygotsky compared with, 13, 30, 31, 33, 34, 35, 39, 40, 41
Piper, D.,115
Plato, 1, 4, 22, 134
Play, 35–36, 63
Plotinus, 4
Popular culture, 131, 158
Positivism, 2–5, 15, 31, 133, 136
Possibilities, 40, 65
Post-Impressionism, 93, 94–95, 113–14
Postmodernism, 45, 125–26, 131, 159, 166, 170
Prawat, R. S., 61, 107, 108, 109, 110, 114, 118, 119
Precognitive theories, 41–43, 49
Preoperational thought stage (Piaget), 27
Presiosi, Donald, 97
Progressive education, 37, 103–4
Project Zero (Harvard University), 20, 49, 59–62

Psychology: and cognitive revolution, 58; and critique of symbol processing, 64; gestalt, 23; and imagination, 133, 136–38, 142; and obstacles to arts learning, 123–24; and psychological studies of mental imagery, 136–38; scientific, 2, 4–5, 15, 16; uneasy connection between art and, 1–13
Psychomotor domain (Bloom), 19, 22, 48
Pylyshyn, Zenon, 136, 137

Quitting, 112, 118–19

Rationalism, 135, 139, 143
Rationality, 148, 150, 155, 159, 167–68
Rauschenberg, Robert, 100
Ray, Man, 153–54
Read, Herbert, 23, 42, 47, 49
Reality: and aesthetic experience, 171; in children's drawings, 47; and cognitive argument for the arts, 156, 167, 171; and cognitive flexibility, 83; and cognitive revolution, 52, 53, 54; construction of, 13; and dualism, 66; and Eisner's forms of representations, 63; and imagination, 137, 139, 153; and integrated cognition theory, 51, 53, 76, 77, 78, 80, 156; and integration of knowledge, 167; and obstacles to arts learning, 122, 131; and purpose of arts, 171; and sociocultural cognition, 13, 53, 77, 80; and symbol processing, 13, 40, 54, 56, 63, 65, 66, 67
"Recognition rule," 94–95
Reductive bias, 91, 93–99
Renoir, Pierre Auguste, 93, 94–95
Representations: and behaviorism, 18; and cognitive argument for the arts, 157, 159, 160; and cognitive flexibility, 82, 83, 88, 90, 92, 96, 99, 100–101, 105, 160; and development in children's drawings, 43, 44–45, 46, 47; Eisner's forms of, 19–20, 62–64, 112, 157–58; and imagination, 63, 135, 138, 139, 153, 159; and integrated cognition theory, 73, 77, 78; multiple, 96; and obstacles to arts learning, 121, 123, 125, 131; and purpose of arts, 171; and symbol processing, 18, 33, 56, 58, 59, 61, 65, 67
Rogoff, B., 36, 71

Rohwer, W. D., 15, 19, 20, 107
Rorty, Richard, 66
Rosch, Eleanor, 140, 141

Scaffolding, 34–35, 38, 78, 81
Schaeffer-Simmern, Henry, 23
Scheffler, Israel, 10, 67–68, 170
Schemata: and cognitive argument for the arts, 160, 168; and cognitive flexibility, 87, 88, 92, 96, 160; and cognitive revolution, 52; and development in children's drawings, 42; image-, 137, 138, 146–48, 149, 150, 168; and imagination, 137, 138, 143, 144, 146–48, 149–52, 168; and integrated cognition theory, 73; of Lakoff and Johnson, 137, 138, 144, 146–48, 149, 150; of Lowenfeld, 42; and obstacles to arts learning, 108; of Piaget, 24–27, 42, 138, 144, 146; and symbol processing, 56. See also Mapping; Structure of knowledge
Schlain, L., 68
Schuell, T., 15
Science: and aesthetic experience, 170; and cognitive argument for the arts, 156, 160, 162, 170; and cognitive flexibility, 89, 100, 103, 105, 160, 162, 163; and imagination, 136–37, 143–44; and integrated cognition theory, 74–77; objectivism in, 5–6; and obstacles to arts learning, 116; and positivism, 2, 4–5; psychology as, 2, 4–5, 15, 16; and purpose of arts, 171; and transition from behaviorism to cognitivism, 156
Scribner, S., 32
Search patterns, 111, 115–18
Sensimotor intelligence stage (Piaget), 27, 108, 138, 149
Sets: overlapping, 83–84, 102
Seurat, Georges, 93, 94–95, 111, 112, 113–14, 115, 116, 117, 119, 132
Shephard, Roger, 136–37
Sherman, Cindy, 96
Short, Georgianna, 82
Simmons, R., 11, 67, 80, 107–8, 109, 112–13, 114, 117, 119
Simon, Herbert, 52, 55, 56, 65
Simplification, 83, 90, 91, 92, 93, 94–95, 99–100, 101, 114

Situated cognition. *See* Sociocultural cognition
Skinner, B. F., 14–15
Sloane, K., 15, 19, 20, 107
Smith, Ralph, 159, 161, 169
Snedden, D., 1
Sociocultural cognition: and abstraction, 69, 71, 72, 77, 80; and categorization, 71, 77; and cognitive argument for the arts, 156, 157; and cognitive revolution, 52–53, 54, 69–72, 79; and implications for arts education, 48–49, 51; and integrated cognition theory, 78, 80–81, 156; and mind, 30, 31, 54, 64; and reality, 13, 53, 77, 80; symbol processing compared with, 70, 71, 72; table summarizing, 80–81. *See also* Vygotsky, Lev
Sociologists: artists compared with, 163–64
Sosnoski, James, 7
Spiral curriculum, 58–59, 100, 103, 104, 105
Spiro, Rand: and cognitive flexibility, 13, 82–91, 92, 94, 95, 96, 100, 103; and differences in structure of knowledge domains, 11, 13; and Koroscik's analysis of misconceptions, 109, 113
Stage theories: and development in children's drawings, 41–43, 47, 48; and features of cognitive developmental theories, 24; and imagination, 146; and obstacles to arts learning, 108; and stages as clusters of ideas, 28. *See also specific theory or theorist*
Steinberg, S., 65
Steiner, Rudolf, 104
Stimulus-response theory. *See* Behaviorism
Strategies: and cognitive argument for the arts, 157, 160; and cognitive flexibility, 86, 88, 97, 105, 160; definition of, 160; and obstacles to arts learning, 110, 111, 112, 115, 117, 118, 119, 130, 131, 132; problems with knowledge-seeking, 115–18
Structure of knowledge: and cognitive argument for the arts, 159–60, 162–64, 166, 167, 168; and cognitive flexibility, 13, 81, 84, 87, 88, 92, 93, 97–105, 159–60, 162–64, 167; and cognitive

revolution, 52, 53, 55, 59, 78, 80; and differences in domains, 10–12; and emergence of cognitive science orientation, 21; and imagination, 139, 142, 143, 144, 146, 147, 168; and integrated cognition theory, 78, 80; and integration of knowledge, 166; and interpretation, 10, 11; and obstacles to arts learning, 107, 114, 117, 128, 130; and overreliance on pre-compiled knowledge, 97–98; and Piaget/symbol processing, 25, 53, 59, 139, 144, 146, 160; and sociological cognition, 31. *See also* Schemata
Styles, artistic, 84–85, 88, 93, 94–95, 100, 109, 113–14, 117, 160
Sully, James, 41, 47
Symbols/symbol processing: and aesthetic experience, 170; and behaviorism, 18; characteristics of, 56–57; and cognitive argument for the arts, 156, 157, 160, 162, 170; and cognitive developmental theories, 49; and cognitive revolution, 52–53, 54, 55–69, 79; critique of, 64–68; and domains of knowledge, 53, 59, 60; and Eisner's forms of representation, 62–64; and Enlightenment philosophy, 68–69; and imagination, 63, 68, 77, 136, 137, 153, 155; and implications for arts education, 51; and integrated cognition theory, 78, 156; as knowledge, 54; and meaning, 56, 57, 60, 63, 65, 68, 72, 79, 81; and mind, 54, 62, 64, 66, 68, 77, 80; and objectivism, 5, 6, 57, 64, 65, 68, 77, 80; and obstacles to arts learning, 107–8; and Parsons's stages in artistic development, 28; and perception, 60, 62, 63, 65, 68, 149; and Project Zero, 59–62; and purpose of arts, 171; and reality, 13, 40, 54, 56, 63, 65, 66, 67; sociocultural cognition compared with, 70, 71, 72; and structure of knowledge, 25, 53, 59, 139, 144, 146, 160; table summarizing, 80–81. *See also* Integrated cognition theory; Piaget, Jean

Taxonomy (Bloom), 19–20, 22, 48
Texts, art education, 22–23
Tharp, R., 33

Thinking, 6, 10, 16–18, 19, 32
Thorndike, Edward L., 5, 10, 16
Transfer of knowledge: and assessment, 12;
    and cognitive flexibility, 83, 87, 88–89,
    102, 103, 105; and cognitive revolution,
    72, 78; and integrated cognition theory,
    78; and obstacles to art learning, 110,
    114, 115, 116, 125, 130, 132; and
    sociocultural cognition, 72
Truth, 8, 55
Tunnel vision, 111, 116
Tyler, Ralph, 19

Understanding: and assessment, 12; and
    bias against arts, 12, 156; and cognitive
    argument for the arts, 156, 159, 160,
    161, 164, 165, 166–67, 168–69; and
    cognitive flexibility, 84, 85, 87, 88, 90,
    91, 94–96, 98, 99, 102, 103, 105, 106,
    160, 161, 167; and cognitive revolution,
    79; definitions of, 12, 152; and
    development in children's drawings,
    43–44; and imagination, 132, 133, 138,
    148, 150, 152, 153; and integrated
    cognition theory, 73–74, 77, 79; and
    integration of knowledge, 159, 164,
    165, 166–67; and obstacles to arts
    learning, 109, 111, 112–13, 114, 116–
    20, 122, 124, 125, 126, 128–32;
    Parsons's developmental stages for, 27–
    28, 29, 30; and purpose of arts, 171;
    and sociocultural cognition, 71; and
    symbol processing, 24, 67

Van Gogh, Vincent, 166
Van Langenhove, Luk, 4
Viola, W., 41
Visual problem solving: drawings as, 43–45

Voneche, J. J., 26, 27
Vygotsky, Lev: and botanical metaphor,
    37; and cognitive revolution, 52;
    contributions of, 12–13, 14; and
    development, 35, 36; difficulties with
    theory of, 39–40; and Eisner's forms of
    representation, 63; and imagination,
    40, 63; and implications for art
    education, 48–49; and integrated
    cognition theory, 75; internalization in
    theory of, 32, 33, 40, 49, 75; and
    knowledge, 39–40; and mediation, 36,
    39, 49; overview of theory of, 30–38;
    Piaget compared with, 13, 30, 31, 33,
    34, 35, 39, 40, 41; and play, 63; recent
    application of theory of, 36. *See also*
    Zone of proximal development

Wadsworth, B., 24–25, 26
Waldorf schools, 104
Waldrop, M. M., 116
Warhol, Andy, 97, 98–99, 102, 166
Watson, John B., 10, 16
Weitz, Morris, 79, 140
Wenger, E., 71–72, 80
Wertsch, J. V., 33, 35
White, Sheldon, 34–35
Wilson, B., 45–46, 49
Winslow, Leon, 104
Wittgenstein, Ludwig, 139, 140
Wodiczko, Krzysztof, 163–64
Wolf, Dennie, 28, 47, 49, 109, 113

Yang, G., 103

Ziff, Paul, 161
Zone of proximal development
    (Vygotsky), 34, 36, 37, 48–49, 81

About the Author

ARTHUR EFLAND received his doctorate in 1965 from Stanford University. He is currently professor emeritus in the Department of Art Education at the Ohio State University. He authored the elementary and secondary guidelines in art education for the state of Ohio, winning an award of excellence from the National Art Education Association in 1982. His book *A History of Art Education: Intellectual and Social Currents in Teaching the Visual Arts* (1990) is frequently cited by scholars in art and general education. He has published in the *Journal of Aesthetic Education, Studies in Art Education, Visual Arts Research,* and *History of Education Quarterly.* His articles on the history of art education in the United States appear in the *International Encyclopedia of Education,* the *Encyclopedia of Curriculum,* and the *Encyclopedia of Art.*